Britain's
Best
Hotels

AA

This product includes mapping data licensed from Ordnance Survey® with the permission of the Controller of Her Majesty's Stationery Office. © Crown copyright 2010. All rights reserved. Licence number 100021153.

Maps prepared by the Mapping Services Department of The Automobile Association.

Maps © AA Media Limited 2010.

Advertising Sales:
advertisementsales@theAA.com

Editorial:
lifestyleguides@theAA.com

Typeset by AA Lifestyle Guides

Printed in E.U by G Canale & C

Managing Editor: Fiona Griffiths

Cover credits
Front Cover: Chewton Glen, Hampshire
Back Cover: (t) Headland Hotel, Devon; (c) Feversham Arms Hotel, North Yorkshire; (b) Chewton Glen, Hampshire

A CIP catalogue record for this book is available from the British Library

ISBN: 978-0-7495-6465-0

Published by AA Publishing, which is a trading name of AA Media Limited, whose registered office is:
Fanum House, Basing View, Basingstoke, Hampshire RG21 4EA
Registered number 06112600

theAA.com/shop

A04114

Britain's Best
Hotels

Contents

Welcome

Britain's Best Hotels covers a selection of the very best hotels in England, Scotland, Wales and the Channel Islands. All establishments are professionally inspected by the AA to ensure the highest standards of hospitality, accommodation and food.

The Best Hotels

This guide covers nearly 300 town and country houses, small and metro hotels. Every establishment has received a star rating and percentage merit score following a visit by an AA inspector. This indicates that you can expect a friendly welcome, comfortable surroundings, excellent food and a good service. Further details about the AA scheme, inspections and awards and rating system can be found on pages 8–9 of this guide.

Before You Travel

Some places may offer special breaks and facilities not available at the time of going to press. If in doubt, it's always worth calling the hotel before you book. See also the useful information provided on pages 10–11, and visit theAA.com for up-to-date establishment and travel information.

Using the Guide

Britain's Best Hotels has been designed to enable you to find an establishment quickly and efficiently. Each entry provides clear information about the type of accommodation, the facilities available and the local area.

Use the contents (page 3) to browse the main gazetteer section by county and the index to find either a location (page 360) or a specific hotel (page 364) by name.

Finding Your Way

The main section of the guide is divided into four parts, covering England, Channel Islands, Scotland and Wales. The counties within each of these sections are ordered alphabetically as are the town or village locations (shown in capital letters as part of the address) within each county. Finally, the establishments are listed alphabetically under each location name. Town names featured in the guide can also be located in the map section at the back of the guide.

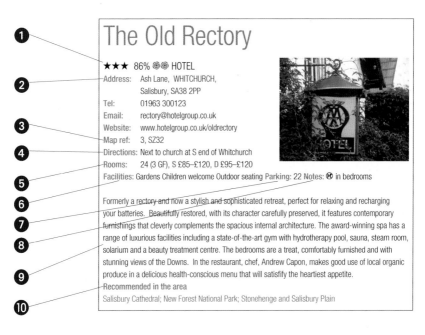

The Old Rectory

★★★ 86% ◉◉ HOTEL

Address:	Ash Lane, WHITCHURCH, Salisbury, SA38 2PP
Tel:	01963 300123
Email:	rectory@hotelgroup.co.uk
Website:	www.hotelgroup.co.uk/oldrectory
Map ref:	3, SZ32
Directions:	Next to church at S end of Whitchurch
Rooms:	24 (3 GF), S £85–£120, D £95–£120
Facilities:	Gardens Children welcome Outdoor seating Parking: 22 Notes: ⊗ in bedrooms

Formerly a rectory and now a stylish and sophisticated retreat, perfect for relaxing and recharging your batteries. Beautifully restored, with its character carefully preserved, it features contemporary furnishings that cleverly complements the spacious internal architecture. The award-winning spa has a range of luxurious facilities including a state-of-the-art gym with hydrotherapy pool, sauna, steam room, solarium and a beauty treatment centre. The bedrooms are a treat, comfortably furnished and with stunning views of the Downs. In the restaurant, chef, Andrew Capon, makes good use of local organic produce in a delicious health-conscious menu that will satisfify the heartiest appetite.

Recommended in the area

Salisbury Cathedral; New Forest National Park; Stonehenge and Salisbury Plain

❶ Stars and symbols

All entries in the guide have been inspected by the AA and, at the time of going to press, belong to the AA hotel scheme. Every establishment in the scheme is classified for quality with a rating of one to five stars (★). Every establishment in Britain's Best Hotels has three, four or five stars and a high merit score (%). The very best hotels in each of these categories have been given red stars (★). Alongside a star rating, each establishment has also been given one of the following descriptive categories:
HOTEL, TOWN HOUSE HOTEL, COUNTRY HOUSE HOTEL, SMALL HOTEL, RESTAURANT WITH ROOMS.
See pages 8–9 for more information on the AA ratings and awards scheme.
Rosette ◉: This is the AA's food award (see page 9 for further details).

❷ Contact Details

The establishment address includes a locator or place name in capitals (e.g. NORWICH). Within each county, entries are ordered alphabetically first by this place name and then by the name of the establishment.

Telephone and fax numbers, and e-mail and website addresses are given where available. See page 10 for information about booking online. The telephone and fax numbers are believed correct at the time of going to press but changes may occur. The latest establishment details are on the Hotel pages at theAA.com.

Website addresses have been supplied by the establishments and lead you to websites that are not under the control of AA Media Limited (AAML). AAML has no control over and accepts no responsibility or liability in respect of the material on any such websites. By including the addresses of third-party websites AAML does not intend to solicit business.

❸ Map reference

Each establishment in this guide is given a map reference for a location which can be found in the atlas section at the back of the guide. It is composed of the map page number (1–13) and two-figure map reference based on the National Grid.

For example: **Map 05 SU48**

05 refers to the page number of the map section at the back of the guide

SU is the National Grid lettered square (representing 100,000sq metres) in which the location will be found

4 is the figure reading across the top and bottom of the map page

8 is the figure reading down each side of the map page

Maps locating each establishment and a route planner are available at theAA.com.

❹ Directions

Where possible, directions have been given from the nearest motorway or major road.

❺ Room Information

The entries show the number of en suite letting bedrooms available. Bedrooms that have a private bathroom adjacent may be included as en suite. Further details of facilities provided in the rooms are listed in the main entry description (see ❾).

Prices: Prices are per room per night (unless otherwise specified) and are provided by the hoteliers in good faith. These prices are indications and not firm quotations. Always check before booking.

❻ Facilities

This section lists a selection of facilities offered by the hotel including sports facilities such as indoor and outdoor swimming pools, golf, tennis and gym; options for relaxation such as spa, jacuzzi and solarium, and services such as satellite TV and Wi-fi. Use the key to the symbols on page 7 to help identify what's available at a particular hotel.

Additional facilities, such as access for the disabled, or notes about other services may be listed here. Some hotels have restricted service during quieter months, and at this time some of the listed facilities will not be available. If unsure, contact the hotel before your visit.

Payment

As most hotels now accept credit or debit cards we only indicate if an establishment does not accept any cards for payment. Credit cards may be subject to a surcharge – check when booking if this is how you intend to pay. Not all hotels accept travellers' cheques.

❼ Parking

This shows the number of parking spaces available. Other types of parking (on road or Park and Ride) may also be possible; check the descriptions for further information.

❽ Notes
This section provides specific details relating to:

Smoking policy: Smoking in public places is now banned in England, Scotland and Wales.

The proprietor can designate one or more bedrooms with ventilation systems where the occupants can smoke, but communal areas must be smoke-free.

Dogs: Although many hotels allow dogs, they may be excluded from some areas of the hotel and some breeds, particularly those requiring an exceptional license, may not be acceptable at all. Under the Disability Discrimination Act 1995 access should be allowed for guide dogs and assistance dogs. Please check the hotel's policy when making your booking.

Children: No children (👶) means children cannot be accommodated, or a minimum age may be specified, e.g. 👶 under 4 means no children under four years old. The main description may also provide details about facilities available for children.

Establishments with special facilities for children may include a babysitting service or baby-intercom system, playroom or playground, laundry facilities, drying and ironing facilities, cots, high chairs and special meals. If you have very young children, check before booking.

Other notes: Additional facilities, such as access for the disabled, or notes about other services.

❾ Description
This may include specific information about the various facilities offered in the rooms, a brief history of the establishment, notes about special features and descriptions of the food where an award has been given (see ❶ above).

❿ Recommended in the Area
These listings give local places of interest and potential day trips and activities.

Key to symbols

★	Black stars (see page 8)
☆	Red stars (see page 9)
%	Merit score
◎	AA Rosette (see page 9)
3, TQ28	Map reference
S	Single room
D	Double room
GF	Ground floor room
Family	Family room
🐕	Dogs allowed
⊗	No dogs allowed (guide dogs for the blind and assist dogs should be allowed)
👶	Children not allowed
Wi-fi	Wireless network available where indicated
STV	Satellite television
⬛	Indoor swimming pool
⬛	Indoor heated swimming pool
⬛	Outdoor swimming pool
⬛	Outdoor heated swimming pool

Best Quality

All entries in Britain's Best Hotels have excelled in several categories set by the AA inspection team. Red stars are awarded to the very best establishments in each star category and signify that the hotel offers the finest accommodation available.

High Standards

Hotels recognised by the AA should:
- have high standards of cleanliness
- keep proper records of booking
- give prompt and professional service to guests, assist with luggage on request, accept and deliver messages
- provide a designated area for breakfast and dinner, with drinks available in a bar or lounge
- provide an early morning call on request
- have good quality furniture and fittings
- provide adequate heating and lighting
- undertake proper maintenance

The hotels in Britain's Best Hotels all have a three, four or five black or red star rating. The following is a brief guide to some of the general expectations for each star classification:

★★★ Three Star
- Management and staff smartly and professionally presented and usually wearing a recognisable uniform
- A dedicated receptionist on duty at peak times
- At least one restaurant or dining room open to residents and non-residents for breakfast and dinner whenever the hotel is open
- Last orders for dinner no earlier than 8pm
- Remote-control television, direct-dial phone
- En suite bath or shower and WC

★★★★ Four Star
- A formal, professional staffing structure with smartly presented, uniformed staff anticipating and responding to your needs or requests
- Usually spacious, well-appointed public areas
- Reception staffed 24 hours by well-trained staff
- Express checkout facilities where appropriate
- Porterage available on request
- Night porter available

- At least one restaurant open to residents and non-residents for breakfast and dinner seven days per week, and lunch to be available in a designated eating area
- Last orders for dinner no earlier than 9pm
- En suite bath with fixed overhead shower and WC

★★★★★ Five Star
- Luxurious accommodation and public areas with a range of extra facilities. First time guests shown to their bedroom
- Multilingual service
- Guest accounts well explained and clearly presented
- Porterage offered
- Guests greeted at hotel entrance, full concierge service provided
- At least one restaurant open to residents and non-residents for all meals seven days per week

- Last orders for dinner no earlier than 10pm
- High-quality menu and wine list
- Evening service to turn down the beds
- Remote-control television, direct-dial telephone at bedside and desk, a range of luxury toiletries, bath sheets and robes
- En suite bathroom incorporating fixed overhead shower and WC

★ Inspectors' Choice

Each year the AA selects the best hotels in each rating. These hotels stand out as the very best in the British Isles, regardless of style. The selected Inspectors' Choice hotels in the main section of this guide are identified by red stars. You can find a list of all the AA's red star hotels on theAA.com under Top Hotels.

Types of hotel

The majority of establishments in this guide come under the category of Hotel; other categories are listed below:

Town House Hotel:

A small, individual city or town centre property, which provides a high degree of personal service and privacy.

Country House Hotel:

These are quietly located in a rural area.

Small Hotel:

Has less than 20 bedrooms and is managed by the owner.

Restaurant with rooms:

This category of accommodation is now assessed under the AA's Guest Accommodation scheme. Some of them have been awarded yellow stars, which indicates that they are among the top ten percent of their star rating. Most Restaurants with Rooms have been awarded AA Rosettes for their food.

A small number of hotels in the guide are not rated because their star classification was not confirmed at the time of going to press. Check theAA.com for current information and ratings.

AA Rosette Awards

Out of the many thousands of restaurants in the UK, the AA identifies some 2,000 as the best. The following is an outline of what to expect from restaurants with AA Rosette Awards. For a more detailed explanation of Rosette criteria please see theAA.com

◉ Excellent local restaurants serving food prepared with care, understanding and skill, using good quality ingredients.

◉◉ The best local restaurants, which aim for and achieve higher standards, better consistency and where a greater precision is apparent in the cooking. There will be obvious attention to the selection of quality ingredients.

◉◉◉ Outstanding restaurants that demand recognition well beyond their local area.

◉◉◉◉ Amongst the very best restaurants in the British Isles, where the cooking demands national recognition.

◉◉◉◉◉ The finest restaurants in the British Isles, where the cooking stands comparison with the best in the world.

Useful Information

If you're unsure about any of the facilities offered, always check with the establishment before you visit or book accommodation.

Hints on booking your stay

It's always worth booking as early as possible, particularly for the peak holiday period from the beginning of June to the end of September. Bear in mind that Easter and other public holidays may be busy too, and in some parts of Scotland, the ski season is a peak holiday period.

Some hotels will ask for a deposit or full payment in advance, especially for one-night bookings. And some hotels charge half-board (bed, breakfast and dinner) whether you require the meals or not, while others may only accept full-board bookings. Not all hotels will accept advance bookings for bed and breakfast, overnight or short stays. Some will not take reservations from mid week.

Once a booking is confirmed, let the hotel know at once if you are unable to keep your reservation. If the hotel cannot re-let your room you may be liable to pay about two-thirds of the room price (a deposit will count towards this payment). In Britain a legally binding contract is made when you accept an offer of accommodation, either in writing or by telephone, and illness is not accepted as a release from this contract. You are advised to take out insurance against possible cancellation, for example AA Single Trip Insurance. Visit theAA.com or call 0845 092 0606 for details.

Booking online

Booking a place to stay can be a very time-consuming process, but you can search quickly and easily online for a place that best suits your needs. Simply visit our website (www.theAA.com/travel) to search for a hotel, then click on Book online on the hotel's own page to check availability.

Prices

The AA encourages the use of the Hotel Industry Voluntary Code of Booking Practice, which aims to ensure that guests know how much they will have to pay and what services and facilities are included, before entering a financially binding agreement. If the price has not previously been confirmed in writing, guests should be given a card stipulating the total obligatory charge when they register at reception.

The Tourism (Sleeping Accommodation Price Display) Order of 1977 compels hotels, travel accommodation, guest houses, farmhouses, inns and self-catering accommodation with four or more letting bedrooms, to display in entrance halls the minimum and maximum price for one or two persons, but they may vary without warning.

Facilities for disabled guests

The final stage (Part III) of the Disability Discrimination Act (access to Goods and Services) came into force in October 2004. This means that service providers may have to make permanent adjustments to their premises. For further information, see the government website www.disability.gov.uk

Please note: AA inspectors are not accredited to make inspections under the National Accessibility Scheme. We indicate in the descriptions if an establishment has ground floor rooms; and if a hotel tells us that they have disabled facilities this is also included in the text.

The establishments in this guide should all be aware of their responsibilities under the Act. We recommend that you always telephone in advance to ensure that the establishment you have chosen has appropriate facilities.

Other useful websites to visit include:
www.holidaycare.org.uk
www.dptac.gov.uk/door-to-door

Licensing Laws

Licensing laws differ in England, Wales, Scotland, the Republic of Ireland, the Isle of Man, the Isles of Scilly and the Channel Islands. Public houses are generally open from mid morning to early afternoon, and from about 6 or 7pm until 11pm, although closing times may be earlier or later and some pubs are open all afternoon. Unless otherwise stated, establishments listed are licensed. Hotel residents can obtain alcoholic drinks at all times, if the licensee is prepared to serve them. Non-residents eating at the hotel restaurant can have drinks with meals. Children under 14 may be excluded from bars where no food is served. Those under 18 may not purchase or consume alcoholic drinks. Club license means that drinks are served to club members only. Forty-eight hours must lapse between joining and ordering.

Fire Safety

The Fire Precautions Act does not apply to the Channel Islands, Republic of Ireland, or the Isle of Man, which have their own rules. As far as we are aware, all hotels listed have applied for and not been refused a fire certificate.

Bank and Public Holidays 2010

New Year's Day	1st January
New Year's Holiday (Scotland)	4th January
Good Friday	2nd April
Easter Monday	5th April
May Day Bank Holiday	3rd May
Spring Bank Holiday	31st May
August Holiday (Scotland)	2nd August
Late Summer Holiday	30th August
St Andrew's Day (Scotland)	30th November
Christmas Day	25th December
Boxing Day	26th December

theAA.com

- Go to theAA.com to find more AA listed guest houses, hotels, pubs and restaurants – There are around 12,000 establishments on the site.

- Route Planner on the home page leads to the AA's famous route planner

- Simply enter your postcode and the establishment postcode given in this guide and click 'Get Route'. Check your details and then click 'Get Route' again and you will have a detailed route plan to take you from door-to-door.

- Use the Travel section to search for Hotels & B&Bs or Restaurants & Pubs by location or establishment name. Scroll down the list of finds for the interactive map and local routes.

The QUEST to be BEST

What makes a truly great hotel? Do you need to have an amazing location, a cool design, the best facilities, the most luxurious rooms and a gourmet restaurant to become one of the finest hotels in the land? Or is there more to it than that? By Fiona Griffiths

Simon Rhatigan should know – his hotel, The Feversham Arms in Helmsley, North Yorkshire, was named AA Hotel of The Year 2009/2010.

Indeed, he has spent millions over the last five years on doing the place up – adding the luxurious Verbena Spa, knocking rooms together to form suites, building a new kitchen and bringing in a talented chef – but, he says, facilities and aesthetics are only part of the picture.

"There was a time when if you were really good at food or you had great facilities you would get customers through the door, but the customer satisfaction threshold is much higher now, and you have to be good at everything," says Rhatigan.

"What's defining the industry more and more is service, atmosphere, and individualisation of customers.

"For a guest it's all about the feeling that the staff know you and will do things for you in the way that you like. That's what gives you a sense of connection with a hotel – a sense that it's a place for you."

'AA Hotel of the Year' The Feversham Arms and owner Simon Rhatigan

The Best Western Castle Green Hotel in Kendal and managing director Tim Rumney

Tim Rumney, managing director at The Best Western Castle Green Hotel in Kendal, Cumbria, would doubtless agree with that.

He's adamant that it's the way the staff interact with guests that makes the real difference in any hotel.

"What we try and do here is employ people who have a personality and aren't afraid to show the customer what excites them about working in a hotel," says Rumney.

"We endeavour to give our staff the authority to make decisions within their job role, and I think that ability to respond quickly to customers' needs makes the difference between a hotel that delivers things that are fairly functional and run-of-the-mill, and a hotel that can deliver exceptional service."

He gives the example of a conference guest who had arrived for a two-day stay and, having packed in a hurry, had forgotten to bring any underwear.

The guest happened to mention this – and his need to go to the shops to buy boxer shorts – to a member of the hotel's conference team.

"So while he was in the conference she went out and bought a pack of boxer shorts, and when he came out for a coffee she gave them to him,"

explains Rumney.

"He thought it was absolutely fantastic. In some hotels she'd have needed to get a purchase order and permission to leave the building to do that."

He adds: "At the end of the day, the product is very important – the quality of the rooms and bathrooms – but it's what we can add to the experience by being flexible and pre-empting the guests' requirements that makes a difference to the way they perceive their stay."

Andrew Stembridge, managing director at the Chewton Glen in New Milton, Hampshire, has a similar tale about a member of his housekeeping team who went out of her way to help some guests who were lost and couldn't find the hotel's spa.

"After their stay they wrote to tell me that they travel all over the world, staying in top hotels, and they had high expectations of Chewton Glen. Everything met their expectations but the one thing that made their stay was when they were wandering, lost, in the corridors and bumped into a room attendant, who put down her pile of towels and literally walked them all the way to the spa.

"It doesn't sound like anything much, but if you're a guest in a hotel – whether you're there for three hours or three days – someone should make your stay special," says Stembridge.

He adds: "I'm a great believer in good, old-fashioned hospitality and in creating a culture where all the staff are being hospitable.

"So room attendants aren't thinking, 'our job

is just to clean rooms', and chefs aren't thinking their job is just to cook what's on the menu. If a guest comes into your restaurant and just wants an omelette, why can't they have an omelette?"

Henrik Muehle, managing director of the St James's Hotel and Club in London, says a great hotel needs a great host.

"I believe in today's times a general manager, or managing director, should be a host, not stuck in an office," he says.

"If you go into any of the great hotels, with

It's about "good, old-fashioned hospitality" – Andrew Stembridge at The Chewton Glen

fantastic service, you see the general manager around – in the restaurant, in the bar, at the reception, on the door – actually communicating with the client. If you do that, people will come back because of the host and because they feel they're being looked after, not because it's a fantastic rate."

Claire Macdonald, who runs Kinloch Lodge on the Isle of Skye with her family, says "hospitality and warmth" are fundamental to any successful hotel.

"You could have

The perfect host – Henrik Muehle managing director of the St James's Hotel and Club

15

The fire is warm and so is the welcome at Claire Macdonald's Kinloch Lodge

the most beautifully done up establishment, with superb food, but it counts for nothing if there isn't a real warmth of both the welcome and care during your visit. It sounds so basic but it's often so lacking in Britain," she says.

"I feel one thing that's very important, although it sounds so little, is fresh flowers – not just one arrangement but lots dotted about. In a private home if people are coming to visit we put fresh flowers out, and it should be the same in a hotel."

She adds: "I also believe that breakfast is as important as dinner. People tend to home in on dinner and forget about breakfast, but gosh, when you're away one of the treats of being away is breakfast."

For Paul Milsom, owner of Milsoms Kesgrave Hall near Ipswich, Suffolk, and Maison Talbooth and Milsoms in Dedham, Essex, it takes many ingredients to elevate a hotel from good to great – and those ingredients have multiplied over the last 20 years.

"All great hotels need a superb location, a special building, a strong food and beverage offering, and large, spacious bedrooms. Increasingly important are additional facilities like spas, and you can see the importance of interior design now which wasn't the case 20 years ago," he says.

"However, it's the little touches – the attention to detail – that are often the things that really 'make' customer stays, and those things tend to happen because of the passion and drive of the people running the hotel."

Paul Milsom and one of the stylish bedrooms at Milsoms Kesgrave Hall

ENGLAND

Embleton Bay, Northumberland, with Dunstanburgh Castle beyond

BEDFORDSHIRE

The Rose Garden at Luton Hoo

Luton Hoo Hotel, Golf and Spa

★★★★★ 87%  HOTEL

Address: The Mansion House, LUTON, LU1 3TQ
Tel: 01582 734437
Fax: 01582 485438
Email: reservations@lutonhoo.com
Website: www.lutonhoo.com
Map ref: 3, TL02
Directions: M1 junct 10A, 3rd exit to A1081 towards Harpenden/St Albans. Hotel less than a mile on left
Rooms: 228 (65 GF) (50 fmly) D £220-£850 (incl. bkfst) **Facilities:** Wi-fi Ⓣ Tennis Spa Gym Golf
Parking: 263 **Notes:** ⊁ on request

The Grade I listed mansion house at Luton Hoo has played host to royalty and dignitaries over the centuries. Painstakingly restored to its former glory, the property stands proudly within magnificent grounds. Boasting over 1,000 acres of parklands designed by the celebrated landscape architect Capability Brown, the estate comprises formal gardens, woodland trails, a 50-acre lake, all-weather and Victorian lawn tennis courts, as well as an 18-hole, par 73 golf course. The spa, using Luton Hoo's own organic product range, provides relaxation and calm for all guests. The opulent bedrooms and suites are all beautifully furnished, have individual character and come well equipped; the suites in the mansion are particularly impressive. Exquisite fine dining is offered in the Wernher Restaurant, with rich furnishings and tapestries setting the mood, while the Adam's Brasserie provides a less formal dining option.

At the foot of the estate, on the banks of the river Lea, the Warren Weir Suite offers an exclusive use venue for meetings, events and weddings. Ideally situated, the hotel is just 10 minutes' drive from London Luton Airport and has excellent links to the M1 and M25.

Recommended in the area

Whipsnade Wild Animal Park and Tree Cathedral; Berkhamsted Castle; Woburn Abbey

The Inn at Woburn

★★★ 81% ◉◉ HOTEL

Address: George Street, WOBURN, Milton Keynes,
MK17 9PX
Tel: 01525 290441
Fax: 01525 290432
Email: inn@woburn.co.uk
Website: www.woburn.co.uk/inn
Map ref: 3, SP93
Directions: M1 junct 13, left to Woburn, at Woburn
left at T-junct, hotel in village
Rooms: 57 (21 GF) (4 fmly) S £105-£145 D £135-£205 Parking: 80

Occupying centre stage in what has been described as "a Georgian town of village proportions", this former coaching inn is part of the estate belonging to the Duke of Bedford, whose home, Woburn Abbey, has been the family seat for nearly 400 years. The village is noted for its fine architecture, antique and gift shops, tea rooms, restaurants and the parkland that surrounds it. Rooms, from singles to executive king, have satellite TV, radio and direct-dial telephone, trouser press and hot-drinks maker. Across the courtyard are seven cottages, five with their own individual sitting room. Olivier's is the hotel's two AA Rosette-awarded restaurant, where contemporary English and Continental cuisine is offered, typified by carpaccio of Woburn venison with roasted beetroot and basil dressing; and daily specials, all of which make extensive use of local produce. Brunch and snack menus, available according to the hour, offer sandwiches, salads, wraps and a 'dish of the day'. The informal Tavistock Bar is a convivial place to relax with a cask-conditioned ale or a fine wine. A concierge service will arrange everything from a restaurant booking to a birthday cake.

Recommended in the area

Woburn Safari Park; Woburn Abbey

Donnington Castle

The Bear Hotel

★★★ 80% ◉◉ HOTEL

Address: 41 Charnham Street, HUNGERFORD, RG17 0EL
Tel: 01488 682512
Fax: 01488 684357
Email: info@thebearhotelhungerford.co.uk
Website: www.thebearhotelhungerford.co.uk
Map ref: 3, SU36
Directions: M4 junct 14, A338 to Hungerford for 3m, left at T-junct onto A4, hotel on left
Rooms: 39 (24 GF) (2 fmly) **S** £82.50-£150 **D** £92.50-£185 **Facilities:** Wi-fi **Parking:** 68

Standing since the 13th century alongside the old London to Bath coaching route (known more prosaically today as the A4), this ancient inn was once owned by Henry VIII, and visited by the famously peripatetic Elizabeth I. We can only guess at the level of comfort in the rooms back then, although we can say with certainty that guests of yesteryear would have been flabbergasted by today's beds with Egyptian cotton sheets, refreshing showers, custom-designed furniture, flat-screen TVs with 12 channels and movies on demand, plus broadband and Wi-fi. There are several places to eat and drink, starting with the Brasserie, where the regularly changing menu might offer roast monkfish with braised faggots and Parma ham, and slow-cooked pork belly, parsley mash, caramelised apple sauce, crackling and red wine sauce. Then there's the Riverside Terrace, overlooking the River Dunn, a contemporary new bar, and finally the snug for a cappuccino while you read the papers. Bear Island makes an ideal venue for a barbecue or just lying in the sun, while business facilities are available in Bear Island House and the Riverside Suite.

Recommended in the area

Newbury Racecourse; Highclere Castle; Kennet & Avon Canal; Lambourne Downs and Avebury Stones

Donnington Valley Hotel & Spa

★★★★ 83% ◉◉ HOTEL

Address: Old Oxford Road, Donnington, NEWBURY,
RG14 3AG
Tel: 01635 551199
Fax: 01635 551123
Email: general@donningtonvalley.co.uk
Website: www.donningtonvalley.co.uk
Map ref: 3, SU46
Directions: M4 junct 13, take A34 signed Newbury.
Take exit signed Donnington/Services, at rdbt
take 2nd exit signed Donnington. Left at next rdbt. Hotel 2m on right **Rooms:** 111 (36 GF) (3 fmly)
Facilities: Wi-fi ☺ Spa Gym Sauna Golf **Parking:** 150 **Notes:** ⊗ in bedrooms

The AA's Hotel of the Year (England) 2007–2008 for consistently high standards of hospitality and service, this fine country hotel has recently had a £14-million redevelopment. Set in rolling Berkshire countryside, it boasts its own 18-hole golf course and a sumptuous state-of-the-art spa. The bedrooms are in elegant contemporary style with luxury linens, marble bathrooms and indulgent little extras.

Recommended in the area

Donnington Castle; The Watermill Theatre; Highclere Castle

The Vineyard at Stockcross

★★★★★ HOTEL

Address: Stockcross, NEWBURY, RG20 8JU
Tel: 01635 528770
Fax: 01635 528398
Email: general@the-vineyard.co.uk
Website: www.the-vineyard.co.uk
Map ref: 3, SU46
Directions: from M4 take A34 towards Newbury, exit
at 3rd junct for Speen. Right at rdbt then right again
at 2nd rdbt.

Rooms: 49 (15 GF) **Facilities:** Wi-fi ☺ Spa Gym Sauna **Parking:** 100 **Notes:** ⊗ in bedrooms

Owned by Sir Peter Michael, who also owns the Peter Michael Winery in California, this hotel offers the ultimate in indulgence, from the luxurious bedrooms and suites to the gourmet dining experience. Renowned chef Daniel Galmiche recently joined The Vineyard, and at the time of going to press the restaurant's Rosette award had not been confirmed. Naturally, the wine list is superb, offering a choice of over 2,000 international wines, including Peter Michael wines, of course.

Recommended in the area

Highclere Castle; The Watermill Theatre; Newbury Racecourse

Oakley Court Hotel

★★★★ 79% ◉ HOTEL

Address: Windsor Road, Water Oakley, WINDSOR,
SL4 5UR
Tel: 01753 609988 & 609900
Fax: 01628 637011
Email: reservations@oakleycourt.com
Website: www.principal-hayley.com
Map ref: 3, SU97
Directions: M4 junct 6, A355, then A332 towards
Windsor, right onto A308 towards Maidenhead. Pass
racecourse, hotel 2.5m on right
Rooms: 118 (28 GF) (5 fmly)
Facilities: Wi-fi ⓣ Tennis Spa Gym **Parking:** 120 **Notes:** ⊗ in bedrooms

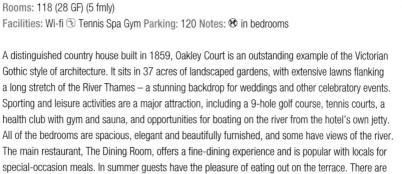

A distinguished country house built in 1859, Oakley Court is an outstanding example of the Victorian
Gothic style of architecture. It sits in 37 acres of landscaped gardens, with extensive lawns flanking
a long stretch of the River Thames – a stunning backdrop for weddings and other celebratory events.
Sporting and leisure activities are a major attraction, including a 9-hole golf course, tennis courts, a
health club with gym and sauna, and opportunities for boating on the river from the hotel's own jetty.
All of the bedrooms are spacious, elegant and beautifully furnished, and some have views of the river.
The main restaurant, The Dining Room, offers a fine-dining experience and is popular with locals for
special-occasion meals. In summer guests have the pleasure of eating out on the terrace. There are
also conference facilities for up to 500 delegates, with the option of private dining. In addition, the hotel
has a choice of sumptuous lounges in which to relax. The service is efficient, friendly and welcoming,
helping to make any stay here a truly memorable one.

Recommended in the area

Legoland; Windsor Castle; Ascot Racecourse

BUCKINGHAMSHIRE

John Milton's 17th century cottage and gardens in Chalfont St Giles

Swans on the River Thames at Marlow

Crowne Plaza Marlow

★★★★ 80% HOTEL

Address: Field House Lane, MARLOW, SL7 1GJ
Tel: 0870 444 8940 & 01628 496800
Fax: 0870 444 8950
Email: enquiries@crowneplazamarlow.co.uk
Website: www.crowneplaza.co.uk
Map ref: 3, SU88
Directions: A404 exit to Marlow, left at mini rdbt, left into Field House Lane
Rooms: 168 (56 GF) (47 fmly) **S** £70-£250
D £70-£250 **Facilities:** STV Wi-fi ⓧ Spa Gym Sauna Steam Room
Parking: 300 **Notes:** ⊗ in bedrooms

Crowne Plaza Marlow lies in the heart of the Thames Valley countryside, yet is perfectly positioned for easy access to the M40, M4 and M25. The en suite bedrooms are light, contemporary and spacious. There are excellent facilities for leisure and business travellers alike including Quad Club with 80-metre pool, technogym, dance studio and beauty. Guests can dine in the Glaze Restaurant, or unwind in the Agua Bar.
Recommended in the area
Windsor Castle; Henley-on-Thames; Adams Park

Danesfield House Hotel & Spa

★★★★ 85% ◉◉◉◉ HOTEL

Address: Henley Road, MARLOW-ON-THAMES,
SL7 2EY
Tel: 01628 891010
Fax: 01628 890408
Email: reservations@danesfieldhouse.co.uk
Website: www.danesfieldhouse.co.uk
Map ref: 3, SU88 **Directions:** (2m from Marlow on
A4155 towards Henley) **Rooms:** 84 (27 GF) (3 fmly)
S £135-£330 **D** £135-£345 (incl. bkfst)
Facilities: STV Wi-fi ⓣ Tennis Spa Gym Sauna Steam Room **Parking:** 100 **Notes:** ⊗ in bedrooms

This magnificent mansion is set within 65 acres of landscaped gardens overlooking the River Thames
and beyond towards the Chiltern Hills. The third building since 1664 to have occupied this site, the
current house and gardens were designed and built at the end of the 19th century. Today, visitors
can begin their stay by taking afternoon tea on the south-facing terrace or within the impressive
Grand Hall, before retiring to one of the traditionally furnished en suite bedrooms, where comfort is
of the essence. All of the rooms come well equipped with amenities such as satellite TV and in-room
movies, private fridge, bathrobes and Molton Brown toiletries. A valet service is also available. Further
rest and relaxation can be found at Danesfield Spa, reached by a connecting bridge from the hotel.
Specially commissioned artworks create the perfect backdrop, and there's a 20-metre ozone-cleansed
pool, sauna, steam room and spa bath, and treatments from ESPA and CARITA. The award-winning
restaurant, Adam Simmonds at Danesfield House, offers superb, imaginative fine dining and an
extensive and far-ranging wine list, while those seeking a more informal atmosphere can head for the
Orangery Brasserie.

Recommended in the area

Windsor Castle; Marlow and Henley boutique shopping; river cruises; clay pigeon shooting

Corpus Christi College, Cambridge University

Arundel House Hotel

★★★ 81% HOTEL

Address: Chesterton Road, CAMBRIDGE, CB4 3AN
Tel: 01223 367701
Fax: 01223 367721
Email: info@arundelhousehotels.co.uk
Website: www.arundelhousehotels.co.uk
Map ref: 3, TL45
Directions: City centre on A1303
Rooms: 103 (14 GF) (7 fmly) **S** £75-£125 **D** £95-£150 (incl. bkfst) **Facilities:** Wi-fi **Parking:** 70 **Notes:** ⊗ in bedrooms

By definition, a fine location in the city of Cambridge would surely be one that overlooks the River Cam and open parkland. The Arundel House Hotel does just that. This privately owned hotel, once a row of very fine Victorian townhouses, is only a short walk from the historic centre and its shops, restaurants and pubs. All bedrooms are en suite, with either a bath, shower, or both. They also have tea and coffee making facilities, TV, radio, direct dial telephone, Wi-fi and room safes. Relax in a comfortable armchair in the bar, then move into the adjacent restaurant, decorated in refreshing spring colours of yellow, orange and green, with generous upholstered chairs, crisp white and yellow linen and beautiful oak dressers and bookcases. A wide range of imaginative dishes features on the fixed price, à la carte, vegetarian and children's menus, all freshly prepared in the hotel's scrupulously clean, award-winning kitchens. Another time, try the all-day Conservatory Brasserie, which offers main meals, snacks and cream teas. The charming garden outside its doors is surprisingly tranquil, despite the proximity of the city centre. While retaining its original façade, the Coach House behind the main building has been completely rebuilt to provide three conference rooms and 22 bedrooms.

Recommended in the area

Kings College, Cambridge; Imperial War Museum, Duxford; Angelsey Abbey (NT)

Bell Inn Hotel

★★★ 79% ◉ HOTEL

Address: Great North Road, STILTON, PE7 3RA
Tel: 01733 241066 & 242626
Fax: 01733 245173
Email: reception@thebellstilton.co.uk
Website: www.thebellstilton.co.uk
Map ref: 3, TL18
Directions: A1(M) junct 16, follow Stilton signs. Hotel in village centre
Rooms: 22 (3 GF) (1 fmly) **S** £73.50-£110.50 **D** £100.50-£130.50 (incl. bkfst) **Facilities:** Wi-fi **Parking:** 30 **Notes:** ⊗ in bedrooms

Just off the Great North Road, this lovely 17th-century coaching inn has served the famous and infamous alike – film star Clark Gable, and highwayman Dick Turpin, for example. The magnificent inn sign is an exact replica of the original and, together with its wrought-iron bracket, weighs an astonishing two and three-quarter tons. Curiously, Stilton cheese has never been made in the village; in coaching days it was extensively sold in the local market, and the name simply stuck. The Bell Inn's recently refurbished en suite bedrooms, including two with four-posters and several with jacuzzis, are arranged around the old courtyard. For dining, guests have a choice – the beamed Galleried Restaurant, with its AA Rosette-awarded menu of modern British cuisine; the softly lit Bistro, offering internationally influenced dishes; and the stone-floored Village Bar, serving bar meals and snacks. Browse over the menus in a comfortable leather armchair in the first-floor Dick Turpin's room, so named because legend says he escaped to his horse, Black Bess, from the window. In favourable weather eat, or just have a drink, in the courtyard.

Recommended in the area

Peterborough Cathedral; Imperial War Museum, Duxford; Flag Fen

Ely Cathedral

Crown Lodge Hotel

★★★ 82% ⊛ HOTEL

Address: Downham Road, Outwell, WISBECH,
PE14 8SE
Tel: 01945 773391 & 772206
Fax: 01945 772668
Email: office@thecrownlodgehotel.co.uk
Website: www.thecrownlodgehotel.co.uk
Map ref: 3, TF40
Directions: On A1122/A1101 approx 5m
from Wisbech

Rooms: 10 (10 GF) (1 fmly) **S** £70-£80 **D** £90-£100 (incl. bkfst) **Facilities:** Wi-fi **Parking:** 57

Off the beaten track, yet easily found in the Fenland village of Outwell, Crown Lodge Hotel overlooks the banks of Well Creek, which meanders through Outwell and Upwell. This delightful rural setting belies the contemporary style and state-of-the-art facilities awaiting you. Bedrooms are smart, well-equipped and comfortable. There's a brasserie-style restaurant, an open-plan bar and a comfortable lounge where you can relax while choosing your freshly prepared meal, sourced largely from local suppliers.
Recommended in the area

Ely Cathedral; Welney Wildfowl and Wetlands Trust; Wicken Fen National Nature Reserve

CHESHIRE

View of the Forest of Bowland at Whitewell, tributary of the River Hodder

Cheshire Plain

Alderley Edge Hotel

★★★ 85% ◉◉◉ HOTEL

Address: Macclesfield Road, ALDERLEY EDGE, SK9 7BJ
Tel: 01625 583033
Fax: 01625 586343
Email: sales@alderleyedgehotel.com
Website: www.alderleyedgehotel.com
Map ref: 6, SJ87 **Directions:** Off A34 in Alderley Edge onto B5087 towards Macclesfield. Hotel 200yds on right **Rooms:** 50 (6 GF) **S** £72.50-£130 **D** £110-£145 **Facilities:** STV Wi-fi **Parking:** 90 **Notes:** ⊗ in bedrooms

Built of local sandstone in 1850 by a Manchester cotton king, this hotel in charming grounds has grand views over the Cheshire Plain. Room goodies include bowls of fruit, bathrobes, trouser press and tea-and-coffee-making facilities. During the daytime light dishes are served in the comfortable lounge bar or on the garden terrace, while dinner is served in The Alderley Restaurant – a light and airy conservatory with splendid panoramic views.

Recommended in the area

Jodrell Bank; Quarry Bank Mill; Tatton Park

Mill Hotel & Spa Destination

★★★ 79% HOTEL

Address: Milton Street, CHESTER, CH1 3NF
Tel: 01244 350035
Fax: 01244 345635
Email: reservations@millhotel.com
Website: www.millhotel.com
Map ref: SJ46
Directions: M53 junct 12, onto A56, left at 2nd rdbt (A5268), then 1st left, 2nd left

Rooms: 128 (57 fmly) S £73-£93 D £91-£112 (incl. bkfst) Facilities: STV Wi-fi ⊗ Spa Gym Sauna Parking: 120 Notes: ⊗ in bedrooms

This popular hotel occupies a former corn mill beside the Shropshire Union Canal. The building dates back to 1830, and many original features remain in its present incarnation as an award-winning hotel. The 129 bedrooms come in five different types, and are spread across two wings – linked by a glass-walled bridge – on either side of the canal. The hotel's leisure facilities are extensive and include a health club with 18m pool, sauna, steam room, spa, gym with Technogym equipment and a range of fitness classes. The award-winning Beauty Spa offers a selection of Pevonia treatments, beauty packages and pamper breaks, plus a hair salon. The Mill Hotel & Spa has no less than five dining options, including the Canaletto Restaurant with its special 'dine & dance' evenings on Fridays and Saturdays, and the Flambé Steak Restaurant, serving steaks cooked at the table. Moored alongside the Canaletto Restaurant is the L'eau-t Cuisine restaurant cruiser; climb onboard for a fascinating journey along the Shropshire Union Canal, while enjoying lunch, afternoon tea or dinner. There are regular special gourmet cruises and casino nights. The Peppermill Trattoria and the Real Ale Bar & Deli Counter overlook the canal and offer more informal dining.

Recommended in the area

Chester Cathedral; Chester Zoo; Roman Walking Tours of Chester

CORNWALL

Bedruthan Steps

Falcon Hotel

★★★ 79% HOTEL

Address: Breakwater Road, BUDE, EX23 8SD
Tel: 01288 352005
Fax: 01288 356359
Email: reception@falconhotel.com
Website: www.falconhotel.com
Map ref: 1, SS20
Directions: Off A39 into Bude, follow road to
Widemouth Bay. Hotel on right over canal bridge
Rooms: 29 (7 fmly) Facilities: STV Wi-fi
Parking: 40 Notes: ⊗ in bedrooms

This hotel has been welcoming guests for more than 200 years. The bedrooms and en suite bathrooms
are all furnished and decorated to a very high standard. The air-conditioned restaurant and the
Coachman's Bar both provide modern English cuisine with international twists, fully complemented
by an extensive range of beers and wines. The Beer Terrace has wonderful views over the canal and
harbour and the hotel's walled gardens are a delight. Private functions can be held in the Acland Suite.
Recommended in the area
Clovelly; Tintagel; Boscastle

Falmouth Hotel

★★★ 75% ⊛ HOTEL

Address: Castle Beach, FALMOUTH, TR11 4NZ
Tel: 01326 312671
Fax: 01326 319533
Email: reservations@falmouthhotel.com
Website: www.falmouthhotel.com
Map ref: 1, SW83
Directions: A30 to Truro then A390 to Falmouth.
Hotel on seafront near Pendennis Castle
Rooms: 69 (17 fmly) S £60–£70 D £98–£240
(incl. bkfst) Facilities: ⊗ Spa Gym STV Wi-fi Parking: 120

Falmouth's first Victorian-era hotel has five acres of beautiful gardens, and is opposite a sandy beach.
Many of its comfortable bedrooms, some with balconies, look across Falmouth Bay to Pendennis Point,
while public areas are roomy and elegant. The Falmouth offers a choice of dining experiences, from
fine-dining showcasing the full talents of the chef and his team in the grand Trelawney Restaurant, to
more simple meals in the bar/lounge and on the outdoor terrrace.
Recommended in the area
Pendennis Castle; National Maritime Museum of Cornwall; Gweek Seal Sanctuary

Royal Duchy Hotel

★★★★ 79% ◉◉ HOTEL
Address: Cliff Road, FALMOUTH, TR11 4NX
Tel: 01326 313042
Fax: 01326 319420
Email: info@royalduchy.com
Website: www.royalduchy.com
Map ref: 1, SW83
Directions: On Cliff Rd, along Falmouth seafront
Rooms: 43 (1 GF) (6 fmly) S £88-£122
D £160-£304 (incl. bkfst) Facilities: Wi-fi ⊗ Sauna
Parking: 50 Notes: ⊗ in bedrooms

It could so easily be the Med. Stretching away to the horizon is an azure bay, to the left a castle stands high on a headland, above your head palm fronds quiver in the gentle breeze, while on the umbrella-shaded table your chilled cocktails await. Actually, this is the Gulf Stream-warmed English Channel on Cornwall's southern coast, and the view is that from the hotel terrace. A short stroll away are the beaches, alleyways and quaint streets of Falmouth, a town that seems content to run at a gentler pace than most, and where you can lose yourself in centuries of maritime history. With so much to see, how useful it is to have binoculars provided in the bedrooms, along with bathrobes, slippers, hairdryer, TV, radio, telephone, and tea and coffee tray. In the Terrace Restaurant a talented team of chefs brings diners an appealing variety of AA Rosette-awarded, classical signature dishes, created from top Cornish produce. And from the bar it's but a few steps to the sun lounge where light snacks, lunches and cream teas are served.

Recommended in the area

Lizard Peninsula; Trelissick Garden; St Michael's Mount

The Old Quay House Hotel

★★ ●● HOTEL

Address: 28 Fore Street, FOWEY, PL23 1AQ
Tel: 01726 833302
Fax: 01726 833668
Email: info@theoldquayhouse.com
Website: www.theoldquayhouse.com
Map ref: 1, SX15
Directions: M5 junct 31 onto A30 to Bodmin.
Then A389 through town, then B3269 to Fowey
Rooms: 11 S £130-£300 D £170-£300 (incl. bkfst)
Facilities: STV Wi-fi Notes: ⊗ in bedrooms ⊮ under 12 yrs

Occupying a perfect waterfront location, this boutique hotel's interior combines traditional architecture and 21st–century styling with the sort of flair that one expects in, say, London. How refreshing then to find here an eclectic assembly of 'island-styled' and classic European furnishings and ornaments characterising the bedrooms, seven of which survey the Fowey estuary through floor-to-ceiling glass doors, and bathrooms that feature high quality fittings and luxury amenities. The theme continues downstairs where, from the entrance, your eyes are drawn through to 'Q', the restaurant, and the glittering water beyond. Q's two AA Rosettes and clutch of gushing media reviews are testament to the creativity of head chef Ben Bass, whose modern European menus, complemented by daily specials, and a carefully selected wine list, have made it one of 'the' places to eat in these parts. The Old Quay has a full wedding and civil ceremony licence and is available for receptions and functions. As the hotel does not have parking facilities, summer season guests should drop off their bags and collect a permit for the Harbour Commissioner's car park about 800 yards further on. Winter guests may use a long-term pay-and-display car park about 700 yards away.

Recommended in the area

The Eden Project; Lost Gardens of Heligan; Lanhydrock House (NT)

The Well House

★★ 85% ◉◉◉ HOTEL

Address: St Keyne, Liskeard, nr LOOE, PL14 4RN
Tel: 01579 342001
Fax: 01579 343891
Email: enquiries@wellhouse.co.uk
Website: www.wellhouse.co.uk
Map ref: 1, SX25
Directions: From Liskeard on A38 take B3254 to St Keyne (3m). At church fork left, hotel 0.5m down hill on left **Rooms:** 9 (2 GF) (1 fmly) **D** £155-£215 (incl. bkfst) **Facilities:** ↝ Tennis **Parking:** 30 **Notes:** ⊗ in bedrooms

This luxurious country house hotel sits in impressive grounds within easy reach of many of Cornwall's best attractions, not least its magnificent coastline. The Well House Hotel is privately owned, with an emphasis on providing a quiet and relaxing haven and the highest levels of comfort and care. Guests can have a drink in the intimate bar before enjoying a meal in the elegant restaurant, prepared with great skill by the kitchen team.

Recommended in the area

Eden Project; Coastal walks, moors and tors; Looe, Polperro and Fowey

Mount Haven Hotel

★★★ 79% ◉◉ HOTEL

Address: Turnpike Road, MARAZION, TR17 0DQ
Tel: 01736 710249
Fax: 01736 711658
Email: reception@mounthaven.co.uk
Website: www.mounthaven.co.uk
Map ref: 1, SW44 **Directions:** From A30 towards Penzance. At rdbt take exit for Helston onto A394. Next rdbt right into Marazion, hotel on left
Rooms: 18 (6 GF) (2 fmly) **S** £65-£90 **D** £90-£190 (incl. bkfst) **Facilities:** Wi-fi Spa **Parking:** 30 **Notes:** ⊗ in bedrooms

St Michael's Mount rises dramatically from the bay just a stone's throw from the terrace at this lovely boutique hotel. The Mount Haven's chic and contemporary design is a fusion of western comfort and eastern culture. Try the double deluxe or one of the four-poster rooms with balconies for a particularly romantic break, and don't miss dinner in the Mount Haven Restaurant. A team of dedicated holistic therapists are available to sort out any remnants of stress.

Recommended in the area

West Cornwall beaches; St Michael's Mount, Minack Theatre, coastal walks

Headland Hotel

★★★★ 77% ◉ HOTEL
Address: Fistral Beach, NEWQUAY, TR7 1EW
Tel: 01637 872211
Fax: 01637 872212
Email: office@headlandhotel.co.uk
Website: www.headlandhotel.co.uk
Map ref: 1, SW86
Directions: A30 onto A392 at Indian Queens, approaching
Newquay follow signs for Fistral Beach, hotel adjacent
Rooms: 96 (35 fmly) S £69-£132 D £79-£349 (incl. bkfst)
Facilities: STV Wi-fi ⓧ ↖ Tennis Sauna Parking: 400

Take the laid back beauty of the surfing paradise of Fistral
Beach, mix it with the splendour of the imposing Headland, and you have the perfect location. Once
inside, the range of public rooms include quiet sitting rooms and the impressive Ballroom and Front
Lounge with stunning views over the ocean. The bedrooms range from Courtyard to Best, all tastefully
furnished to a high standard of comfort. The Headland Brasserie is open for breakfast and dinner
daily, and also Sunday lunch, serving top quality local produce prepared imaginatively in elegant
surroundings; or try the Terrace Restaurant with its expansive views over Fistral Beach. Here you can
enjoy a delicious cappuccino with home-made cakes or a full meal including local lobster thermidor.
With a range of short breaks available, from Sheer Indulgence for a touch of romance and relaxation,
to Adrenaline Adventures and Storm Watching Breaks for a more active break, there is something for
most people throughout the year. On site, guests can enjoy a game of tennis, a round of pitch and putt,
a game of croquet or just relax beside the outdoor pool topping up the tan.

Recommended in the area

Eden Project; Lanhydrock (NT); Tate St Ives

Newquay

Hotel Penzance

★★★ 83% ◉◉ HOTEL

Address: Britons Hill, PENZANCE, TR18 3AE
Tel: 01736 363117
Fax: 01736 350970
Email: reception@hotelpenzance.com
Website: www.hotelpenzance.com
Map ref: 1, SW43
Directions: From A30 pass heliport on right, left at next rdbt for town centre. 3rd right onto Britons Hill. Hotel on right

Rooms: 25 (2 GF) **S** £80-£85 **D** £115-£185 (incl. bkfst) **Facilities:** Wi-fi ⌇ **Parking:** 12

Converted from two Edwardian merchants' houses in the 1920s, this boutique hotel stands in a Mediterranean-style garden perched high above the town's rooftops, overlooking the waterfront activity below. Many of the individually styled rooms enjoy sea views. In the restaurant, the seasonally changing menu takes full advantage of local produce in peak condition – fish from Newlyn, meats and dairy produce from nearby farms, plus some Cornish wines.

Recommended in the area

St Michael's Mount; Minack Theatre; Tate St Ives

Driftwood

★ ★ ★ ❀❀❀ HOTEL

Address: Rosevine, PORTSCATHO, TR2 5EW
Tel: 01872 580644
Fax: 01872 580801
Email: info@driftwoodhotel.co.uk
Website: www.driftwoodhotel.co.uk
Map ref: 1, SW83
Directions: A390 towards St Mawes. On A3078 turn left to
Rosevine at Trewithian
Rooms: 15 (1 GF) (3 fmly) **S** £140-£204 **D** £165-£240 (incl.
bkfst) **Facilities:** Wi-fi **Parking:** 30 **Notes:** ⊗ in bedrooms

In seven acres of cliffside gardens, with panoramic views of
Gerrans Bay, stands this peaceful and secluded hotel. Walk down a wooded path to your own little
cove and look out across the very waters that will provide your dinner lobster or crab. Head indoors to
find stylishly contemporary sitting rooms stocked with books, magazines and board games. There's
even a small games room for the children. Comfortable, uncluttered bedrooms are decorated in soft
shades reminiscent of the seashore. Ground floor rooms have their own decked terrace, while tucked
away, overlooking the sea, is a restored weatherboarded cabin with two bedrooms and a sitting room.
A large deck in the sheltered terraced garden is strewn with steamer chairs for taking in the unbroken
sea view. On warm evenings hurricane lamps are lit for pre-dinner drinks and after-dinner coffee. The
three AA Rosette awarded restaurant (from which, no surprise, you can again see the sea) serves fresh,
locally sourced food – and not just fish. Yes, there's John Dory or monkfish, for example, but the menu
will also feature dishes such as roasted Terras Farm duck breast, pastilla of duck leg, endives and
orange and port jus.

Recommended in the area

Falmouth Maritime Museum; Lost Gardens of Heligan; Tate Gallery St Ives

Rose-in-Vale Country House Hotel

★★★ 79%  COUNTRY HOUSE HOTEL

Address: Mithian, ST AGNES, TR5 0QD
Tel: 01872 552202
Fax: 01872 552700
Email: reception@rose-in-vale-hotel.co.uk
Website: www.rose-in-vale-hotel.co.uk
Map ref: 1, SW56 **Directions:** Take A30 S towards
Redruth. At Chiverton Cross at rdbt take B3277 signed St Agnes. In 500mtrs turn at tourist info sign for
Rose-in-Vale. Into Mithian, right at Miners Arms, down hill. Hotel on left
Rooms: 20 (5 GF) (2 fmly) **S** £75-£150 **D** £100-£275 (incl. bkfst)
Facilities: Wi-fi ⤢ **Parking:** 52 **Notes:** ⛔ under 12 yrs

The Rose in Vale is a lovely grade II listed building set in its own wooded valley on the north Cornish
coast near St Agnes. It has a very friendly and relaxed atmosphere, almost like staying in the home of
a good friend rather than a hotel. Although only five minutes from the A30, it has a wonderful feeling of
privacy and seclusion. More energetic guests can take advantage of The Rose in Vale's close proximity
to the coastal path and a number of golf courses. After a day out walking, golfing or exploring, the
hotel is a lovely place to return to, particularly for dinner in the light and airy Valley Restaurant. The
dinner menu changes daily and offers traditional British cuisine based on the very best seasonal and
local ingredients, including fish landed just a short distance away. The Rose in Vale has recently been
refurbished and boasts a range of different-sized and designed bedrooms with every modern comfort.
Some bedrooms come with the added luxuries of four-poster beds and Jacuzzi baths.

Recommended in the area

South West Coastal Path; Eden Project; National Maritime Museum

Carbis Bay Hotel

★★★ 78% ◉ HOTEL
Address: Carbis Bay, ST IVES, TR26 2NP
Tel: 01736 795311
Fax: 01736 797677
Email: carbisbayhotel@btconnect.com
Website: www.carbisbayhotel.co.uk
Map ref: 1, SW54
Directions: A3074, through Lelant. 1m, at Carbis Bay 30yds before lights turn right into Porthrepta Rd to sea & hotel
Rooms: 40 (16 fmly) **Facilities:** ⤳
Parking: 200 **Notes:** ⊗ in bedrooms

This family-run hotel sits on its own golden sandy beach in beautiful Carbis Bay. It was built in 1894 by the famous Cornish architect Sylvanus Trevail, and it retains much of its original character and charm, while offering everything the modern guest could wish for. There are 44 individually furnished rooms, including some with sea views and balconies, as well as some new luxury apartments and cottages tucked away in an idyllic wooded valley on the edge of the beach. For the ultimate seaside break, you can book yourself into one of the hotel's fabulous self-catering beach houses. The Sands is the hotel's fine-dining restaurant, open for breakfast, dinner and Sunday lunch, with stunning views across St Ives Bay. The Conservatory is open all day for morning coffee, lunches – including Sunday lunch – and afternoon tea. During the high season there are regular cabaret nights. If you're lucky enough to stay while the weather is fine, there's a pool and a sun terrace in the tranquil tropical garden. If the weather isn't so good, relax in one of the hotel's spacious lounges, sip a cocktail in the magnificent conservatory, or head to the basement games room for a spot of snooker.

Recommended in the area

Tate Gallery; St Michael's Mount; Mousehole

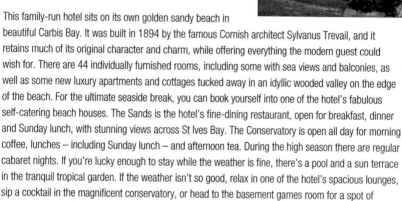

19th-century Truro Cathedral

Alverton Manor

★★★ 81% ◉◉ HOTEL
Address: Tregolls Road, TRURO, TR1 1ZQ
Tel: 01872 276633
Fax: 01872 222989
Email: reception@alvertonmanor.co.uk
Website: www.alvertonmanor.co.uk
Map ref: 1, SW75
Directions: From Carland Cross, take A39 to Truro
Rooms: 33 (3 GF) **Facilities:** Wi-fi **Parking:** 120

Quintessentially English, this grade II listed building has stood on a hillside in Truro since 1880. A convent for many years, it has since been converted into a country-house-style hotel within walking distance of Truro's amenities and ideally placed for exploring west Cornwall. Traditional values are key to everything at Alverton Manor, and this is particularly evident in the restaurant, where the cooking is classic British and the kitchen sources seasonal ingredients from local suppliers. The hotel even rears its own Devon Red cattle, which stars on the menu alongside local free-range chicken, lamb, pork, and plenty of vegetarian options.

Recommended in the area

Cathedral city of Truro; Eden Project; north and south Cornwall coast

The Nare Hotel

★★★★ 85% ◉ COUNTRY HOUSE HOTEL

Address: Carne Beach, VERYAN-IN-ROSELAND, TR2 5PF
Tel: 01872 501111
Fax: 01872 501856
Email: office@narehotel.co.uk
Website: www.narehotel.co.uk
Map ref: 1, SW93 **Directions:** From Tregony follow A3078 for approx 1.5m. Left at Veryan sign, through village towards sea & hotel
Rooms: 37 (7 GF) (7 fmly) S £135-£250 D £246-£460 (incl. bkfst & dinner)
Facilities: Wi-fi ⊗ ⤳ Tennis Spa Gym Sauna **Parking:** 80

Overlooking a superb beach, The Nare is the only four-red-star hotel in Cornwall. It has a delightful country-house ambience and is now in its third generation of family ownership. Those guests looking for total relaxation will certainly find it here, from the comfy sofas in the lounge to the spa treatments and hot tub overlooking the sea. More active types can enjoy a good range of leisure activities including tennis courts, croquet, billiards, two swimming pools, a gym and even a 22-foot yacht for charter. The owners have shied away from the trend for designer hotels, preferring to individually style their rooms in a more traditional but equally luxurious style. Most are spacious and many have a balcony or terrace with wonderful sea views. Suites have a separate lounge and one has a kitchen, too. All rooms enjoy the valet service, including 24-hour room service. For dinner there's a choice of two eating options – the more formal Dining Room and the casual Quarterdeck. Whichever you go for, expect to enjoy plenty of first-class Cornish ingredients, including locally reared beef, seafood from local fishermen, and lots of fresh seasonal vegetables and fruit. The Nare also boasts an extensive wine cellar.

Recommended in the area

Eden Project; Lost Gardens of Heligan; Caerhays Castle

CUMBRIA

Ashness Bridge and Skiddaw Mountain, Lake District National Park

Rothay Manor

★★★ 83% ◉ HOTEL

Address: Rothay Bridge, AMBLESIDE, LA22 0EH
Tel: 015394 33605
Fax: 015394 33607
Email: hotel@rothaymanor.co.uk
Website: www.rothaymanor.co.uk/aa
Map ref: 5, NY30
Directions: In Ambleside follow signs for Coniston (A593). Hotel 0.25m SW of Ambleside opposite rugby pitch
Rooms: 19 (3 GF) (7 fmly) S £95-£145 D £140-£230 (incl. bkfst)
Facilities: STV Wi-fi **Parking:** 45 **Notes:** ⊗ in bedrooms

This traditional Regency country house hotel was built in 1825 and lies in the heart of the Lake District, just a quarter of a mile from Lake Windermere, making it ideally situated for walking, cycling or exploring the local towns and villages. Set in its own landscaped gardens, it offers guests the perfect opportunity to relax and recharge their batteries. Owned and run by the Nixon family for over 40 years, it has a long-standing reputation for its relaxed, comfortable and friendly atmosphere, as well as its excellent food and wine. Bedrooms are all en suite and include a number of suites, family rooms and rooms with balconies, from which to enjoy fine views of the fells. For added privacy, two suites are located in a separate building close to the main hotel. All of the rooms are comfortably equipped and furnished to a very high standard, with TV and tea-and-coffee-making facilities supplied. Public areas include a choice of lounges, a spacious restaurant with an imaginative menu making much use of fresh, local produce, and conference facilities. Guests can also enjoy free use of the Low Wood leisure club, which has an indoor heated pool and is located 1.5 miles from the hotel.

Recommended in the area

Cruises on the Lakes; Hill Top (Beatrix Potter); Holker Hall and Gardens

The Pheasant

★★★ 83% ❀ HOTEL

Address: BASSENTHWAITE, CA13 9YE
Tel: 017687 76234
Fax: 017687 76002
Email: info@the-pheasant.co.uk
Website: www.the-pheasant.co.uk
Map ref: 5, NY23
Directions: Midway between Keswick &
Cockermouth, signed from A66
Rooms: 15 (2 GF) S £83-£88 D £156-£206 (incl.
bkfst) Facilities: Wi-fi Parking: 40 Notes: ⛔ under 12 yrs

A charming old coaching inn in well-tended gardens, at the unspoilt northern end of the Lake District, this is a good example of a traditional Cumbrian hostelry. Its history stretches back over 500 years to its origins as a farmhouse, then from 1778 an alehouse. One of its 19th-century regulars was the famous huntsman John ('With his hounds and his horn in the morning') Peel, who would often celebrate and recount his exploits in the tap room. Now the hotel bar, this mellow, oak-panelled room with exposed beams, wooden settles, polished parquet flooring and log fires remains more or less unchanged, although there's probably been quite a turnover in its great selection of malt whiskies. The individually decorated bedrooms have been sympathetically refurbished to a high standard with en suite bathrooms offering both bath and power shower, and all equipped with phone, tea tray and flat-screen TV. On the daily changing menu in the attractive beamed restaurant might be roast rack of Cumbrian lamb with shepherds pie and minted mash potato, or grilled fillet of sea bass with roast lobster cream sauce. Lighter lunches are available in the lounges or bar. Traditional Cumbrian afternoon tea means home-made scones with rum butter.

Recommended in the area

Rheged Discovery Centre; Muncaster Castle; Skiddaw

Farlam Hall Hotel

★ ★ ★ ❀ HOTEL

Address: BRAMPTON, CA8 2NG
Tel: 016977 46234
Fax: 016977 46683
Email: farlam@relaischateaux.com
Website: www.farlamhall.co.uk
Map ref: 6, NY56
Directions: On A689 (Brampton to Alston). Hotel 2m
on left (not in Farlam village)
Rooms: 12 (2 GF) S £155-£185 D £295-£350 (incl.
bkfst & dinner) Facilities: Wi-fi Parking: 35 Notes: 👶 under 5 yrs

This large, creeper-clad manor house is set in 12 acres of lovely grounds amid beautiful and wild Cumbrian countryside. Dating back to the 16th century, it is mostly a creation of the 1800s, when the Thompson family were in residence, and steam railway enthusiasts will revel in its connection with George Stephenson and his Rocket locomotive (its experimental track once ran through the grounds here). Today it offers warm hospitality from the family owners and 12 luxurious bedrooms, each with an ultra-modern bathroom. Two are ground-floor rooms, and another room is in the converted stables which is reached by an external stone staircase. After a day exploring the fells, there's nothing nicer than to relax in one of the two large drawing rooms, where open fires add to the ambience in cooler weather. The restaurant, also open to non-residents in the evenings, offers a high standard of modern cuisine based on the sound traditional skills of the team of chefs. Dinner is served at 8pm, with a small, daily-changing menu, and guests usually congregate for pre-dinner drinks and canapes in one of the drawing rooms. A smart style of dress is requested. Residents who are around during the day can also get a light lunch. No children under five years.

Recommended in the area

Northern Pennines Area of Outstanding Natural Beauty; Hadrian's Wall; Carlisle Castle and Cathedral

Borrowdale Gates Country House Hotel

★★★ 79% COUNTRY HOUSE HOTEL

Address: GRANGE-IN-BORROWDALE, Keswick, CA12 5UQ

Tel: 017687 77204

Fax: 017687 77195

Email: hotel@borrowdale-gates.com

Website: www.borrowdale-gates.com

Map ref: 5, NY21

Directions: From A66 follow B5289 for approx 4m. Turn right over bridge, hotel 0.25m beyond village

Rooms: 27 (10 GF) **S** £50-£60 **D** £100-£180 (incl. bkfst) **Facilities:** Wi-fi **Parking:** 29

Surrounded by first-class fell-walking country and set in two acres of peaceful, wooded grounds, the Borrowdale Gates Hotel is close to the shores of Derwentwater, with the many attractions of Keswick nearby. The Victorian building has been lovingly refurbished, blending modern comfort with homely charm. Every window is a picture frame for the beauty of the Borrowdale Valley. The dining room looks onto green pastures where Herdwick sheep graze, and across to the slopes of Castle Crag, High Spy, Grange Fell and distant Glaramara. It's a wonderful place to linger over dinner, before curling up with a brandy beside the log fire in the beamed lounge. Each of the bedrooms has fabulous views and comes complete with crisp cotton sheets, feather pillows (unless you prefer a different kind), fluffy white towels and a tray of morning tea and coffee. All are individually designed and some boast a decked balcony or French doors opening onto the gardens. Contemporary country-house cooking with a lightness of touch is the mainstay of the kitchen, with menus making the most of superb Lake District produce.

Recommended in the area

Keswick's Theatre by the Lake; Derwentwater cruises; Beatrix Potter Gallery; Wordsworth House

Autumn in the Lakes

Clare House

★ ⊕ HOTEL
Address: Park Road, GRANGE-OVER-SANDS,
LA11 7HQ
Tel: 015395 33026 & 34253
Fax: 015395 34310
Email: info@clarehousehotel.co.uk
Website: www.clarehousehotel.co.uk
Map ref: 5, SD47
Directions: Off A590 onto B5277, through Lindale into Grange, keep left, hotel 0.5m on left past Crown Hill & St Paul's Church **Rooms:** 18 (4 GF) **S** £84 **D** £168 (incl. bkfst & dinner)
Facilities: Wi-fi **Parking:** 18 **Notes:** ⊗ in bedrooms

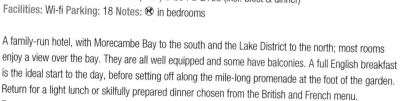

A family-run hotel, with Morecambe Bay to the south and the Lake District to the north; most rooms enjoy a view over the bay. They are all well equipped and some have balconies. A full English breakfast is the ideal start to the day, before setting off along the mile-long promenade at the foot of the garden. Return for a light lunch or skilfully prepared dinner chosen from the British and French menu.
Recommended in the area
Holker Hall; Windermere Steamboat Centre; Cumberland Pencil Museum

Rothay Garden Hotel

★★★★ 80% ◉◉ HOTEL

Address: Broadgate, GRASMERE, LA22 9RJ
Tel: 015394 35334
Fax: 015394 35723
Email: stay@rothaygarden.com
Website: www.rothaygarden.com
Map ref: 5, NY31 **Directions:** Off A591, opposite Swan Hotel, into Grasmere, 300yds on left
Rooms: 30 (8 GF) (3 fmly) S £100-£140 D £140-£300 (incl. dinner) **Facilities:** Wi-fi **Parking:** 38

The award-winning Rothay Garden hotel reopened in 2008 after a major redevelopment. Situated on the edge of picturesque Grasmere village, and nestling in two acres of riverside gardens surrounded by majestic fells, this privately-run hotel provides the comfort, quality and peace and quiet that so many visitors to the Lake District look for. There are 25 beautiful bedrooms, as well as five brand new loft suites. Relax in the hotel's chic lounge bar before dining in the elegant candlelit conservatory restaurant overlooking the gardens. Masterchef Andrew Burton serves a modern European menu which takes fine Lakeland produce as its starting point. Rothay Garden has been owned and operated by Chris Carss for nearly 20 years, and he and his dedicated team will do their utmost to make sure your stay is memorable for all the right reasons. Of course, the beauty of the Lake District is right on your doorstep here. Wordsworth's Grasmere really is the "jewel of the Lakes" and the hotel is ideally situated for visiting Ambleside, Windermere, Keswick and Kendal. Rothay Garden offers special short getaways and holidays all year, including seasonal weekend breaks, four-night midweek value breaks, traditional Christmas and New Year breaks, and a specialist food and wine programme during March and November.

Recommended in the area

Dove Cottage and the Wordsworth Museum; Grasmere Gingerbread Shop; Lake Windermere Steamers

Wordsworth Hotel

★★★★ 78% ◎◎ HOTEL

Address: GRASMERE, LA22 9SW
Tel: 015394 35592
Fax: 015394 35765
Email: enquiry@thewordsworthhotel.co.uk
Website: www.thewordsworthhotel.co.uk
Map ref: 5, NY31
Directions: Off A591 centre of village adjacent to
St Oswald's Church
Rooms: 36 (2 GF) (2 fmly) S £85-£105

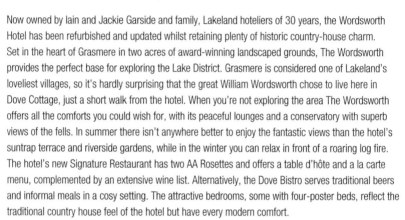

D £170-£290 (incl. bkfst & dinner) Facilities: Wi-fi ☉ Gym Sauna Parking: 60 Notes: ⊗ in bedrooms

Now owned by Iain and Jackie Garside and family, Lakeland hoteliers of 30 years, the Wordsworth
Hotel has been refurbished and updated whilst retaining plenty of historic country-house charm.
Set in the heart of Grasmere in two acres of award-winning landscaped grounds, The Wordsworth
provides the perfect base for exploring the Lake District. Grasmere is considered one of Lakeland's
loveliest villages, so it's hardly surprising that the great William Wordsworth chose to live here in
Dove Cottage, just a short walk from the hotel. When you're not exploring the area The Wordsworth
offers all the comforts you could wish for, with its peaceful lounges and a conservatory with superb
views of the fells. In summer there isn't anywhere better to enjoy the fantastic views than the hotel's
suntrap terrace and riverside gardens, while in the winter you can relax in front of a roaring log fire.
The hotel's new Signature Restaurant has two AA Rosettes and offers a table d'hôte and a la carte
menu, complemented by an extensive wine list. Alternatively, the Dove Bistro serves traditional beers
and informal meals in a cosy setting. The attractive bedrooms, some with four-poster beds, reflect the
traditional country house feel of the hotel but have every modern comfort.

Recommended in the area

Dove Cottage; Hill Top (Beatrix Potter's home); lake cruises

Best Western Castle Green Hotel in Kendal

★★★ 81% ◉◉ HOTEL

Address: KENDAL, LA9 6RG
Tel: 01539 734000
Fax: 01539 735522
Email: reception@castlegreen.co.uk
Website: www.castlegreen.co.uk
Map ref: 6, SD59
Directions: M6 junct 37, A684 towards Kendal. Hotel on right in 5m
Rooms: 100 (25 GF) (3 fmly) S £79-£99 D £98-£138 (incl. bkfst) **Facilities:** STV Wi-fi ⊗ Spa Gym
Parking: 200 **Notes:** ⊗ in bedrooms

The Castle Green, with Kendal on its doorstep, is well placed for exploring the southern end of the beautiful Lake District. Standing in 14 acres of woodlands and gardens, this smart modern hotel offers comfort and convenience in all its en suite rooms. They all look bright and fresh with soft duvets, flat-screen satellite TV and a tempting room service menu. Those wanting more space and a little more luxury might opt for an Executive room, while the two rooms with a four-poster will appeal to those after something different or a little more romantic. The bustling Greenhouse restaurant offers a choice of things to look at – in one direction, through huge panoramic windows, are the landscaped gardens and Kendal Castle; in the other, the chefs at work in the theatre-style kitchen. The produce is the best the region can provide – try Cumbrian lamb, for example, or Morecambe Bay shrimps. Alexander's, in the grounds, is the hotel's genuine real-ale pub, serving hearty meals and snacks. Work out in the leisure club's gym, swim in the indoor pool, or relax in the steam room.

Recommended in the area

Lake District National Park; Abbot Hall Art Gallery; Levens Hall & Topiary Gardens

Burn How Garden House Hotel

★★★ 80% ◉ HOTEL

Address: Back Belsfield Road, Bowness,
WINDERMERE, LA23 3HHv
Tel: 015394 46226
Fax: 015394 47000
Email: info@burnhow.co.uk
Website: www.burnhow.co.uk
Map ref: 6, SD49
Directions: Exit A591 at Windermere, following signs
to Bowness. Pass Lake Piers on right, take 1st left to
hotel entrance **Rooms:** 28 (6 GF) (10 fmly) **S** £60-£95 **D** £95-£145 (incl. bkfst)
Facilities: Wi-fi **Parking:** 30 **Notes:** ⊗ in bedrooms

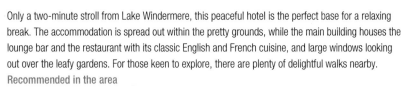

Only a two-minute stroll from Lake Windermere, this peaceful hotel is the perfect base for a relaxing break. The accommodation is spread out within the pretty grounds, while the main building houses the lounge bar and the restaurant with its classic English and French cuisine, and large windows looking out over the leafy gardens. For those keen to explore, there are plenty of delightful walks nearby.
Recommended in the area
Hilltop; Windermere lake cruises, South Lakes Wild Animal Park

---

Cedar Manor Hotel & Restaurant

★★ 83% ◉ HOTEL

Address: Ambleside Road, WINDERMERE, LA23 1AX
Tel: 015394 43192 & 45970
Fax: 015394 45970
Email: info@cedarmanor.co.uk
Website: www.cedarmanor.co.uk
Map ref: 6, SD49 **Directions:** From A591 follow
signs to Windermere. Hotel on left just beyond St
Mary's Church **Rooms:** 11 (3 GF) (2 fmly) **S** £63-£75
D £90-£150 (incl. bkfst) **Facilities:** Wi-fi **Parking:** 11

Built in 1854 as a private country retreat, the Cedar Manor Hotel provides comfortable accommodation for those wishing to relax and enjoy the breathtaking scenery, wonderful walks and wealth of leisure facilities Windermere and the National Park have to offer. The restaurant serves locally sourced produce from a seasonally changing menu, complemented by a carefully selected wine list. Set in mature walled gardens dominated by a 200-year-old cedar tree, the hotel feels peaceful and secluded, yet is just a short stroll away from the shores of Lake Windermere and the centre of Windermere village.
Recommended in the area
Lake Windermere cruises; Blackwell Arts and Crafts House; Beatrix Potter's house

Rowing boats on Lake Windermere

Gilpin Lodge Country House Hotel

★★★★ ◉◉◉ HOTEL

Address: Crook Road, WINDERMERE, LA23 3NE
Tel: 015394 88818
Fax: 015394 88058
Email: hotel@gilpinlodge.co.uk
Website: www.gilpinlodge.co.uk
Map ref: 6, SD49
Directions: M6 junct 36, take A590/A591 to rdbt
north of Kendal, take B5284, hotel 5m on right
Rooms: 20 (11 GF) **S** £180 **D** £290-£440 (incl. bkfst
& dinner) **Facilities:** Wi-fi **Parking:** 40 **Notes:** ⊗ in bedrooms **Notes:** ⚹ under 7 yrs

An elegant, friendly hotel in 20 tranquil acres of gardens, moors and woodland, owned and run by two generations of the Cunliffe family. The en suite bedrooms all have bath and shower, luxury toiletries and bathrobes. Individually and stylishly decorated to a high standard, they are quiet, with delightful views. Each room has a sitting area, TV, direct-dial phone, radio, hair dryer, and beverage tray with home-made biscuits; some rooms also have a trouser press. The Garden Suites have enormous beds, walk-in dressing areas, large sofas, modern fireplaces, flat-screen TVs and sensual bathrooms; glass-fronted lounge areas lead to individual gardens with cedarwood hot tubs. Food is important at Gilpin Lodge. The chefs are passionate about using the finest local ingredients as extensively as possible. It's hard to put a label on the food – classically based, yes, yet thoroughly modern and imaginative, without being too experimental. Tables have fresh flowers, candles at night, crisp white linen, fine china and glass, and gleaming silver. The walk-in wine cellar, featuring over 300 wines from 13 countries, reflects real interest rather than a desire to sell high priced vintages. Residents have free use of a local leisure club, although on-call spa therapists will visit guest rooms.

Recommended in the area

Lake Windermere; Beatrix Potter Gallery; Dove Cottage and Wordsworth Museum

'The Steamer' Lake Windermere

Macdonald Old England Hotel

★★★★ 84% 🏵🏵 HOTEL

Address: Church Street, Bowness, WINDERMERE,
LA23 3DF
Tel: 0844 879 9144
Fax: 015394 43432
Email: sales.oldengland@macdonald-hotels.
co.uk
Website: www.macdonaldhotels.co.uk
Map ref: 6, SD49
Directions: Through Windermere to Bowness,
straight across at mini-rdbt . Hotel behind church on right
Rooms: 106 (14 GF) (3 fmly) **S** £96-£200 **D** £106-£210 (incl. bkfst)
Facilities: STV Wi-fi 🏊 Spa Gym **Parking:** 90 **Notes:** ⊗ in bedrooms

A local landmark, this ivy-clad Victorian mansion stands on the shores of Lake Windermere. Mature
gardens lead to the waterfront and the hotel's own jetties. The newly refurbished bedrooms, most with
lake views, come with thoughtful extras. The Vinland Restaurant is well known for its excellent cuisine.
Recommended in the area
Windermere Steamboat Museum; Lake District National Park; Lakeside and Haverthwaite Railways

Washington Central Hotel

★★★ 83% HOTEL

Address: Washington Street, WORKINGTON,
CA14 3AY
Tel: 01900 65772
Fax: 01900 68770
Email: kawildwchotel@aol.com
Website: www.washingtoncentralhotelworkington.
com
Map ref: 5, NY02
Directions: M6 junct 40, A66 to Workington.
Left at lights, hotel on right
Rooms: 46 (4 fmly) S £85 D £125 (incl. bkfst)
Facilities: Wi-fi ⊗ Gym Sauna **Parking:** 14 **Notes:** ⊗ in bedrooms

Enjoying a prominent town centre location, this distinctive red-brick hotel is within walking distance of most amenities, including shops, cinema and parks, while only a little further afield are the delights of the Lake District National Park. Public areas include several lounges, a spacious bar, a popular coffee shop and Caesar's leisure club, which has a 20-metre swimming pool surrounded by frescoes. The well-maintained and comfortable en suite bedrooms are equipped with TV, safe, hairdryer, trouser press, work desk, and coffee-and-tea-making facilities. The executive accommodation includes a four-poster suite with hi-fi system and luxurious lounge. In the wood-panelled Carlton Restaurant the best local ingredients are used in dishes such as rack of Lakeland fell-bred lamb on rosemary crushed potatoes, and Solway sea bass. For special occasions, book the eight-cover Clock Tower Restaurant, not just for the food, but for views towards Scotland.

Recommended in the area

Western Lakes; Scafell and Wasdale; Keswick; Solway Firth; Cockermouth

DERBYSHIRE

Ladybower Reservoir, Derwent Valley, Peak District National Park

Chatsworth House

Wind in the Willows Hotel

★★ 83% HOTEL

Address: Derbyshire Level, GLOSSOP, SK13 7PT
Tel: 01457 868001
Fax: 01457 853354
Email: info@windinthewillows.co.uk
Website: www.windinthewillows.co.uk
Map ref: 7, SK09
Directions: 1m E of Glossop on A57, turn right opp
Royal Oak, hotel 400yds on right
Rooms: 12 S £88 D £135 (incl. bkfst) **Facilities:**
Wi-fi **Parking:** 16 **Notes:** ⊗ in bedrooms ⋈ under 10 yrs

The Wind in the Willows is a privately owned country-house hotel which has retained its original charms, including oak panelled rooms, traditional furnishings and open log fires. It sits in five acres of land on the edge of the Peak District National Park. The Dining Room has an excellent reputation for traditional cuisine, freshly prepared using local produce, and complemented by carefully selected wines. Glossop private golf course lies adjacent to the hotel and many other outdoor activities can be found nearby.

Recommended in the area

The Peak District National Park; Chatsworth House; Kinder Scout

Losehill House Hotel & Spa

★★★ 81% ◎ HOTEL

Address: Edale Road, HOPE, S33 6RF
Tel: 01433 621219
Fax: 01433 622501
Email: info@losehillhouse.co.uk
Website: www.losehillhouse.co.uk
Map ref: 6, SK18
Directions: A6187 into Hope. Take turn opposite
church into Edale Rd. 1m, left & follow signs to hotel
Rooms: 21 (3 GF) (4 fmly) **S** £120-£150
D £150-£210 (incl. bkfst) **Facilities:** Wi-fi ⏲ Spa **Parking:** 20 **Notes:** ⊗ in bedrooms

Nestled between historic Losehill and Win Hill, this wonderful Arts and Crafts period house-turned-luxury-hotel occupies a secluded spot in the Peak District National Park. The surrounding countryside is undoubtedly some of the best for walking and outdoor activities in Britain, and the views across the Vale of Edale are nothing short of spectacular. The house has been expertly restored and decorated throughout in a relaxing, contemporary style. All 21 en suite bedrooms are attractively furnished and come with TVs and DVD players and extensive countryside views. The spa offers the ultimate in relaxation, with its indoor pool, sauna, outdoor hot tub and a wide range of treatments. Head to the drawing room to enjoy a pre-dinner drink – and to drink in more of that stunning vista – before settling down to eat in the delightful restaurant, with its nightly-changing table d'hote menu based around locally sourced produce. There are more panoramic views to be enjoyed here, and everything is homemade by a talented kitchen team. Light, healthy lunches are now available during the week – perfect for spa guests – but if you're looking to indulge, try the traditional afternoon tea.

Recommended in the area

Caves at Castleton; The Pennine Way; The Peak District National Park; Chatsworth house

The Red House Country Hotel

★★ 85% ◎ HOTEL

Address: Old Road, Darley Dale, MATLOCK,
DE4 2ER
Tel: 01629 734854
Email: enquiries@theredhousecountryhotel.co.uk
Website: www.theredhousecountryhotel.co.uk
Map ref: 7, SK35
Directions: Off A6 onto Old Rd signed Carriage
Museum, 2.5m N of Matlock
Rooms: 9 (2 GF) **S** £54-£64 **D** £91-£108 (incl. bkfst)
Facilities: Wi-fi **Parking:** 12 **Notes:** ⊗ in bedrooms ✦ under 12 yrs

Built in 1891 and set in pretty Victorian lawned gardens, the family-owned Red House Country
Hotel offers guests a chance to relax in peaceful, comfortable surroundings, while at the same time
providing a good base for exploring the Peak District. Guests arriving in the afternoon are treated
to complimentary afternoon tea, along with cakes and biscuits. Each of the well-equipped en suite
bedrooms has its own unique features, and all supply a hairdryer, hospitality tray with home-made
biscuits, telephone, TV and Wi-fi. Some rooms enjoy glorious views of the gardens and Derwent Valley,
and two ground-floor rooms are located in the adjacent 19th-century coach house. Public areas
include two comfortable lounges with original features where you can enjoy refreshments and pre-
dinner drinks. The AA Rosette-awarded restaurant maintains an excellent reputation for high-quality
food. Smart casual dress is requested in the evenings. The hotel is particularly proud of its hearty
breakfasts, which include home-made muesli, kippers from the Summer Isles Smokehouse and home-
baked bread.

Recommended in the area

The Peak District National Park; Chatsworth House; Haddon Hall

The Peacock at Rowsley

★★★ ◉◉ HOTEL

Address:	Bakewell Road, ROWSLEY, Bakewell, DE4 2EB
Tel:	01629 733518
Fax:	01629 732671
Email:	reception@thepeacockatrowsley.com
Website:	www.thepeacockatrowsley.com

Map ref: 7, SK26
Directions: A6, 3m before Bakewell
Rooms: 16 (5 fmly) S £75-£95 D £145-£230 (incl. bkfst) Facilities: Wi-fi Parking: 25 Notes: ⚫ under 10 yrs

Within Britain's oldest national park, this is a perfect base for taking exhilarating walks across lonely moorland, for exploring beautiful secluded valleys and pretty villages, and for fishing – the hotel owns fly fishing rights on the Wye and Derwent, the latter flowing through the garden. In 2004 Keira Knightley, Matthew Macfadyen and other actors and crew stayed here while filming *Pride and Prejudice* at Haddon Hall. The bedrooms are luxurious, most with king- or super king-size beds, and each has been styled by the international designer, India Mahdavi, who has blended antique furniture with contemporary decor. One room has a four-poster bed, another has an antique bed from Belvoir Castle. Modern facilities include Wi-fi, and there are soft drinks as well as tea-and-coffee-making supplies. The main restaurant overlooks the garden and has an interesting menu that might include starters like duck liver ballotine with hazelnuts and figs, or smoked eel with apple purée, celeriac remoulade and a quail's egg. Main courses are equally imaginative, with recent offerings including shoulder of lamb with roast sweetbread, black olive gnocchi, fennel and goat's cheese. There's also a cosy bar, with an open fire and stone walls, serving real ales, cocktails and simple dishes.

Recommended in the area

Haddon Hall; Chatsworth House; Peak District National Park

DEVON

Grimspound, Dartmoor National Park

Northcote Manor

★★★ ◎◎ COUNTRY HOUSE HOTEL
Address: BURRINGTON, Umberleigh, EX37 9LZ
Tel: 01769 560501
Fax: 01769 560770
Email: rest@northcotemanor.co.uk
Website: www.northcotemanor.co.uk
Map ref: 2, SS61
Directions: Off A377 opposite Portsmouth Arms, into hotel drive. Do not enter Burrington village
Rooms: 11 S £110-£170 D £160-£260 (incl. bkfst)
Facilities: Wi-fi Tennis Croquet **Parking:** 30

This beautiful early 18th-century hotel stands in 20 acres of mature grounds and woodlands, complete with a reinstated Victorian water garden and ancient apple orchards. Bedrooms exude comfort and style and have luxurious touches, from designer bath products to fluffy bathrobes, creating a haven of tranquillity. The restaurant's seasonal menu offers well-prepared, locally sourced dishes such as Ruby Red beef and Exmoor lamb with exceptional wines to accompany each course.

Recommended in the area
Rosemoor RHS garden; Dartington Crystal; North Devon coast

Royal Castle Hotel

★★★ 80% HOTEL
Address: 11 The Quay, DARTMOUTH, TQ6 9PS
Tel: 01803 833033
Fax: 01803 835445
Email: enquiry@royalcastle.co.uk
Website: www.royalcastle.co.uk
Map ref: 2, SX85
Directions: in centre of town, overlooking Inner Harbour **Rooms:** 25 (3 fmly) S £90-£95 D £130-£199 (incl. bkfst) **Facilities:** Wi-fi **Parking:** 17

With its stylish décor, original antiques and quirky features, the Royal Castle Hotel is a truly special place to stay while exploring beautiful Dartmouth. Positioned around an Elizabethan inner courtyard, the 25 non-smoking bedrooms all have individual charm and great character. The restaurant has lovely river views and you'll often find local crab and oysters on the menu, as well as spit-roasts. The hotel's cellar is well-stocked and there are two character bars to choose from, both with lots of intimate cosy corners and open fires in winter.

Recommended in the area
Dartmouth River cruises; wine and cheese tasting at Sharpham Vineyard; Dittisham village

Langstone Cliff Hotel

★★★ 78% HOTEL
Address: Dawlish Warren, DAWLISH, EX7 0NA
Tel: 01626 868000
Fax: 01626 868006
Email: reception@langstone-hotel.co.uk
Website: www.langstone-hotel.co.uk
Map ref: 2, SX97
Directions: 1.5m NE off A379 Exeter road to
Dawlish Warren
Rooms: 66 (10 GF) (52 fmly)
Facilities: STV Wi-fi ☜ ⅋ Tennis Gym **Parking:** 200

It was the Rogers family who welcomed the first guests here in
1947. They're still here – although it's generations two and three running the show now – and some
of those original guests are still coming. Such loyalty is understandable: the views of the sea from the
lawn, veranda and lounges are breathtaking, and a two-mile stretch of beach is five minutes' walk
away. The service is attentive, the public rooms spacious, the lounges are comfortable and the bars
friendly. Bedrooms are frequently refurbished and all are en suite, with TV, radio, baby-listening, phone
and other amenities. Many are designed as family rooms and some have balconies. The extensive
breakfast menu in the Lincoln Restaurant gets guests off to a good start, and during the day everything
from pastries and light snacks through to full meals are available. Dinner is chosen from a fixed price
menu or the carvery, and many of the sensibly priced wines are available by the glass. There are indoor
and outdoor heated pools, a hard tennis court, compact leisure centre and full-size snooker table. An
18-hole golf course is nearby, but you can practise your swing beforehand in the hotel grounds.
Recommended in the area
Paignton Zoo; Powderham Castle; Miniature Pony Centre

The Horn of Plenty

★★★ 85% ◉◉◉ HOTEL

Address: GULWORTHY, PL19 8JD
Tel: 01822 832528
Fax: 01822 834390
Email: enquiries@thehornofplenty.co.uk
Website: www.thehornofplenty.co.uk
Map ref: 1, SX47
Directions: From Tavistock take A390 W for 3m. Right at Gulworthy Cross. In 400yds turn left, hotel in 400yds on right
Rooms: 10 (4 GF) (3 fmly) **S** £110-£190 **D** £120-£200 (incl. bkfst) **Parking:** 25

A former AA Hotel of the Year, The Horn of Plenty continues to provide first rate food and accommodation in a glorious location. Surrounded by a designated Area of Outstanding Natural Beauty, it has fine grounds of its own and is just off the western edge of Dartmoor. Joint proprietor (with Paul Roston) is master chef Peter Gorton, who trained at some of the finest restaurants in the UK and abroad and provides the culinary highlight to any stay here. The dinner menu might include such starters as roast pigeon wrapped in potato on a foie gras salad with a port and red wine dressing, or steamed red mullet on a crab cake with ginger and spring onions. Recent main courses have featured spiced duck breast with a cherry compote and port sauce, and pan-fried sea bass with a white wine saffron sauce. Remember to look up from the food occasionally to enjoy the view of the Tamar Valley from the glass-fronted dining room. The hotel's bedrooms are luxurious and include fresh flowers, bottled water, home-made shortbread biscuits and towelling robes, and bathrooms have a range of beauty products. Some rooms are in the coach house, and these have balconies overlooking the walled gardens.

Recommended in the area

Morwelham Quay; Buckland Abbey (NT); Plymouth

Sidmouth

Combe House – Devon

★★★ ◎◎ COUNTRY HOUSE HOTEL

Address: Gittisham, HONITON, EX14 3AD
Tel: 01404 540400
Fax: 01404 46004
Email: stay@combehousedevon.com
Website: www.combehousedevon.com
Map ref: 2, ST10
Directions: Off A30 1m S of Honiton, follow Gittisham Heathpark signs. From M5 exit 29 for Honiton.

Rooms: 16 (1 fmly) S £159-£364 D £179-£384 (incl. bkfst) Facilities: Wi-fi Parking: 39

This independent, privately owned Elizabethan manor is set in 3,500 acres of Devon estate. It has a lovely, relaxed atmosphere, almost like staying in the country home of a good friend. The public rooms feature oak panelling, old portraits and huge open fireplaces, while all of the spacious bedrooms are recently refurbished. Food is the big attraction; Combe House's Master Chefs create modern British dishes using produce from local farms within a few miles' radius and the hotel's own gardens.

Recommended in the area

Southwest Coastal Path; Killerton Gardens & Knightshayes Court (NT); Darts Farmshop; Topsham

Ilsington Country House Hotel

★★★ 86% ◎◎ COUNTRY HOUSE HOTEL

Address: Ilsington Village, ILSINGTON, Newton
         Abbot, TQ13 9RR
Tel: 01364 661452
Fax: 01364 661307
Email: hotel@ilsington.co.uk
Website: www.ilsington.co.uk
Map ref: 2, SX77
Directions: M5 onto A38 to Plymouth. Exit at Bovey Tracey. 3rd exit from rdbt to 'Ilsington', then 1st right. Hotel in 5m by Post Office

Rooms: 25 (8 GF) (4 fmly) S £95-£110 D £140-£174 (incl. bkfst)
Facilities: Wi-fi ⊗ Spa Gym Sauna Parking: 100

A friendly, family-owned hotel set in 10 acres of Dartmoor's southern slopes, offering tranquillity and far-reaching views. The air-conditioned restaurant serves local fare and classic dishes featuring fresh market produce. Scrumptious Devonshire cream teas are served in the conservatory or garden.

Recommended in the area

Castle Drogo; Buckfast Abbey; Dartmoor National Park

Becky Falls, Dartmoor National Park

The White Hart Hotel

★★★ 81% ⊛ HOTEL

Address: The Square, MORETONHAMPSTEAD, TQ13 8NF
Tel: 01647 441340
Fax: 01647 441341
Email: enquiries@whitehartdartmoor.co.uk
Website: www.whitehartdartmoor.co.uk
Map ref: 2, SX78
Directions: A30 towards Oakhampton. At Whiddon Down take A382 for Moretonhampstead **Rooms:** 28 (4 GF) (6 fmly)
S £50-£75 **D** £90-£120 (incl. bkfst)

The White Hart Hotel has been standing at the heart of Moretonhampstead – gateway to the Dartmoor National Park – since 1639. These days it's a perfect blend of contemporary style and old-world charm. The 28 beautifully furnished bedrooms all have bags of character, while the hotel's brasserie is a warm and welcoming setting for some fine British and European cooking. Meals can also be taken in the cosy bar, washed down, perhaps, by a pint of local real ale.

Recommended in the area

Cathedral city of Exeter; Becky Falls; Drago Castle

Tides Reach Hotel

★★★ 82% ◉ HOTEL

Address: South Sands, SALCOMBE, TQ8 8LJ
Tel: 01548 843466
Fax: 01548 843954
Email: enquire@tidesreach.com
Website: www.tidesreach.com
Map ref: 2, SX73
Directions: Off A38 at Buckfastleigh to Totnes.
Then A381 to Salcombe, follow signs to South Sands
Rooms: 35 (7 fmly) S £77-£150 D £128-£310 (incl.
bkfst & dinner) **Facilities:** Wi-fi ⊗ Spa Gym Sauna **Parking:** 100 **Notes:** 🐾 under 8yrs

The Tides Reach Hotel sits in an idyllic spot overlooking a quiet, sandy cove on the shores of the beautiful Salcombe Estuary. The views from the public rooms and the 35 bedrooms are fabulous, but you needn't merely look out across the water – there are plenty of opportunities to get out on the water. A short walk or ferry ride along the estuary will bring you to the picturesque sailing resort of Salcombe, while right in front of the hotel you can enjoy safe swimming and various watersports.

The Tides Reach Hotel has been owned by the Edwards family for three generations, which probably has a lot to do with its friendly, homely atmosphere. The accommodation is tastefully furnished and there are several different room types, including many with balconies. The conservatory-style Garden Room Restaurant offers a daily-changing modern British menu featuring top-quality Devon produce, especially fish and seafood. Expect the likes of hand-picked Salcombe crab or Bigbury Bay mussels to begin, followed by line-caught Salcombe sea bass or rib of prime South Devon beef. During your stay make sure you find time to visit the spa, take a dip in the indoor pool and relax in the peaceful garden with its centrepiece ornamental lake.

Recommended in the area

Overbeck's sub-tropical gardens and house (NT); Dartmoor National Park; South West Coastal Path

Exmoor National Park

Saunton Sands Hotel

★★★★ 78% HOTEL
Address: SAUNTON, EX33 1LQ
Tel: 01271 890212 & 892001
Fax: 01271 890145
Email: reservations@sauntonsands.com
Website: www.sauntonsands.com
Map ref: 1, SS43
Directions: Off A361 at Braunton, signed Croyde
B3231, hotel 2m on left
Rooms: 92 (39 fmly) S £90-£129 D £170-£364

Facilities: Wi-fi 🕸 ⚓ Tennis Spa Gym Sauna Parking: 142 Notes: ⊗ in bedrooms

From the front of this majestic hotel, high above Braunton Burrows, three things account for what you can see – sea, sand and sky, stretching far into the distance. It's an inspiring view, probably best savoured from a seat on the terrace, while inside other moods may be satisfied in one of the public rooms – a quiet corner in which to read or snooze maybe, or the bar for freshly ground coffee, or perhaps a peaty malt. Imagine then the views from the many bedrooms that face the beach and the sometimes gentle, sometimes roaring Atlantic Ocean. Wherever your room, it will be equipped to the standard expected from a luxury hotel. In the restaurant, daily changing dinner menus make the most of seasonal local produce, while the Terrace Lounge offers snacks, hot and cold meals throughout the day, and traditional afternoon cream teas. At night these areas become the social heart of the hotel, with live music and entertainment. Just below the hotel is The Sands Café Bar, a more relaxed place for a daytime drink or light bite, or freshly cooked pastas and grills in the evening.

Recommended in the area

Exmoor National Park; Tarka Trail; Hartland Heritage Coast

Riviera Hotel

★★★★ 82% ◉ HOTEL

Address: The Esplanade, SIDMOUTH, EX10 8AY
Tel: 01395 515201
Fax: 01395 577775
Email: enquiries@hotelriviera.co.uk
Website: www.hotelriviera.co.uk
Map ref: 2, SY18
Directions: M5 junct 30 & follow A3052
Rooms: 26 (6 fmly) **S** £125-£185 **D** £250-£350
(incl. bkfst & dinner) **Facilities:** Wi-fi **Parking:** 27

The Riviera Hotel, with its fine Regency façade and alluring blend of old-fashioned service and present-day comforts, is splendidly positioned at the centre of Sidmouth's esplanade, overlooking Lyme Bay. With its mild climate and the beach just on the doorstep, the setting echoes the south of France and is ideal for those in search of relaxation and quieter pleasures. Glorious sea views can be enjoyed from the recently redesigned en suite bedrooms, all of which are fully appointed and have many thoughtful extras. In the elegant bay-view dining room guests are offered a fine choice of dishes from extensive menus, with local seafood being a particular speciality. Wedding parties and business conferences can be accommodated, and the hotel can arrange sporting activities in the area, including golfing with concessionary fees at the nearby Sidmouth Golf Club and Woodbury Park Golf and Country Club. Arrangements can also be made for riding, and pheasant and duck shooting on local estates. The hotel has a long tradition of hospitality and is perfect for unforgettable holidays, long weekends, or a memorable Christmas break.

Recommended in the area

Bicton Gardens; Killerton House and Gardens; Exeter Cathedral

Westcliff Hotel

★★★ 80% HOTEL

Address: Manor Road, SIDMOUTH, EX10 8RU
Tel: 01395 513252
Fax: 01395 578203
Email: stay@westcliffhotel.co.uk
Website: www.westcliffhotel.co.uk
Map ref: 2, SY18
Directions: Exit A3052 to Sidmouth then to seafront & esplanade, turn right, hotel directly ahead
Rooms: 40 (5 GF) (1 fmly) S £60-£120 D £65-£260 (incl. bkfst & dinner) **Facilities:** Wi-fi ⸚ **Parking:** 40

The privately-owned Westcliff Hotel is set in two beautiful acres of lawns and gardens, right in the middle of the Jurassic Coast, a World Heritage Site since 2001. In fact, the Westcliff's position gives it a natural advantage, sheltering it from every wind but the south. Regency Sidmouth is known as the 'Jewel of the West Country' and its town centre, promenade and beaches are just a short walk away. Locally renowned for excellent food and courteous and efficient service, the Westcliff Hotel offers elegant lounges and a cocktail bar open on to the heated outdoor swimming pool (June to September). The different types of bedroom are well proportioned, tastefully furnished and equipped with all the usual amenities. Most have sea views, some from their own private balconies. In fact, only a few of the single and standard rooms do not face the sea. The Harding's restaurant offers a tempting choice of both à la carte and fixed price menus, and views of the red cliffs for which this part of Devon is famous. The Westcliff Hotel is open all year round.

Recommended in the area

Bicton Gardens; Crealy Adventure Park; Otterton Mill; Jurassic Coast (World Heritage Site); Sidmouth

Corbyn Head Hotel & Orchid Restaurant

★★★ 77% ◉◉◉ HOTEL

Address: Torbay Road, Sea Front, TORQUAY, TQ2 6RH
Tel: 01803 213611
Fax: 01803 296152
Email: info@corbynhead.com
Website: www.corbynhead.com
Map ref: 2, SX96
Directions: Follow signs to Torquay seafront, turn right on seafront. Hotel on right with green canopies
Rooms: 45 (9 GF) (4 fmly)
Facilities: Wi-fi ⚡ Gym Sauna **Parking:** 50

This establishment is sited in a magnificent setting on Torbay's waterfront just a minute's leisurely walk to Livermead Beach. The rooms are all en suite; most have sea views, and many have private balconies. Guests staying seven nights on the standard tariff receive a free extra night's accommodation, and there are accommodation packages at Christmas, New Year and throughout the year. The three AA Rosette air-conditioned Orchid Restaurant offers fine dining on the top floor of the hotel, with magnificent views over Torbay. Smart casual wear is requested here. The traditional English cuisine of the Harbour View Restaurant, made with only the finest local produce, is constantly changing, while the Regency Lounge and the Continental Coffee Bar open onto the Poolside Terrace and offer wonderful views to guests enjoying morning coffee and afternoon tea. The Corbyn Head Hotel also offers free on-site parking.

Recommended in the area

Paignton Zoo; Kent's Cavern, Torquay; Babbacombe Model Village

Grand Hotel

★★★★ 76% ● HOTEL

Address: Sea Front, TORQUAY, TQ2 6NT
Tel: 01803 296677
Fax: 01803 213462
Email: reservations@grandtorquay.co.uk
Website: www.grandtorquay.co.uk
Map ref: 2, SX96
Directions: A380 to Torquay. At seafront turn right, then 1st right. Hotel on corner, entrance 1st on left
Rooms: 132 (3 GF) (32 fmly) **S** £60-£100

D £120-£220 (incl. bkfst) **Facilities:** Wi-fi ⓧ ⸎ Tennis Spa Gym Sauna **Parking:** 57

Standing proud on the seafront in Torquay – the heart of the English Riviera – The Grand Hotel offers high standards of accommodation, service, food and facilities. The Edwardian building has been modernised over the years but has lost nothing of its grandeur in its lounges and public rooms. The Gainsborough restaurant is the hotel's fine dining venue, recently awarded an AA Rosette for its accomplished modern cooking based around locally-sourced ingredients.
Recommended in the area
English Riviera beaches; Greenway (Agatha Christie's home); Paignton Zoo

Orestone Manor Hotel & Restaurant

★★★ 86% ●● HOTEL

Address: Rockhouse Lane, Maidencombe,
TORQUAY, TQ1 4SX
Tel: 01803 328098
Fax: 01803 328336
Email: info@orestonemanor.com
Website: www.orestonemanor.com
Map ref: 2, SX96
Directions: A38 onto A380 then B3192

Rooms: 12 (1 GF) (3 fmly) **S** £90-£149 **D** £135-£225 (incl. bkfst) **Facilities:** Wi-fi ⸎ **Parking:** 40

With stunning views across the Torbay coastline, Orestone Manor was the home of painter John Calcott Horsley, RA, best known for painting the first Christmas card. A colonial theme runs through the house with spacious bedrooms all beautifully decorated. The restaurant makes good use of local produce.
Recommended in the area
Dartmoor; South Devon Railway; Berry Pomeroy Castle

DORSET

Eypes Mouth, Golden Cap Estate

Jurassic Coast

BridgeHouse

★★★ 80% HOTEL

Address: 3 Prout Bridge, BEAMINSTER, DT8 3AY
Tel: 01308 862200
Fax: 01308 863700
Email: enquiries@bridge-house.co.uk
Website: www.bridge-house.co.uk
Map ref: 2, SY40
Directions: Off A3066, 100yds from town square
Rooms: 14 (5 GF) (1 fmly) S £76-£108 D £116-
£200 (incl. bkfst) Facilities: Wi-fi Parking: 20

Sitting beside a bridge, this small hotel offers the perfect blend of historic charm and 21st century luxury. The building is medieval but its interior has been sympathetically updated throughout by owners Mark and Joanna Donovan, so expect beautiful, characterful public areas, new bathrooms for each of the 13 stylish bedrooms, and all the latest technology. The Georgian dining room offers a traditional menu featuring plenty of top-notch Dorset produce, while lighter dishes are available in the conservatory and a brasserie menu is served al fresco in the beautiful walled garden.

Recommended in the area

The Jurassic Coast; Abbotsbury Swannery; Mapperton House and Gardens

Best Western Connaught Hotel

★★★ 82% ◉ HOTEL

Address:	West Hill Road, West Cliff,
	BOURNEMOUTH, BH2 5PH
Tel:	01202 298020
Fax:	01202 298028
Email:	reception@theconnaught.co.uk
Website:	www.theconnaught.co.uk
Map ref:	3, SZ19

Directions: Follow Town Centre West & BIC signs

Rooms: 83 (10 fmly) **S** £40-£80 **D** £60-£120 (incl. bkfst) **Facilities:** STV Wi-fi ⊗ Spa Gym Sauna **Parking:** 66 **Notes:** ⊗ in bedrooms

Built around 1850 as a gentleman's residence, this award-winning, environmentally-friendly hotel is centrally located on the West Cliff in an acre of grounds. All of the attractions of the town centre are less than five minutes' walk away, as are the beach and the Bournemouth International Centre with its busy programme of concerts and events. Accommodation is stylish and well-equipped, with a variety of rooms and suites, including family suites, available in the main hotel as well as in the neighbouring Connaught Lodge. All rooms are en suite, most have Wi-fi and some have private balconies or terraces overlooking the private garden terrace. The Spa Centre with its 18m pool, sauna, aroma steam room and massage therapy room adds to the relaxation factor, while for those feeling more energetic there are two gyms. The hotel was highly commended in the 'Best Large Hotel in Bournemouth' and 'Best Restaurant in Bournemouth' categories at the Bournemouth Tourism Awards in 2009. It was also the first hotel in the town to be awarded a silver shield through the Green Tourism Business Scheme for its commitment to the environment. 'Green' activities include recycling as much waste as possible, switching to low energy lighting and using local ingredients in the AA Rosetted Blakes restaurant.

Recommended in the area

Bournemouth Pier; Lower Gardens; Bournemouth Oceanarium

Bournemouth Pier

Chine Hotel

★★★ 81% ⊛ HOTEL

Address: Boscombe Spa Road, BOURNEMOUTH, BH5 1AX
Tel: 01202 396234 & 0845 337 1550
Fax: 01202 391737
Email: reservations@fjbhotels.co.uk
Website: www.fjbhotels.co.uk
Map ref: 3, SZ19 **Directions:** Follow BIC signs, A338/Wessex Way to St Pauls rdbt. 1st exit, to next rdbt, 2nd exit signed Eastcliff, Boscombe, Southbourne. Next rdbt, 1st exit into Christchurch Rd. After 2nd lights, right into Boscombe Spa Rd
Rooms: 88 (8 GF) (16 fmly) **S** £45-£105 **D** £90-£210 (incl. bkfst & dinner)
Facilities: STV Wi-fi ⊛ ⌇ Gym Sauna **Parking:** 55 **Notes:** ⊗ in bedrooms

The newly refurbished Chine sits in three acres of secluded, mature gardens with magnificent sea views. A short walk through the hotel gardens quickly brings you to miles of sandy beaches, but if it's not beach weather, you can always escape to the Roman Spa. For dining, choose between the Sea View restaurant, where you can gaze out over Poole Bay, or the new Gallery Brasserie.
Recommended in the area Bournemouth shopping centre; Poole Quay; New Forest National Park

Hermitage Hotel

★★★ 82% ❀ HOTEL
Address: Exeter Road, BOURNEMOUTH,
BH2 5AH
Tel: 01202 557363
Fax: 01202 559173
Email: info@hermitage-hotel.co.uk
Website: www.hermitage-hotel.co.uk
Map ref: 3, SZ19
Directions: A338 Ringwood, follow signs for BIC and pier. Hotel directly opposite
Rooms: 74 (7 GF) (9 fmly)
Facilities: Wi-fi Parking: 58 Notes: ⊗ in bedrooms

Occupying an impressive location overlooking the seafront, The Hermitage Hotel provides the ideal place to stay while visiting Bournemouth for business or pleasure. The Bournemouth International Centre, with its packed progamme of concerts, exhibitions and events, is just across the road from the hotel, while the beach and pier are merely a short stroll away. The town centre is also just a few minutes walk from the hotel, as are the pretty Lower Gardens and the Pavilion theatre. Privately owned and operated, The Hermitage has 74 en suite bedrooms furnished in an elegant and classic style. Most have spectacular sea views and all are equipped with flat-screen TVs and complimentary Wi-fi. There's a lift to all floors and plenty of on-site parking which is free to guests. The Hermitage is one of only a handful of hotels in Bournemouth to hold an AA Rosette for the quality of its cooking. The well-appointed dining room offers a regularly changing menu featuring plenty of local and regional produce, such as pan-seared Portland scallops, roasted rump of Hampshire lamb and Barford Farm ice creams. Light lunches and traditional afternoon tea are served in the comfortable lounge.

Recommended in the area

Bournemouth Beach; Bournemouth Oceanarium; Compton Acres

Hotel Miramar

★★★ 82% HOTEL

Address: East Overcliff Drive, East Cliff,
BOURNEMOUTH, BH1 3AL
Tel: 01202 556581
Fax: 01202 291242
Email: sales@miramar-bournemouth.com
Website: www.miramar-bournemouth.com
Map ref: 3, SZ19
Directions: Wessex Way rdbt turn into St Pauls
Rd, right at next rdbt. 3rd exit at next rdbt, 2nd exit

at next rdbt into Grove Rd. Hotel car park on right **Rooms:** 43 (6 fmly) **S** £49.95-£75.95 **D** £99.90-£151.95 (incl. bkfst & dinner) **Facilities:** Wi-fi **Parking:** 80

Hotel Miramar boasts one of the most spectacular vantage points in Bournemouth, looking out across the glittering waters of the bay, with the Needles and the Isle of Wight to the east, the giant chalk stacks of Old Harry Rocks to the west, and the Purbeck Hills of Hardy's Wessex beyond. It may not be in the countryside, but Hotel Miramar is the epitome of an English country house with its rambling facade of Grecian-style pillars and curved balconies overlooking the terraces and sweeping lawns that appear to stretch down to the water's edge. Inside, the hotel's Edwardian origins are reflected in the elegant decor. The Miramar's 43 en suite bedrooms are all individually designed and equipped with every modern-day comfort, while retaining many period features. Several bedrooms enjoy breathtaking views across the bay and some have private balconies. The attractive restaurant looks out towards the sea and is a popular spot for Sunday lunch, when a pianist is on hand to entertain. The table d'hote menu changes daily and and is complemented by fine wines from a well stocked cellar. Meals can also be taken on the pretty terrace during the summer months.

Recommended in the area

Bournemouth seafront; Compton Acres; Christchurch Priory

Langtry Manor

★★★ 81% ❀ HOTEL

Address:	Derby Road, East Cliff, BOURNEMOUTH, BH1 3QB
Tel:	0844 3725 432
Fax:	01202 290115
Email:	lillie@langtrymanor.com
Website:	www.langtrymanor.co.uk
Map ref:	3, SZ19

Directions: A31/A338, 1st rdbt by rail station turn left. Over next rdbt, 1st left into Knyveton Rd. Hotel opposite

Rooms: 20 (3 GF) (2 fmly) S £69-£129 D £98-£218 (incl. bkfst) Parking: 30

This warm, inviting boutique hotel is steeped in history and romance and designed with Edwardian elegance and contemporary style in mind. The house was built in 1877 by King Edward VII for his mistress, the actress Lillie Langtry, and in its new life as a hotel it has a fittingly romantic theme, with many rooms featuring four-poster beds and Jacuzzi baths. Langtry's restaurant has a rather special ambience and with its high ceilings, huge stained glass windows, Tudor tapestries, grand fireplace and minstrels' gallery it's a regal setting for some fine contemporary cooking. On Saturday nights the hotel is known for its six-course Edwardian banquets, complete with a short performance entitled the "Life of Lillie". Family owned and run, Langtry Manor is tucked away in a quiet street in the East Cliff area of Bournemouth, with the cosmopolitan shops, bars and theatres of the town, plus the new surf reef, just a leisurely stroll away. Stonehenge, the New Forest National Park and the Jurassic Coast are within an hour's drive, making Langtry Manor the perfect base for exploring this beautiful part of southern England.

Recommended in the area

Bournemouth beach and seafront; Boscombe Surf Reef; Lulworth Cove

Captain's Club Hotel and Spa

★★★★ 80% ◉◉ HOTEL

Address: Wick Ferry, Wick Lane, CHRISTCHURCH,
BH23 1HU

Tel: 01202 475111

Fax: 01202 490111

Email: enquiries@captainsclubhotel.com

Website: www.captainsclubhotel.com

Map ref: 3, SZ19

Directions: B3073 to Christchurch. On Fountain rdbt
take 5th exit (Sopers Ln) 2nd left (St Margarets Ave)
1st right onto Wick Ln

Rooms: 29 (12 fmly) S £125-£169 D £169-£229 (incl. bkfst)

Facilities: Wi-fi Spa Sauna Parking: 41

Sleek, smooth and ultra modern, Captain's Club Hotel is a testament to designer flair. This strikingly contemporary boutique hotel resides on the banks of the River Stour, just a short walk from the centre of historic Christchurch. There are many relaxing and fun ways to spend your time here – amongst them enjoying a soothing spa treatment, a trip across the bay aboard the hotel's 34-foot luxury motor cruiser, a stroll along the quayside to Christchurch Priory (which boasts choir stalls older than those in Westminster Abbey), or simply sitting back in a so-comfortable armchair to drink in the superb vista through floor-to-ceiling windows. All 29 bedrooms and suites have a contemporary maritime theme and are light and airy with stunning riverside views, air-conditioning, flat-screen TV, DVD player and free high-speed wireless broadband. The modern maritime theme and fabulous river views continue in Tides Restaurant, where the cuisine reflects the feel of the hotel: uncomplicated, fresh, innovative and ultimately satisfying.

Recommended in the area

Christchurch Priory and harbour; Isle of Wight; New Forest National Park

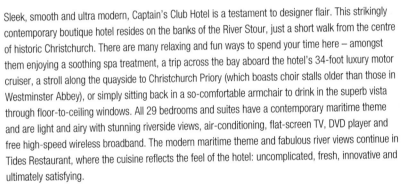

Harbour Heights Hotel

★★★★ 80% ◉◉ HOTEL

Address: 73 Haven Road, Sandbanks, POOLE,
BH13 7LW
Tel: 01202 707272 & 0845 337 1550
Fax: 01202 708594
Email: enquiries@fjbhotels.co.uk
Website: www.fjbhotels.co.uk
Map ref: 3, SZ09
Directions: Follow signs for Sandbanks, hotel on left
after Canford Cliffs
Rooms: 38 (2 fmly) D £100-£190 (incl. bkfst)
Facilities: STV Wi-fi **Parking:** 50 **Notes:** ⊗ in bedrooms

The hotel was built in 1920 and completely renovated in 2003, and offers contemporary elegance with a classic Rhode Island twist. The two-AA Rosette harbar bistro offers an impressive menu using local produce wherever possible. The bar and restaurant extend onto a tiered landscaped terrace with panoramic views over Poole Harbour. The hotel is ideally situated for the many local attractions.

Recommended in the area

Tank Museum; Swanage Railway; Purbeck Heritage Coast

Haven Hotel

★★★★ 76% ◉◉ HOTEL

Address: Banks Road, Sandbanks, POOLE,
BH13 7QL
Tel: 01202 707333 & 0845 337 1550
Fax: 01202 708796
Email: reservations@fjbhotels.co.uk
Website: www.fjbhotels.co.uk
Map ref: 3, SZ09
Directions: B3965 towards Poole Bay, left onto the
Peninsula. Hotel 1.5m on left next to Swanage Toll
Ferry point **Rooms:** 77(4 fmly) S £100-£165 D £200-£420 (incl. bkfst)
Facilities: STV Wi-fi ⊗ ⊀ Tennis Spa Gym Sauna **Parking:** 160 **Notes:** ⊗ in bedrooms

The Haven is idyllically located at the very tip of the exclusive Sandbanks peninsular with uninterrupted views of Poole Harbour. Most rooms have balconies and views across to the Purbeck Hills, Studland Beach or Brownsea Island. The waterside La Roche restaurant showcases some of Dorset's finest produce on its seasonally changing menus.

Recommended in the area

Jurassic Coast; Brownsea Island; Purbeck Hills; Compton Acres; Corfe Castle

Corfe Castle

Sandbanks Hotel

★★★★ 76% ☺ HOTEL

Address: 15 Banks Road, Sandbanks, POOLE, BH13
7PS

Tel: 01202 707377 & 0845 337 1550

Fax: 01202 708885

Email: reservations@fjbhotels.co.uk

Website: www.fjbhotels.co.uk

Map ref: 3, SZ09

Directions: A338 from Bournemouth onto Wessex
Way, to Liverpool Victoria rdbt. Left, then 2nd exit
onto B3965 **Rooms:** 110 (4 GF) (31 fmly) **S** £75-£155 **D** £150-£310 (incl. bkfst)
Facilities: STV Wi-fi ☺ Spa Gym Sauna **Parking:** 120 **Notes:** ☺ in bedrooms

The Sandbanks is situated on a Blue Flag beach, looking across Poole Bay to the famous Old Harry
Rocks. The view can be enjoyed from the terrace, the newly refurbished lounges, the Seaview
Restaurant and many of the bedrooms. Depending on the time of year several watersports are offered.
Experienced staff are available to assist with all aspects of business or social events.

Recommended in the area

Poole Quay; Alice in Wonderland Park; Jurassic Coastal Path

CO DURHAM

Castle Bridge, Barnard Castle, River Tees

Headlam Hall

★★★ 85% ◉ HOTEL

Address: Headlam, Gainford, DARLINGTON,
DL2 3HA

Tel: 01325 730238

Fax: 01325 730790

Email: admin@headlamhall.co.uk

Website: www.headlamhall.co.uk

Map ref: 6, NZ21

Directions: 2m N of A67 between Piercebridge &
Gainford **Rooms:** 40 (10 GF) (4 fmly) **S** £90–£115 **D**
£115–£190 (incl. bkfst) **Facilities:** STV Wi-fi ⊗ Tennis Spa Gym Sauna **Parking:** 80

A fine 17th-century mansion set amid beautiful grounds and gardens in a tranquil part of Teesdale. A glorious haven for anyone conducting business in the Middlesbrough-Stockton-Darlington conurbation to the east, it is also perfect for exploring rural Co Durham and the Yorkshire Dales. There is also the option of taking in a round of golf on the hotel's own nine-hole course, a dip in its spacious indoor pool with water-jet feature, a work-out in the gym or a pampering spa treatment. The spa also has a sauna, steam room and air-conditioned exercise studio. Not surprisingly, the hotel is a popular venue for functions and conferences. The bedrooms come in a variety of sizes, some with elegant period furniture, others in cosy cottage style. All have contemporary touches and facilities including Sky TV and free wireless broadband. The public areas are richly decorated and include a cocktail bar and the elegant drawing room overlooking the main lawn. The restaurant, spread across four very different dining areas, serves modern British cuisine along the lines of pink bream fillet with lemon and sun-blushed tomato couscous and red pepper oil, and crispy breast of Gressingham duck with duck leg hash, carrot puree and black cherry sauce.

Recommended in the area

Raby Castle; Bowes Museum; High Force waterfall

Facade of Audley End House near Saffron Walden

De Rougemont Manor

★★★★ 73% HOTEL

Address: Great Warley Street, BRENTWOOD, CM13 3JP
Tel: 01277 226418 & 220483
Fax: 01277 239020
Email: info@derougemontmanor.co.uk
Website: www.derougemontmanor.co.uk
Map ref: 4, TQ59
Directions: M25 junct 29, A127 to Southend then B186 towards Great Warley
Rooms: 79 (16 GF) (6 fmly) S £89–£139 D £99–£159 (incl. bkfst)
Facilities: STV Wi-fi ⚡ Tennis Gym **Parking:** 133 **Notes:** ⊗ in bedrooms

A multi-gabled, oak-beamed Victorian mansion standing on a hilltop overlooking this perhaps surprisingly rural part of Essex and, 27 miles away, the high-rises of the City of London. Within its 12 wooded acres is a rather famous and quite delightful Italian garden. In the early part of the last century the property, known then as Goldings, was the home of philanthropist Evelyn Heseltine, whose daughter Muriel married Major General Cecil De Rougement, whose names the present owners, a local family, have commemorated in the hotel's name and in its refurbished Heseltines Restaurant. The well-appointed bedrooms are all different shapes and sizes, and each is tastefully decorated and furnished in either oak or beechwood in keeping with the hotel's period style. All have satellite flat-screen TV, hairdryer, direct-dial telephone, alarm clock, radio, tea-and-coffee-making facilities and trouser press, and most have jacuzzi baths. Heseltines offers an extensive regular menu with daily specials, all dishes prepared from fresh, seasonal ingredients. Such is its layout that it can cater for large gatherings as well as smaller, more intimate private meals and get-togethers.

Recommended in the area

Weald Country Park; Romford Market; Southend-on-Sea; Lakeside; Bluewater

Maison Talbooth

★★★ ⊛ COUNTRY HOUSE HOTEL

Address: Stratford Road, DEDHAM, CO7 6HN
Tel: 01206 322367
Fax: 01206 322752
Email: maison@milsomhotels.com
Website: www.milsomhotels.com
Map ref: 4, TM03
Directions: A12 towards Ipswich, 1st turn signed
Dedham, follow to left bend, turn right.
Hotel 1m on right
Rooms: 12 (5 GF) (1 fmly) S £150-£275 D £190-£325 (incl. bkfst)
Facilities: STV Wi-fi ◬ Tennis Spa Parking: 20 Notes: ⊗ in bedrooms

This impressive Victorian country house sits in a peaceful rural location in the heart of Constable country, amid pretty landscaped grounds overlooking the River Stour. Recently refurbished, it now boasts three principal suites, each with its own hot tub on a private terrace. All of the spacious en suite bedrooms are individually decorated, with tasteful furnishings, co-ordinated fabrics and thoughtful extras such as super-king-size beds, goose-feather duvets, fluffy towels and mini-bars; many rooms have fine views over Dedham Vale. The hotel features a day spa with three treatment rooms, plus an outdoor hot tub. In the Pool House there's a dining area complete with kitchen, which can be used for house parties and meetings, while other public areas include a comfortable drawing room where guests may take afternoon tea or snacks. A new addition is the Garden Room Restaurant, a light and airy room with a high-vaulted ceiling and large windows. Here, guests can enjoy everything from breakfast to a light lunch through to dinner, and even dancing if the house is booked for exclusive use. It's no wonder the hotel is a popular venue for weddings.

Recommended in the area

Sir Alfred Munnings Museum; Beth Chatto Gardens; Colchester Castle

milsoms

★★★ 78%  SMALL HOTEL

Address: Stratford Road, Dedham, COLCHESTER, CO7 6HW

Tel: 01206 322795

Fax: 01206 323689

Email: milsoms@milsomhotels.com

Website: www.milsomhotels.com

Map ref: 4, TM03 **Directions:** 6m N of Colchester off A12, follow Stratford St Mary/Dedham signs. Turn right over A12, hotel on left

Rooms: 15 (4 GF) (3 fmly) S £90-£110 D £110-£155 **Facilities:** STV Wi-fi **Parking:** 70

Milsoms is situated in the heart of Constable country in the Dedham Vale, and makes a perfect base for exploring the countryside on the north Essex/Suffolk border. The hub of milsoms is the contemporary bar and brasserie, where food is served all day and the whole a la carte menu is available from noon until late. The restaurant spills out onto the terrace which is covered with a huge architectural sail. Fifteen stylish, individually designed en suite bedrooms complete the milsoms picture.

Recommended in the area

The Painters Trail – Constable, Gainsborough and Munnings; Suffolk Heritage Coast; Stour Valley

The Pier at Harwich

★★★ 82%  HOTEL

Address: The Quay, HARWICH, CO12 3HH

Tel: 01255 241212

Fax: 01255 551922

Email: pier@milsomhotels.com

Website: www.milsomhotels.com

Map ref: 4, TM23

Directions: Opposite lifeboat station on Quay

Rooms: 14 (1 GF) (5 fmly) S £80-£95 D £105-£185 (incl. bkfst) **Facilities:** STV Wi-fi

Parking: 10 **Notes:** ⊗ in bedrooms

Beside the quay in Harwich old town and located in two historic buildings, The Pier enjoys spectacular views of the ever-changing scenery of the east coast's busiest harbour. Bedrooms are stylish with many individual touches and all have private bathrooms, satellite TV, minibars and tea and coffee tray. There are two fabulous restaurants, the first-floor Harbourside, with views of the Stour and Orwell estuaries and the harbour below, specialises in locally caught seafood while the Ha'penny Bistro offers relaxed brasserie-style food. The hotel can arrange sailing days on a renovated traditional fishing smack.

Recommended in the area Sailing; Ha'penny Pier and Museum; Redoubt Fort; Martello Tower

St Mary's Church, Painswick

Swan Hotel

★★★ 82% ❀ HOTEL

Address: BIBURY, GL7 5NW

Tel: 01285 740695

Fax: 01285 740473

Email: info@swanhotel.co.uk

Website: www.cotswold-inns-hotels.co.uk/swan

Map ref: 3, SP10

Directions: 9m S of Burford A40 onto B4425. 6m N of Cirencester A4179 onto B4425

Rooms: 22 (1 fmly) Facilities: Wi-fi Parking: 22

With beautifully landscaped gardens bisected by the River Coln, within one of England's prettiest villages, the picturesque, ivy-clad Swan Hotel truly presents a Cotswolds idyll. Starting life as coaching inn in the 17th century, it is now furnished in country-house style to create a relaxing atmosphere and its ornamental garden is surrounded by a crystal-clear moat. The cosy lounges, decorated in country house style, offer a peaceful place to relax, each having a feature fireplace, and the convivial bar serves real ales. There's a touch of eccentricity about the bedrooms, most of which have river views; each is individually styled and all boast a lavish bathroom, perhaps with a large hot-tub bath. There are also some new, two-storey self-contained suites a short walk from the main building, with separate sitting rooms and a private garden. The Whooper Suite, in a Cotswold stone cottage, offers the ultimate luxury and stunning views. The Gallery Restaurant serves modern European-style cuisine in a romantic setting, with original oil paintings by a Dartmoor artist on the walls. The freshest local produce goes into dishes such as roast venison and baby turnips, with a pancetta and thyme port glaze, or brill poached in red wine shallots and rosemary, with sweet potato purée and goats' cheese ravioli.

Recommended in the area

Cirencester; Cotswold Wildlife Park; Chedworth Roman Villa

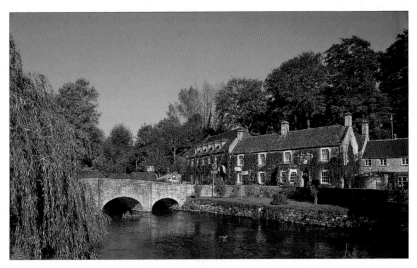

Forest of Dean, bluebells

Buckland Manor

★★★ ◉◉ COUNTRY HOUSE HOTEL
Address: BUCKLAND, WR12 7LY
Tel: 01386 852626
Fax: 01386 853557
Email: info@bucklandmanor.co.uk
Website: www.bucklandmanor.co.uk
Map ref: 3, SP03
Directions: Off B4632 (Broadway to Winchcombe
road) Rooms: 13 (4 GF) (2 fmly) S £270-£470
D £280-£480 (incl. bkfst) Facilities: STV Tennis
Parking: 30 Notes: ⊗ in bedrooms ⚲ under 12 yrs

This grand 13th-century Cotswold manor house is surrounded by pretty, well-kept gardens featuring a stream, waterfalls, a croquet lawn and tennis courts. Everything here is geared to encourage rest and relaxation. Inside you'll find log fires and comfy armchairs aplenty, while the en suite bedrooms are roomy and beautifully furnished. In the elegant dining room, with views over the rolling hills, great emphasis is placed on local produce, including herbs from the garden, and the wine list is a treat.
Recommended in the area
Hidcote Manor Gardens; Sudeley Castle; Stratford-upon-Avon

Corse Lawn House Hotel

★★★ ◉◉ HOTEL

Address: CORSE LAWN, GL19 4LZ
Tel: 01452 780771
Fax: 01452 780840
Email: enquiries@corselawn.com
Website: www.corselawn.com
Map ref: 2, SO82 **Directions:** On B4211 5m SW of
Tewkesbury **Rooms:** 19 (5 GF) (2 fmly) **S** £95-£100
D £150-£170 (incl. bkfst)
Facilities: STV Wi-fi ⊗ Tennis **Parking:** 62

This privately owned and run hotel occupies an elegant Queen Anne grade II listed house, and is idyllically situated beside an ornamental pond in the picture-postcard village of Corse Lawn. The house has been carefully extended and refurbished over the years to offer 21st century comforts in a beautiful period setting. The Hine family and their staff provide a very personal welcome, the Dining Room and Bistro have won many accolades (including a Notable Wine List award from the AA), and swimming, tennis and croquet are all within the grounds. All in all, it adds up to a seriously relaxing stay.

Recommended in the area

The Cotswolds; Forest of Dean; The Malverns

Washbourne Court Hotel

★★★ 88% ◉◉ HOTEL

Address: LOWER SLAUGHTER, GL54 2HS
Tel: 01451 822143
Fax: 01451 821045
Email: info@washbournecourt.co.uk
Website: www.vonessenhotels.co.uk
Map ref: 3, SP12
Directions: Exit A429 at 'The Slaughters' sign, between
Stow-on-the-Wold & Bourton-on-the-Water.
Hotel in village centre
Rooms: 30 (9 GF) **S** £135-£225 **D** £135-£350 (incl. bkfst)
Facilities: Wi-fi **Parking:** 40

Standing beside the River Eye in one of the Cotswolds' prettiest villages, Washbourne Court is a stylish, luxury, country-house hotel dating back to the 17th century. The en suite bedrooms are all beautifully furnished to the highest standards, while the stunning mirror-panelled Eton's Restaurant serves superb modern British and French cuisine.

Recommended in the area

Batsford Arboretum; Bourton-on-the-Water; Cotswold Falconry Centre

Manor House Hotel

★★★★ 75% ◉◉ HOTEL

Address: High Street, MORETON-IN-MARSH,
GL56 0LJ
Tel: 01608 650501
Fax: 01608 651481
Email: info@manorhousehotel.info
Website: www.cotswold-inns-hotels.co.uk/manor
Map ref: 3, SP23
Directions: Off A429 at south end of town. Take East
St off High St, hotel car park 3rd on right
Rooms: 35 (1 GF) (3 fmly) **Facilities:** Wi-fi **Parking:** 24

The Manor House was bequeathed to the Dean and Chapter of Westminster in 1539 by Henry VIII, when it was a traditional coaching inn at the heart of the busy market town of Moreton-in-Marsh. Today the attractive Cotswold stone building retains plenty of 16th century character, blending seamlessly with 21st century style and technology. The bedrooms, including four-poster rooms and suites, are elegantly furnished with a country-house look, and have lots of period features like open fireplaces and window seats. Each comes with flat-screen TV, tea-and-coffee-making facilities and luxurious Molton Brown toiletries in the bathroom. There's also a one-bedroom cottage in the grounds with its own private garden and terrace with hot tub – perfect for longer stays or a truly indulgent escape. The cooking in the Mulberry Restaurant is modern British and takes its lead from fresh, seasonal, local produce. Dinner might begin with peppered Cerney goats cheese with carpaccio of beetroot and beetroot sorbet for example, followed, perhaps, by belly of pork and tenderloin with Scotch egg, French beans and celeriac. The Beagle Bar & Brasserie offers a more informal dining option, as well as serving afternoon tea and cocktails.

Recommended in the area

Royal Shakespeare Company; Stratford-Upon-Avon; Batsford Arboretum; Hidcote Manor Gardens

Cotswold Water Park

Cotswold Water Park Hotel

★★★★ 76% HOTEL

Address: Lake 6 Spine Road East, SOUTH CERNEY,
GL7 5FP
Tel: 0800 374692 & 01285 864000
Fax: 01285 864001
Email: waterpark@four-pillars.co.uk
Website: www.cotswoldwaterpark.co.uk
Map ref: 3, SU09
Directions: Off A419, 3m from Cirencester
Rooms: 219 (115 GF) (29 fmly) S £70-£119
D £70-£133 **Facilities:** STV Wi-fi ☜ Spa Gym **Parking:** 200 **Notes:** ⊗ in bedrooms

This luxurious hotel, which opened in 2007, is set in 55 acres of idyllic parkland. It looks out over a large lake – one of more than 140 in the Cotswold Water Park – and its restaurants, spa, and many of the 318 bedrooms have views of the water. The hotel's design is contemporary but inspired by the surrounding environment, with much use of wood, stone and other natural materials. All rooms come with free broadband access, and there are some suites and apartments with kitchens for longer stays.

Recommended in the area

Keynes Country Park; Watersports on the lakes; nature reserves

103

Stonehouse Court

★★★ 79% ◉ HOTEL
Address: STONEHOUSE, Stroud, GL10 3RA
Tel: 0871 871 3240 & 01453 794 950
Fax: 0871 871 3241
Email: info@stonehousecourt.co.uk
Website: www.stonehousecourt.co.uk
Map ref: 2, SO80
Directions: M5 junct 13, off A419. Follow signs for Stonehouse, hotel on right 0.25m after 2nd rdbt
Rooms: 36 (6 GF) (2 fmly) S £80-£95 D £100-£180 (incl. bkfst)
Facilities: Wi-fi Gym Parking: 200

This handsome 17th century manor house sits in six acres of stunning grounds overlooking the Stroud Water Canal and surrounded by the rolling hills of the Stroud Valley. If you're looking for peace and tranquillity, you'll find it here: the gardens are truly stunning – the perfect spot for a gentle stroll, a glass of Pimms on a sunny summer's day, or a game of croquet. An arched gateway leads from the end of the garden through to the canal and the countryside beyond. The house itself, which was built in 1601 on the site of an earlier manor, is elegantly furnished in a traditional English country-house style. It really does feel like a home from home, and that has much to do with the staff, who are friendly, professional and caring. Enjoy a drink on the terrace or in the cosy lounge before taking your seat in Henry's Restaurant, an informal space which combines the charm of the Tudor house with contemporary style. The menu here is modern European and may take in the likes of tian of Cornish white crab with green apple and wasabi horseradish, followed by roast rack of Forest of Dean lamb with pancetta and Gruyere boulangere potato, lamb faggot, roasted plum tomatoes and a balsamic jus.

Recommended in the area

Canal boat trips; Gloucester Cathedral; Cheltenham

Calcot Manor

★★★★ ◉◉ HOTEL
Address: Calcot, TETBURY, GL8 8YJ
Tel: 01666 890391
Fax: 01666 890394
Email: reception@calcotmanor.co.uk
Website: www.calcotmanor.co.uk
Map ref: 2, ST89
Directions: 3m West of Tetbury at junct A4135/A46
Rooms: 35 (17 GF) (13 fmly) S £216-£241
D £240-£265 (incl. bkfst)
Facilities: STV Wi-fi ◉ ✕ Spa Gym Sauna **Parking:** 150 **Notes:** ⊗ in bedrooms

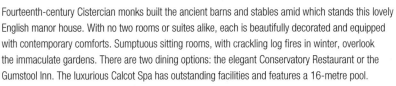

Fourteenth-century Cistercian monks built the ancient barns and stables amid which stands this lovely English manor house. With no two rooms or suites alike, each is beautifully decorated and equipped with contemporary comforts. Sumptuous sitting rooms, with crackling log fires in winter, overlook the immaculate gardens. There are two dining options: the elegant Conservatory Restaurant or the Gumstool Inn. The luxurious Calcot Spa has outstanding facilities and features a 16-metre pool.
Recommended in the area
Slimbridge Wildfowl Trust; Westonbirt Arboretum; Tetbury

Lords of the Manor

★★★★ ◉◉◉ COUNTRY HOUSE HOTEL
Address: UPPER SLAUGHTER, GL54 2JD
Tel: 01451 820243
Fax: 01451 820696
Email: enquiries@lordsofthemanor.com
Website: www.lordsofthemanor.com
Map ref: 3, SP12
Directions: 2m W of A429. Turn off A40 onto A429, take 'The Slaughters' turn. Through Lower Slaughter for 1m to Upper Slaughter. Hotel on right

Rooms: 26 (9 GF) (4 fmly) S £191 D £191-£362 (incl. bkfst) **Facilities:** Wi-fi **Parking:** 40

A 17th century honey-coloured rectory in eight acres of gardens and parkland, the Lords is the next best thing to a private retreat. Reception rooms have been preserved with style and character, their log fires blazing throughout the winter, and French windows thrown open to the terrace in summer. Some of the bedrooms overlook the gardens and lake, others the Victorian courtyard. Room extras include DVD player and luxury toiletries. The restaurant serves some of the county's finest food.
Recommended in the area
Bourton Model Village; Cotswold Farm Park; Broadway

Albert Square, Manchester

Egerton House Hotel

★★★ 78% HOTEL

Address: Blackburn Road, Egerton, BOLTON, BL7 9SB

Tel: 01204 307171

Fax: 01204 593030

Email: reservation@egertonhouse-hotel.co.uk

Website: www.egertonhouse-hotel.co.uk

Map ref: 6, SD70

Directions: M61, A666 (Bolton road), pass ASDA on right. Hotel 2m on, just past war memorial on right

Rooms: 29 (7 fmly) **Facilities:** Wi-fi **Parking:** 135

Notes: ⊗ in bedrooms

This beautiful privately-owned country-house hotel enjoys a secluded location in three acres of developed gardens just three miles away from Bolton. A family home for over 200 years, Egerton House has a warm and welcoming feel and plenty of character, making it a delightful retreat with the beauty of the Lancashire Hills right on the doorstep. Indeed, once you've settled into the cosy lounge with its open fire and lovely views of the grounds, it would be easy to forget the outside world exists. All 29 en suite rooms at Egerton House are non-smoking and come with flat-screen TV with Freeview, tea-and-coffee-making facilities, iron and ironing board and trouser press. Wi-fi access is available in the lounge. Dinner and Sunday lunch are served in The Dining Room, a smart and contemporary space where the focus of the table d'hote menu is high-quality regional produce put to use in classic English and French dishes. Whether you're staying for business or pleasure, you can expect first-class, friendly service from a dedicated team. The hotel is an ideal venue for meetings, private gatherings and weddings, and took home the 'Hotel of the Year' award in the Lancashire Life Magazine Food & Wine Awards 2009-2010.

Recommended in the area

Bolton Museum, Art Gallery & Aquarium; Smithills Hall; Trafford Centre

The Saddleworth Hotel

★★★★ 80% ◉◉ COUNTRY HOUSE HOTEL

Address: Huddersfield Road, DELPH, Saddleworth,
OL3 5LX
Tel: 01457 871888
Fax: 01457 871889
Email: enquiries@thesaddleworthhotel.co.uk
Website: www.thesaddleworthhotel.co.uk
Map ref: 7, SE00
Directions: A6052 Delph. At White Lion PH left on local road,
left after 0.5m onto A62, hotel 0.5m on right
Rooms: 13 (1 GF) (3 fmly) **S** £90-£120
D £160-£300 (incl. bkfst)
Facilities: STV Wi-fi ⚘ **Parking:** 142 **Notes:** ⊗ in bedrooms

Once a coaching station on one of the busiest routes across the Pennine Hills, the Saddleworth Hotel sits in nine acres of beautiful gardens and woodland in the picturesque Castleshaw Valley. The house was built in the 17th century and has been lovingly restored and sympathetically updated by the live-in owners. There are many interesting period features, including the panelling and fireplace in the Great Hall which were taken from historic Weasenham Hall in East Anglia, and the wrought iron French doors leading to the garden which date back to 1795 and were recovered from a Newmarket stud, but originally came from a chateau in Bordeaux. All 12 bedrooms have their own individual character and are elegantly furnished and equipped with all the latest technology, while the luxury continues in the en suite marble bathrooms. Now approaching its 50th successful year, The Saddleworth Hotel is a popular venue for parties, weddings, fine dining and afternoon tea. The restaurant serves a combination of traditional English and Continental cuisine, complemented by a choice of over 100 fine wines.

Recommended in the area

Roman fortress; Standedge Tunnel; Pennine Way

The Midland

★★★★ 85% ◉◉ HOTEL

Address: Peter Street, MANCHESTER, M60 2DS
Tel: 0161 236 3333
Fax: 0161 932 4100
Email: midlandsales@qhotels.co.uk
Website: www.qhotels.co.uk
Map ref: 6, SJ89
Directions: M602 junct 3, follow Manchester Central Convention Complex signs, hotel opposite.
Rooms: 312 (11 fmly) S £95-£250 D £95-£250
Facilities: STV Wi-fi ⊛ Gym Sauna Notes: ⊗ in bedrooms

In May 1904 at this terracotta-coloured Edwardian hotel, then just a year old, Mr Rolls met Mr Royce for the first time. It stands as proudly now as it did that day, when they agreed to make and sell cars. Its central position makes it easily accessible by road, rail and tram networks, and the Bridgewater Hall, MEN Arena, shops and theatres are all within walking distance. Now transformed by a £15 million restoration programme it is, without doubt, one of Manchester's finest hotels. Through the magnificent lobby are the elegant public areas, extensive function and meeting rooms and a choice of bars, the Wyvern and the Octagon Lounge. Dining is also a matter of choice, including modern French cuisine with a British influence in the hotel's two-Rosette restaurant, The French. The leisure club houses a gym, swimming pool, sauna, solarium, aerobic studio and squash court. State-of-the-art conference facilities can cater for up to 700 delegates. All bedrooms and suites are equipped with air-conditioning, tea-and-coffee-making facilities, mini-bar, Wi-fi, in-house movies and flat-screen TVs.

Recommended in the area

Salford Quays; Lowry Galleries; Old Trafford Football Stadium

Best Western Hotel Smokies Park

★★★ 80% HOTEL

Address:	Ashton Road, Bardsley, OLDHAM, OL8 3HX
Tel:	0161 785 5000
Fax:	0161 785 5010
Email:	sales@smokies.co.uk
Website:	www.smokies.co.uk
Map ref:	7, SC90
Directions:	On A627 between Oldham & Ashton-under-Lyne
Rooms:	73 (22 GF) (2 fmly) S £56-£86 D £62-£102 (incl. bkfst)
Facilities:	STV Wi-fi Gym Sauna Parking: 120 Notes: ⊗ in bedrooms

Best Western Hotel Smokies Park is located in Oldham, a short drive from Manchester city centre. It has 73 en suite, no-smoking rooms, including 10 Executive and Superior suites, with all the modern facilities you would expect. The rooms are delightfully furnished, spacious, and come complete with multi-channel TV, direct-dial telephone, hairdryer, ironing facilities and hospitality tray. The hotel's stylish and contemporary restaurant, Brasserie 1, serves an international menu based around fresh ingredients which are locally sourced as much as possible. For a more informal alternative, Bar 1 offers an excellent choice of drinks alongside a menu of lighter dishes and bar snacks. For active guests, there's an on-site gym, plus a steam room and sauna to relax in after a workout. Complimentary Wi-fi is available throughout the hotel and parking is free. Best Western Smokies Park is also well placed for hosting conferences and events, with space and facilities for up to 400 delegates.

Recommended in the area

Daisy Nook Country Park; Portland Basin Museum; Bramall Hall

A path leading into Breamore wood

Esseborne Manor

★★★ 79% ® HOTEL

Address: Hurstbourne Tarrant, ANDOVER, SP11 0ER
Tel: 01264 736444
Fax: 01264 736725
Email: info@esseborne-manor.co.uk
Website: www.esseborne-manor.co.uk
Map ref: 3, SU34
Directions: Halfway between Andover & Newbury on A343, just 1m N of Hurstbourne Tarrant
Rooms: 19 (6 GF) (2 fmly) **S** £90-£130
D £125-£180 (incl. bkfst) **Facilities:** STV Wi-fi Tennis **Parking:** 50

A long drive leads to this privately-owned Victorian country-house hotel, set in three acres of gardens high on the hill above the lovely Bourne Valley. The surrounding high downland makes this a perfect spot for country walks, with lots of delightful village pubs for refreshment along the way. All the bedrooms, overlooking the gardens and farmlands beyond, are individually decorated, and some have jacuzzis and four-poster beds. Feature rooms include Lymington, with a luxurious Victorian bath overlooking the croquet lawn; Ferndown, with a canopy bed and a private patio; and the Honeymoon Suite, with a separate lounge and rococo-style king-size bed. The Dining Room, with its fabric-lined walls, provides a warm and elegant setting for the chef's fine English cuisine, using local produce and herbs from the hotel's own gardens. A choice of fixed-price menus is offered, including a Menu du Vin that includes a specially selected glass of wine with each course. There's also an extensive wine list should you prefer to select your own. The dinner menu might include such main courses as slow-roast pheasant, steak and Guinness pie with pot-au-feu vegetables, and fillet of cod with crushed new potato and tomato fondue.

Recommended in the Area

Highclere Castle; Winchester; Broadlands

Montagu Arms Hotel

★★★ ◉◉ HOTEL

Address: Palace Lane, BEAULIEU, SO42 7ZL
Tel: 01590 624467 & 0845 123 5613
Fax: 01590 612188
Email: reservations@montaguarmshotel.co.uk
Website: www.montaguarmshotel.co.uk
Map ref: 3, SU30
Directions: M27 junct 2, turn left at rdbt, follow signs for Beaulieu. Continue to Dibden Purlieu, then right at rdbt. Hotel on left
Rooms: 22 (3 fmly) **S** £140 **D** £180 **Facilities:** Wi-fi **Parking:** 86 **Notes:** ✖ in bedrooms

In the heart of a lovely New Forest village, the Montagu Arms manages to achieve the impression of almost total seclusion, despite the flow of visitors that flock to the area during the tourist season. Dating back to 1742, the building has changed over the years but still exudes English country-house character, with beautiful oak panelling, open fireplaces and pretty gardens. Aptly for its forest setting, the bedrooms are each named after a species of tree and each is individually styled and luxurious. Many have a four-poster bed and some also have a sofa bed, making them ideal for families. The public areas include a comfortable lounge with an adjoining conservatory and the lively, oak-panelled Monty's Bar and Brasserie, offering classics such as sausage and mash and ploughman's lunches. The award-winning Terrace Restaurant overlooks the beautiful gardens and, as the name suggests, it does indeed have a terrace for alfresco dining on warmer days. Guests are offered complimentary use of the Thai spa at sister hotel Careys Manor in Brockenhurst. There you can relax in the hydrotherapy pool and thermal rooms, invigorate yourself in the sensory showers, and perhaps book yourself a treatment from a wide list of options.

Recommended in the area

National Motor Museum; Bucklers Hard; Exbury Gardens

Balmer Lawn

★★★★ 75% ◉ HOTEL

Address: Lyndhurst Road, BROCKENHURST, SO42 7ZB
Tel: 01590 623116
Fax: 01590 623864
Email: info@balmerlawnhotel.com
Website: www.balmerlawnhotel.com
Map ref: 3, SU30
Directions: Just off A337 from Brockenhurst towards Lymington
Rooms: 54 (10 fmly) **S** £99-£110 **D** £150-£180 (incl. bkfst)
Facilities: Wi-fi ⊗ ꝛ Tennis Spa Gym Sauna **Parking:** 100

This imposing, four-storey hotel was built about 1800 as a New Forest hunting lodge. And so it remained until the First World War, when it became a field hospital, then, during the Second, an Army staff college. Namedroppers on the staff may mention King George V, Russian royalty, Churchill and Eisenhower as past guests. Individually designed en suite rooms meet the needs of all, from families to business travellers, providing hospitality tray, direct dial phone, TV, hairdryer and trouser press. Family rooms offer a games console (business guests may consider this unfair!). Many rooms offer views of the forest. With an AA Rosette for fine dining, the comfortable Beresford's Restaurant offers high standards of food, wine and service. At weekends there is live entertainment, with jazz on Sundays. Leisure facilities include indoor and outdoor heated pools, spa bath, sauna, air-conditioned gym, squash court, all-weather tennis court and table tennis. Conference rooms are well equipped, many with broadband access. The hotel is a good base for walking, cycling, riding and mountain-biking through the beautiful open heathland of the New Forest National Park.

Recommended in the area

Beaulieu Palace, Abbey and Motor Museum; Bucklers Hard; Hurst Castle

Careys Manor Hotel

★★★★ 79% ◉◉ HOTEL

Address: BROCKENHURST, SO42 7RH
Tel: 01590 624467
Fax: 01590 622799
Email: stay@careysmanor.com
Website: www.careysmanor.com
Map ref: 3, SU30
Directions: M27 junct 3, M271, A35 to Lyndhurst. A337 towards Brockenhurst. Hotel on left after 30mph sign **Rooms:** 80 (32 GF) **S** £149–£189 **D** £198–£358 (incl. bkfst) **Facilities:** Wi-fi ⊗ Spa Gym Sauna **Parking:** 180 **Notes:** ⊗ in bedrooms ⋈ under 16 yrs

Careys Manor and SenSpa is an award-winning hotel located deep in the heart of the beautiful New Forest National Park. With three restaurants, there is plenty to choose from – whether you prefer fine dining in the two AA-Rosetted Manor Restaurant, the relaxed atmosphere of Blaireau's French Bistro, or want to enjoy authentic Thai cuisine in the Zen Garden Restaurant. All use only the finest ingredients sourced in line with an ethical food policy of buying local, free-range and organic produce where possible. SenSpa, the £6 million Thai spa, offers state-of-the-art facilities including a large hydrotherapy pool, herbal sauna, crystal steam room, ice room, experience showers and much more besides. A range of indulgent natural treatments includes a variety of massages such as traditional Thai and Swedish massage, Ayurvedic head massage, Oriental foot massage and Thai herbal poultice, and a range of unique pure spa treatments. Many of SenSpa's therapists are from Thailand and bring with them experience and knowledge to help create an authentic Thai spa. In short, English tradition combined with contemporary oriental sophistication, making it the ideal place to enjoy a relaxing break.

Recommended in the area

Beaulieu Palace and Motor Museum; Hurst Castle; Exbury Gardens

Rhinefield House

★★★★ ◉◉ HOTEL

Address: Rhinefield Road, BROCKENHURST,
SO42 7QB
Tel: 01590 622922
Fax: 01590 622800
Email: rhinefieldhouse@handpicked.co.uk
Website: www.handpicked.co.uk
Map ref: 3, SU30
Directions: A35 towards Christchurch. 3m from
Lyndhurst turn left to Rhinefield, 1.5m to hotel
Rooms: 50 (18 GF) (10 fmly) S £115-£175 D £125-185 (incl. bkfst)
Facilities: STV Wi-fi ⊗ ⅄ Tennis Gym Sauna
Parking: 100 Notes: ⊗ in bedrooms

A stunning country house hotel set in 40 acres of peaceful and secluded gardens in the heart of the
New Forest. Standing at the end of a long sweeping drive, shaded by Canadian redwood and copper
beech trees and lined with rhododendrons, it's the ideal retreat for a romantic break. Rhinefield
House is a member of Hand Picked Hotels, an exclusive collection of country house hotels renowned
for superb food, fine wines and excellent service in stylish surroundings. All 50 of its comfortable,
elegant bedrooms are named after different places or the flora and fauna of the New Forest, while
the excellent facilities include indoor and outdoor swimming pools. Guests can dine al fresco on the
terrace overlooking the beautiful lake and grounds, or choose from either the award-winning Armada
Restaurant with its magnificent fireplace carving of the Armada (which took nine years to complete
from a solid block of oak some 4ft thick) or the Brasserie, offering contemporary dining in stylish
surroundings and views across the ornamental ponds.

Recommended in the area

New Forest National Park; National Motor Museum; Lymington

Old Thorns Manor Hotel

★★★ 82% HOTEL

Address: Griggs Green, LIPHOOK, GU30 7PE
Tel: 01428 724555
Fax: 01428 725036
Email: sales@oldthorns.com
Website: www.oldthorns.com
Map ref: 3, SU82
Directions: Griggs Green exit off A3 hotel
0.5m off exit **Rooms:** 83 (14 GF) (2 fmly) **S** £75-£170
D £99-£195 (incl. bkfst)
Facilities: STV Wi-fi ⊗ Tennis Spa Gym **Parking:** 100

Originally a 17th century farmhouse, the Old Thorns was bought
by the Kenwood family (of Kenwood mixer fame) and developed into a beautiful country estate. It's
been run as a luxury hotel for some years, but thanks to a £20 million redevelopment – which began in
2007 – it is well on track to becoming one of England's premier resort hotels. In the early 1980's the
legendary Peter Alliss designed the 18-hole Old Thorns championship golf course, which remains his
favourite to this day. Through the current investment programme golfers will benefit from an improved
shop, a new coffee shop, bars and dining facilities. Already completed is the new Alliss wing, which has
added 49 stylish bedrooms to the original 33, all with flat-screen TV's, Wi-fi, refreshments facilities,
trouser press and high quality contemporary furnishings. Also new to the hotel are some luxury
penthouse apartments and spacious family rooms, plus a revamped spa, fitness studio, restaurants and
bars. The new-look Old Thorns retains much of its original charm and blends in seamlessly with the
surrounding 400-acre estate. Despite its countryside location on the border of Hampshire with West
Sussex and Surrey, the hotel is just 30 minutes from the M25.

Recommended in the area

Hollycombe Working Steam Museum; Go Ape!; Bird World

New Forest National Park

Westover Hall Hotel

★★★ 88% ◉◉ COUNTRY HOUSE HOTEL

Address: Park Lane, MILFORD ON SEA, SO41 0PT
Tel: 01590 643044
Fax: 01590 644490
Email: info@westoverhallhotel.com
Website: www.westoverhallhotel.com
Map ref: 3, SZ29
Directions: M3 & M27 W onto A337 to Lymington,
follow signs to Milford-on-Sea onto B3058, hotel
outside village centre towards cliff

Rooms: 15 (2 GF) (2 fmly) S £145 D £290 (incl. bkfst & dinner) Facilities: Wi-fi Parking: 50

A beautiful, Grade II-listed Victorian country house hotel, 150 metres from the beach, with views of the Isle of Wight and The Needles. Bedrooms have private bathrooms, tasteful furnishings and luxury Italian bed linen. There is also a 'Beach Retreat' adjacent to the hotel with two suites. Top quality New Forest produce is used to great effect in Westover Hall's fine dining restaurant, One Park Lane, as well as in the more informal Vista Bistro.

Recommended in the area

Beaulieu Palace & Motor Museum; Hurst Castle; Hengistbury Head

Chewton Glen Hotel & Spa

★★★★★ ◎◎◎ COUNTRY HOUSE HOTEL

Address: Christchurch Road, NEW MILTON,
BH25 5QS
Tel: 01425 275341
Fax: 01425 272310
Email: reservations@chewtonglen.com
Website: www.chewtonglen.com
Map ref: 3, SZ29
Directions: A35 from Lyndhurst for 10m, left at staggered junct. Follow tourist sign for hotel through Walkford, take 2nd left
Rooms: 58 (9 GF) **S** £329-£1295 **D** £329-£1295
Facilities: Wi-fi ③ ⟋ Tennis Spa Gym Sauna **Parking:** 100 **Notes:** ⊗ in bedrooms

The sea is just 10 minutes' walk from this superb 18th-century country-house hotel. Bedrooms are individually styled with luxurious fabrics and furnishings. All bedrooms enjoy the benefits of air conditioning, satellite television, radio, DVD and CD players, and direct-dial telephone. There are also a number of suites, some duplex, and all with secluded private gardens. Guests can enjoy the health and beauty treatments, both traditional and modern, of the elegant high-tech spa, where everything from a massage to a facial or a body polish is offered. The restaurant offers a wide variety of cuisines, using as much fresh local produce as possible and vegetarian and low-calorie dishes can be provided. The nearby New Forest offers wild mushrooms, vegetables and game; seafood may come from Christchurch and Lymington nearby. The wine list is drawn from a cellar of over 600 bins. Short residential packages are available including: Gourmet Dining Breaks, Spa Breaks and Celebration Breaks. Children of all ages are welcome at the hotel.

Recommended in the area

New Forest National Park; National Motor Museum, Beaulieu; Buckler's Hard historic village

Tylney Hall Hotel

★ ★ ★ ★ 🏵🏵 HOTEL

Address: ROTHERWICK, Hook, RG27 9AZ
Tel: 01256 764881 **Fax:** 01256 768141
Email: sales@tylneyhall.com
Website: www.tylneyhall.com
Map ref: 3, SU75 **Directions:** M3 junct 5, A287 to
Basingstoke, over junct with A30, over railway bridge,
towards Newnham. Right at Newnham Green. Hotel
1m on left **Rooms:** 112 (21 GF) (1 fmly)
D £210-£505 (incl. bkfst)
Facilities: STV Wi-fi 🕭 ⅀ Tennis Spa Gym Sauna **Parking:** 120 **Notes:** 🛏 on request

A grand, Victorian Grade II listed house, Tylney Hall sits peacefully in 66 acres of rich, rolling Hampshire
countryside, with the tree-lined approach setting the scene for this idyllic destination. This sense of
calm is echoed throughout the grounds, where the lake, manicured lawns and magnificently restored
water gardens were originally laid out by the famous gardener Gertrude Jekyll. The level of comfort is
typified by 112 bedrooms and suites, all individually furnished and meticulously maintained. Palatial
lounges offer the perfect location to enjoy a quiet drink or afternoon tea overlooking the grounds.
Award-winning cuisine is served in the Oak Room Restaurant, where a modern cooking style with
classic hallmarks combines with the best local produce. Rest and relaxation is never far away, with
the luxurious health spa offering the latest treatments in tranquil surroundings, plus a gymnasium,
saunas, and indoor and outdoor pools. There is also an 18-hole golf course close by. With a range of
private function rooms, including the self-contained Hampshire Suite, Tylney Hall is a popular venue for
weddings, meetings and events. Tylney Hall's storybook setting is at odds with its convenient location,
close to the M25, 40 minutes from Heathrow Airport and with good links into London.
Recommended in the area
Jane Austen's House; Milestones Museum; Watercress Line heritage steam railway line

The Royal Hotel

★★★★ 76% ◉◉ HOTEL

Address: Belgrave Road, VENTNOR, PO38 1JJ
Tel: 01983 852186
Fax: 01983 855395
Email: enquiries@royalhoteliow.co.uk
Website: www.royalhoteliow.co.uk
Map ref: 3, SZ57
Directions: A3055 into Ventnor follow one-way system, after lights left into Belgrave Rd. Hotel on right
Rooms: 54 (8 fmly) S £105-£170 D £170-£190 (incl. bkfst)
Facilities: Wi-fi ⚲ **Parking:** 50
Notes: ⊗ in bedrooms

The Royal Hotel has been a destination for the discerning traveller for more than 150 years. Grand yet intimate, this beautiful early Victorian hotel has 54 bedrooms and is set in stunning sub-tropical gardens. The tone is English country house with a contemporary twist, using silks, velvets and elegant toile de jouy fabrics. Many of The Royal's principal bedrooms have delightful views over the garden or Ventnor Bay, and all are individually styled and equipped with flat-screen TVs and direct-dial telephones. A visit to the hotel's elegant two-Rosette restaurant, with its high ceilings and crystal chandeliers, is an absolute must. Passion, time and culinary invention go into putting together a constantly changing seasonal menu, which makes the most of excellent local produce. To sum up, The Royal Hotel offers award-winning dining, warm, attentive service and a fabulous location – quite simply the perfect destination for a family holiday or stylish getaway.

Recommended in the area:

Coastal walks; Ventnor Botanic Garden; Appuldurcombe House

Freshwater Bay

George Hotel

★★★ ❀❀ HOTEL

Address: Quay Street, YARMOUTH, Isle of Wight,
PO41 0PE
Tel: 01983 760331 **Fax:** 01983 760425
Email: res@thegeorge.co.uk
Website: www.thegeorge.co.uk
Map ref: 3, SZ38 **Directions:** Between castle & pier
Rooms: 19 (1 GF) S £100–£162.50
D £190–£267.50 (incl. bkfst) **Facilities:** STV
Notes: ⊗ in bedrooms ⋈ under 10 yrs

This delightful 17th-century hotel enjoys a wonderful location at the water's edge, adjacent to the castle and quay. The entrance is large and light, with stone flags and a sweeping staircase. The cosy lounge is traditional – tapestry cushions and velvet curtains. Dining is in the Brasserie, a bright room with wonderful views over the Solent. Menus are seasonal, contemporary style with a European influence, and fish features regularly. Bedrooms are individually furnished with many thoughtful extras – some have balconies with sea views. The George offers an exciting programme of events throughout the year.

Recommended in the area

Osborne House; Carisbrooke Castle; Ventnor Botanic Gardens

HEREFORDSHIRE

Hereford Cathedral

Bridge at Wilton

★★★★ ◉◉ RESTAURANT WITH ROOMS
Address: HR9 6AA
Tel: 01989 562655 Fax: 01989 567652
Email: info@bridge-house-hotel.com
Website: www.bridge-house-hotel.com
Map ref: 2, SO52 Directions: Off junct A40 &
A49 into Ross-on-Wye, 300yds on left. Hotel on right
Rooms: 8 S £75-£80 D £100-£120
Facilities: Wi-fi Parking: 30
Notes: ⊗ in bedrooms 🚼 under 14 yrs

There are eight attractively furnished en suite bedrooms at this smart Georgian country house beside a medieval bridge. It's a delightful spot, with well established gardens stretching down to the banks of the River Wye, but it's the food – served in the rustic chic dining room – that's the star attraction here. The modern British cooking is founded on top-quality local produce, including vegetables and herbs from the garden. Typical dishes include twice-baked Hereford hop souffle with rhubarb compote and beetroot vinaigrette, and loin of Gorsley lamb with crab tortellini, curried parsnip nage and mint oil.
Recommended in the area
Ross-on-Wye shopping; Symonds Yat; Goodrich Castle

Wilton Court Hotel

★★★ 81% ◉◉ HOTEL
Address: Wilton Lane, ROSS-ON-WYE, HR9 6AQ
Tel: 01989 562569
Fax: 01989 768460
Email: info@wiltoncourthotel.com
Website: www.wiltoncourthotel.com
Map ref: 2, SO52
Directions: M50 junct 4 onto A40 towards
Monmouth at 3rd rdbt turn left signed Ross-on-Wye
then take 1st right, hotel on right

Rooms: 10 (1 fmly) S £80-£135 D £105-£155 (incl. bkfst) Facilities: Wi-fi Parking: 24

From the outside, the distinctive architecture of this riverside hotel declares its Tudor origins, while Helen and Roger Wynn's collection of decorative Oriental curios serves to make its Elizabethan interior doubly fascinating. The old walled gardens are filled with mature shrubs, and well-trimmed lawns slope down to the River Wye. Bedrooms overlook either the river or gardens. You can eat in the cosy bar or the more formal Mulberry Restaurant. The conservatory extension is a delightful spot, and there's al fresco dining in the courtyard during the summer.
Recommended in the area Royal Forest of Dean; Hereford Cathedral; Hay-on-Wye

The reservoir control wheel at Tringford

The Grove

★★★★★ 89% ◉◉◉ HOTEL

Address: Chandler's Cross, RICKMANSWORTH,
WD3 4TG
Tel: 01923 807807
Fax: 01923 221008
Email: info@thegrove.co.uk
Website: www.thegrove.co.uk
Map ref: 3, TQ09
Directions: From M25 follow A411 signs towards
Watford. Hotel entrance on right.
Rooms: 227 (35 GF) (32 fmly) **Facilities:** STV Wi-fi ⓢ ⤳ Tennis Spa Gym Sauna
Parking: 400 **Notes:** ⊗ in bedrooms

The history of the Grove, a magnificent 18th-century stately home set within 300 acres of park and woodland, is rich and interesting. In its heyday, having been the seat of the Earls of Clarendon, it was a venue for lavish country house parties, which royalty attended. Today, the hotel calls its mix of traditional elegance with hip, contemporary design, 'groovy grand'. The guest rooms range from the merely luxurious in the West Wing, to the positively palatial in the individually designed Mansion suites, many with open fires and four-poster beds. There is a choice of three dining venues, each with an outdoor terrace. Head for three-Rosetted Colette's for fine dining in elegant surroundings, The Glasshouse for buffet-style food, and The Stables for simply presented, contemporary home-made meals. The award-winning Sequoia spa is a tranquil sanctuary - a place to retreat, rest, workout and re-energise. The 18-hole golf course is playable all year and hosted the 2006 World Championships. The Grove is just 17 minutes by train from London Euston, and three minutes from the M25 in the heart of the Hertfordshire countryside, making it the perfect venue for a weekend escape with the family.

Recommended in the area

Whipsnade Wild Animal Park; St Albans Cathedral; Knebworth House

St Michael's Manor

★★★★ 77% ◉◉ HOTEL

Address: Fishpool Street, ST ALBANS, AL3 4RY
Tel: 01727 864444
Fax: 01727 848909
Email: reservations@stmichaelsmanor.com
Website: www.stmichaelsmanor.com
Map ref: 3, TL10
Directions: From St Albans Abbey follow Fishpool Street towards St Michael's village. Hotel 0.5m on left
Rooms: 30 (4 GF) (3 fmly) **S** £145-£240 **D** £180-£345 (incl. bkfst)
Facilities: STV Wi-fi **Parking:** 75 **Notes:** ⊗ in bedrooms

This magnificent 16th century country manor house was lovingly converted into a hotel in the 1960s by the Newling Ward family, who still own and run it today. Many of the individually designed bedrooms share outstanding views over the five-acre gardens, complete with private lake. The conservatory-style restaurant, lounge, bar and patio also benefit from lovely garden views. With such a green and tranquil setting, it's hard to believe that the city centre and its main attractions, including the Roman area and abbey, are a mere 10-minute walk away. The restaurant's award-winning modern British cuisine draws food lovers from afar. There's a full a la carte menu or you can order from the table d'hote Lake Menu which changes weekly and offers excellent value at £20 for three courses including coffee. St Michael's Manor is also a popular venue for cream teas and Sunday lunches. The hotel offers the perfect blend of classical charm, romance and a relaxing atmosphere, making it ideal for weddings, conferences, weekends away and short breaks.

Recommended in the area

St Albans Cathedral and Abbey; Verulamium Museum; Hatfield House

KENT

Saxon Shore Way

Eastwell Manor

★★★★ ◉◉ HOTEL

Address: Eastwell Park, Boughton Lees, ASHFORD, TN25 4HR
Tel: 01233 213000
Fax: 01233 635530
Email: enquiries@eastwellmanor.co.uk
Website: www.eastwellmanor.co.uk
Map ref: 4, TR04
Directions: On A251, 200yds on left when entering Boughton Aluph **Rooms:** 62 (2 fmly)
Facilities: STV Wi-fi ⊗ ⤳ Tennis Golf Spa Gym Sauna **Parking:** 200 **Notes:** ⊗ in bedrooms

Eastwell Manor, dating back to the Norman Conquest, lies in 62 acres of grounds, including a formal Italian garden, lawns and parkland. In the 16th century Richard Plantagenet lived here, and Queen Victoria and King Edward VII were frequent visitors. Its age is apparent in the lounges, restaurant and bar, with their original fireplaces, carved panelling and fine antiques. Twenty-three individually designed bedrooms are named after previous owners. The 19 luxury mews cottages in the grounds have been converted from Victorian stables. They are en suite with kitchen, sitting room and dining facilities and are also available on a self-catering basis. Complimentary Wi-fi is available throughout. The informal, all-day Brasserie in The Pavilion looks out across the countryside, while the more formal dining destination is the Manor Restaurant with a French and modern British menu. The Pavilion Spa houses a 20-metre pool in a Roman-baths-style setting, hydrotherapy pool, sauna, Jacuzzi, steam room and technogym. The beauty and therapy area, Dreams, pampers both men and women. There is also a 20-metre outdoor heated swimming pool, all-weather tennis court and the 'Eastwell 9' Golf Course (2,132 yards, par 32).

Recommended in the area

Canterbury Cathedral; Sissinghurst Castle; Leeds Castle; Godinton House

Leeds Castle

Thistle Brands Hatch

★★★★ 80% HOTEL
Address: BRANDS HATCH, Dartford, DA3 8PE
Tel: 0871 376 9008
Fax: 0871 376 9108
Email: brandshatch@thistle.co.uk
Website: www.thistle.com/brandshatch
Map ref: 4, TQ56
Directions: Follow Brands Hatch signs, hotel on left
of racing circuit entrance
Rooms: 121 (60 GF) (5 fmly)
Facilities: Wi-fi ⊗ Spa Gym Sauna **Parking:** 200

Obviously a premier choice for motor racing fans since it stands right at the entrance to the famous
Brands Hatch circuit, this hotel is also ideally located for visiting all the delights of the 'Garden of
England'. This is a modern building, offering standard, deluxe and executive rooms, 15 meeting rooms,
and leisure facilities that include an indoor swimming pool, health treatments and fitness equipment. A
highlight of a stay here is a meal in Genevieves Restaurant, while The Racing Bar also serves food.
Recommended in the area
Lullingstone Castle; Knole (NT); North Downs Way

Rowhill Grange Hotel & Utopia Spa

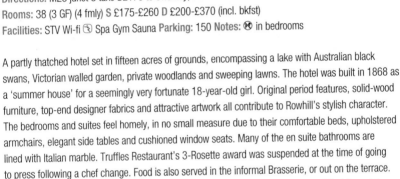

★★★★ 82% HOTEL
Address: WILMINGTON, Dartford, DA2 7QH
Tel: 01322 615136
Fax: 01322 615137
Email: admin@rowhillgrange.co.uk
Website: www.rowhillgrange.co.uk
Map ref: 4, TQ57
Directions: M25 junct 3 take B2173 to Swanley, then B258 to Hextable
Rooms: 38 (3 GF) (4 fmly) S £175-£260 D £200-£370 (incl. bkfst)
Facilities: STV Wi-fi ⊗ Spa Gym Sauna **Parking:** 150 **Notes:** ⊗ in bedrooms

A partly thatched hotel set in fifteen acres of grounds, encompassing a lake with Australian black swans, Victorian walled garden, private woodlands and sweeping lawns. The hotel was built in 1868 as a 'summer house' for a seemingly very fortunate 18-year-old girl. Original period features, solid-wood furniture, top-end designer fabrics and attractive artwork all contribute to Rowhill's stylish character. The bedrooms and suites feel homely, in no small measure due to their comfortable beds, upholstered armchairs, elegant side tables and cushioned window seats. Many of the en suite bathrooms are lined with Italian marble. Truffles Restaurant's 3-Rosette award was suspended at the time of going to press following a chef change. Food is also served in the informal Brasserie, or out on the terrace. In the Utopia spa, one of the world's top 50 according to a national newspaper, qualified therapists offer beauty treatments, massage and aromatherapy. The indoor swimming pool is surrounded by a convincing Tuscan trompe l'oeil.

Recommended in the area

Leeds Castle; Brands Hatch; Bluewater Shopping Centre

The Pantiles

The Brew House Hotel

★★★★ 77% ⊛ HOTEL

Address: 1 Warwick Park, ROYAL TUNBRIDGE WELLS, TN2 5TA

Tel: 01892 520587 & 552591

Fax: 01892 534979

Email: reception@brewhousehotel.com

Website: www.brewhousehotel.com

Map ref: 4, TQ53 **Directions:** A267, 1st left onto Warwick Park, hotel immediately on left

Rooms: 10 D £120-£175 (incl. bkfst)

Facilities: STV Wi-fi **Parking:** 8 **Notes:** ⊗ in bedrooms

This luxurious privately-owned hotel is adjacent to the historic Pantiles and a short walk from the town centre with its interesting boutiques, bars and restaurants. There are 10 individually designed bedrooms complete with all the latest technology and impressive, state-of-the-art bathrooms. Mood lighting and chic furnishings create a relaxed atmosphere in the popular, modern restaurant, brasserie and bar and service is friendly and professional.

Recommended in the area

The Pantiles; Groombridge Place Gardens & Enchanted Forest; Penshurst Place and Gardens

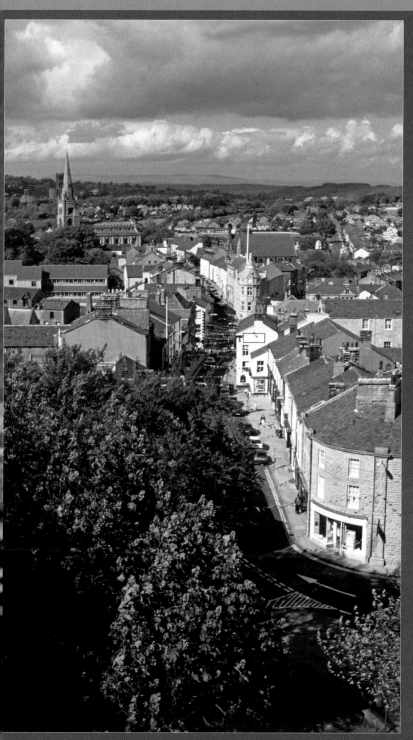

Clitheroe

Blackpool Pleasure Beach

Barton Grange Hotel

★★★★ 77% HOTEL

Address: Garstang Road, BARTON, Preston,
PR3 5AA
Tel: 01772 862551
Fax: 01772 861267
Email: stay@bartongrangehotel.com
Website: www.bartongrangehotel.co.uk
Map ref: 6, SD53 **Directions:** M6 junct 32, follow
Garstang (A6) signs for 2.5m. Hotel on right
Rooms: 51 (4 GF) (4 fmly) **S** £65-£95 **D** £75-£115
Facilities: STV Wi-fi ⊗ Gym Sauna **Parking:** 250 **Notes:** ⊗ in bedrooms

Guests return again and again to this family-run hotel. Bedrooms and public areas have a smart
contemporary look, while retaining the traditional charm of the late Victorian house. With something for
everyone and a relaxed, friendly atmosphere, The Walled Garden Bistro serves traditional, wholesome
food with a twist. You can get active in the indoor pool or gym, or relax in the sauna, but make sure you
fit in a visit to the family's garden centre just two miles down the road.

Recommended in the area

National Football Museum at Preston; Beacon Fell Country Park; Blackpool

Best Western Carlton Hotel

★★★ 78% ❀ HOTEL

Address: 282 North Promenade, BLACKPOOL,
FY1 2EZ
Tel: 01253 628966
Fax: 01253 752587
Email: mail@carltonhotelblackpool.co.uk
Website: www.bw-carltonhotel.co.uk
Map ref: 5, SD31
Directions: M6 junct 32/M55 follow signs for North Shore.
Between Blackpool Tower & Gynn Sq
Rooms: 58 S £40-£75 D £60-£120 (incl. bkfst)
Facilities: STV Wi-fi **Parking:** 43 **Notes:** ❸ in bedrooms

Built at the turn of the century, the Best Western Carlton Hotel is easily accessible and pleasantly situated on the quieter North Promenade of Blackpool. It overlooks 12 miles of sandy beaches on the stunning Fylde Coast, with panoramic views of the Irish Sea, but is still within walking distance of the town centre, the Golden Mile and the award-winning Hounds Hill Shopping Centre. The hotel boasts two very different dining experiences: Caesars, serving traditional British cuisine, and the AA Rosetted Jali Fine Indian Dining, which has picked up a 'quality assured' award from Taste Lancashire. Whichever you choose, expect high standards of service from a team of experienced, friendly staff, and an intimate atmosphere. All bedrooms at the Best Western Carlton are non-smoking, attractively decorated and equipped to the highest standard with en suite facilities and complimentary Wi-fi. Some rooms also benefit from sea views, and there is lift access to all floors. The hotel offers full conference and banqueting facilities to suit any kind of meeting or function, while a team of dedicated and professional staff is on hand to ensure that every event is a success.

Recommended in the area

Blackpool Tower, Winter Gardens, Pleasure Beach

Rosehill House Hotel

★★★ 78% HOTEL

Address: Rosehill Avenue, BURNLEY, BB11 2PW
Tel: 01282 453931
Fax: 01282 455628
Email: rhhotel@provider.co.uk
Website: www.rosehillhousehotel.co.uk
Map ref: 6, SD83 Directions: 0.5m S of town centre, off A682
Rooms: 34 (4 GF) (3 fmly) Facilities: STV Wi-fi
Parking: 52 Notes: ⊗ in bedrooms

This elegant mansion is set in a quiet residential area of
town. Many original features of the Victorian house have been
retained, giving the hotel a unique charm and character. There
are 31 individually designed bedrooms with all the modern-day comforts you'd expect, including
complimentary Wi-fi. Dugdales Restaurant, with its wood-panelled dining room and airy Victorian
conservatory, offers a very affordable a la carte menu. For guests looking to unwind, there's a snooker
room and a park next door with a children's play area, tennis and opportunities for walking and jogging.
Recommended in the area
Gawthorpe Hall (NT); Panopticon; Padiham shopping

Pines Hotel

★★★ 82% ⊛ HOTEL

Address: 570 Preston Rd, Clayton-Le-Woods, CHORLEY,
              PR6 7ED
Tel: 01772 338551
Fax: 01772 629002
Email: mail@thepineshotel.co.uk
Website: www.thepineshotel.co.uk
Map ref: 6, SD61 Directions: A6 towards Preston/Whittle-le-
Woods. Approx 2.5m, hotel on right Rooms: 35 (14 GF) (2 fmly)
Facilities: STV Wi-fi Parking: 120 Notes: ⊗ in bedrooms

Privately owned and run since 1963, the Victorian Pines Hotel
sits in four acres of formal, mature gardens. The elegant en
suite bedrooms are stylish and individually designed, offering high levels of comfort, and some have
four-posters and Jacuzzi baths. The hotel boasts a smart conservatory bar and the aptly named
Rosette Restaurant, as well as extensive function rooms, making this a popular venue for weddings and
conferences. Regular cabaret and party nights take place in the Dixon Suite.
Recommended in the area
Astley Hall Museum; Yarrow Valley Country Park; Chorley market

Northcote

★★★★ 80% ◉◉◉ SMALL HOTEL

Address: Northcote Road, LANGHO, Blackburn,
BB6 8BE
Tel: 01254 240555
Fax: 01254 246568
Email: reservations@northcote.com
Website: www.northcote.com
Map ref: 6, SD73
Directions: M6 junct 31, 9m to Northcote. Follow
Clitheroe (A59) signs, Hotel on left before rdbt
Rooms: 14 (4 GF) (2 fmly) S £170-£210 D £200-£250 (incl. bkfst)
Facilities: STV Wi-fi **Parking:** 50 **Notes:** ⊗ in bedrooms

Built in the 1880s, Northcote still has the ambience of a Victorian family home and the focus is on eating well, as, no doubt, it was when it belonged to a textile baron. Its former ownership explains its proximity to Lancashire's industrial heartland to the south, but stretching northwards across the River Ribble is Longridge Fell and the Forest of Bowland. The excellent road network also makes it easy to reach the Yorkshire Dales and Blackpool. Proprietors Nigel Haworth and Craig Bancroft describe their venture as a restaurant with rooms, and the food is certainly a very good reason to come here. Nigel is a staunch supporter of the county's many artisan food producers and, with their ingredients and organic fruit, vegetables and herbs from the manor's own gardens, creates memorable culinary delights. The bedrooms have individual, contemporary decor that is stunning in its originality and the quality of the fabrics and wall coverings. Each room has a high-tech sound system with iPod connector, TV with 200 satellite stations, DVD and CD player and complimentary Wi-fi. Cosy bathrobes are provided, along with Molton Brown hair and skin-care products.

Recommended in the area

Clitheroe; Ribble Valley; Gawthorpe Hall (NT)

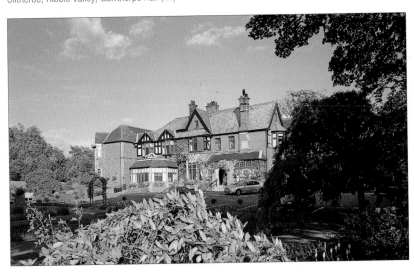

Best Western Premier Leyland Hotel

★★★★ 77% HOTEL

Address: Leyland Way, LEYLAND, Preston,
PR25 4JX
Tel: 01772 422922
Fax: 01772 622282
Email: leylandhotel@feathers.uk.com
Website: www.feathers.uk.com
Map ref: 6, SD52
Directions: M6 junct 28 turn left at end of slip road, hotel 100mtrs on left
Rooms: 93 (31 GF) (4 fmly) S £60-£150 D £70-£160 (incl. bkfst)
Facilities: STV Wi-fi ⊗ Gym Sauna Parking: 150

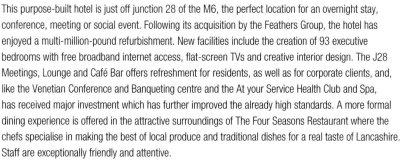

This purpose-built hotel is just off junction 28 of the M6, the perfect location for an overnight stay, conference, meeting or social event. Following its acquisition by the Feathers Group, the hotel has enjoyed a multi-million-pound refurbishment. New facilities include the creation of 93 executive bedrooms with free broadband internet access, flat-screen TVs and creative interior design. The J28 Meetings, Lounge and Café Bar offers refreshment for residents, as well as for corporate clients, and, like the Venetian Conference and Banqueting centre and the At your Service Health Club and Spa, has received major investment which has further improved the already high standards. A more formal dining experience is offered in the attractive surroundings of The Four Seasons Restaurant where the chefs specialise in making the best of local produce and traditional dishes for a real taste of Lancashire. Staff are exceptionally friendly and attentive.

Recommended in the area

Blackpool Pleasure Beach; Camelot Theme Park; Martin Mere

Martin Mere Wetland Centre

Bedford Hotel

★★★ 79% HOTEL

Address: 307-313 Clifton Drive South, LYTHAM ST
ANNES, FY8 1HN
Tel: 01253 724636
Fax: 01253 729244
Email: reservations@bedford-hotel.com
Website: www.bedford-hotel.com
Map ref: 5, SD32 **Directions:** From M55 follow
signs for airport to last lights. Left through 2 sets of
lights. Hotel 300yds on left

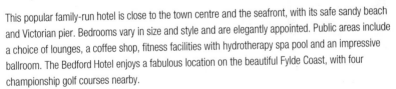

Rooms: 45 (6 GF) **Facilities:** STV Wi-fi Gym **Parking:** 25 **Notes:** ⊗ in bedrooms

This popular family-run hotel is close to the town centre and the seafront, with its safe sandy beach
and Victorian pier. Bedrooms vary in size and style and are elegantly appointed. Public areas include
a choice of lounges, a coffee shop, fitness facilities with hydrotherapy spa pool and an impressive
ballroom. The Bedford Hotel enjoys a fabulous location on the beautiful Fylde Coast, with four
championship golf courses nearby.

Recommended in the area

Beach, pier and promenade; Royal Lytham and St Annes Golf Club; Blackpool

Bradgate Country Park

Belvoir Castle

Best Western Premier Yew Lodge Hotel

★★★★ 80% 🏵🏵 HOTEL

Address: Packington Hill, KEGWORTH, DE74 2DF
Tel: 01509 672518
Fax: 01509 674730
Email: info@yewlodgehotel.co.uk
Website: www.yewlodgehotel.co.uk
Map ref: 3, SK42 **Directions:** M1 junct 24. Follow signs to Loughborough & Kegworth on A6. On entering village, 1st right, after 400yds hotel on right
Rooms: 100 (22 fmly) **Facilities:** STV Wi-fi 🐾 Spa Gym Sauna **Parking:** 180

Situated at the heart of Kegworth village, the Best Western Premier Yew Lodge has recently completed a £7 million development programme. The award-winning Orchard restaurant serves British food with a fusion twist, while the Library offers superb wines. Reeds is a stunning health club and spa complete with pool, state-of-the-art fitness suite and beauty salon.

Recommended in the area

The National Forest; Donington Park; Belvoir Castle

Belmont Hotel

★★★ 80% HOTEL

Address: De Montfort Street, LEICESTER, LE1 7GR
Tel: 0116 254 4773
Fax: 0116 247 0804
Email: info@belmonthotel.co.uk
Website: www.belmonthotel.co.uk
Map ref: 3, SK50
Directions: from A6 take 1st right after rail station. Hotel 200yds on left
Rooms: 77 (9 GF) (7 fmly) S £70–£120 D £80–£130
Facilities: Wi-fi Gym **Parking:** 75

Owned by the Bowie family for over 70 years, this well-established, elegant town house hotel stands in the city's green and tranquil New Walk conservation area. Yet the main shops and railway station are only minutes away via a tree-lined walkway laid out in 1785 to connect the town with Victoria Park, once a racecourse. Over the years many changes have been made to the fabric of the building, but always with a sympathetic eye to its past. Individually designed, well-equipped bedrooms offer Wi-fi, TV with Freeview, radio, hospitality tray, hairdryer, direct-dial telephone, modem point and ironing facilities. The Executive rooms additionally offer a business desk, second phone and a more spacious bathroom. From the kitchen, making use of the freshest, highest quality ingredients, comes good British and Continental cuisine, served in Cherry's Restaurant. In the hotel's own words, though, its 'heart' is Jamie's Lounge Bar, where you can order a lighter meal, or just have a coffee or glass of wine from a comprehensively international wine list. The Belmont is much in demand for weddings and business meetings; the largest of the nine conference rooms holds 175 delegates.

Recommended in the area

Rockingham Castle; National Space Centre; Foxton Locks; Highcross shopping quarter; Curve Theatre

Hotel Maiyango

★★★★ 78% @ SMALL HOTEL

Address: 13-21 St Nicholas Place, LEICESTER,
LE1 4LD
Tel: 0116 251 8898
Fax: 0116 242 1339
Email: reservations@maiyango.com
Website: www.maiyango.com
Map ref: 3, SK50 **Directions:** B4114 (Narborough
Rd) to city centre, right onto A47 (Hinkley Rd), keep
right into St Nicholas Place
Rooms: 14 **S** £145-£185 **D** £145-£185 (incl. bkfst) **Facilities:** Wi-fi **Notes:** ⊗ in bedrooms

Hotel Maiyango is a stunning boutique hotel setting a new standard for city centre accommodation in the heart of Leicester. The 14 contemporary rooms and suites provide relaxed, luxury surroundings whether for a business stay or a romantic weekend escape. The hotel is thoughtfully designed with bespoke handmade furniture, beautiful commissioned artwork and intimate lighting throughout, and there are lots of little extra touches to make any stay here a memorable one. Maiyango Restaurant has won many awards, including 'gold' in the 'Taste of England' category in the East Midlands Tourism awards, and runner-up in the Enjoy England Taste Awards 2009. As well as great food, expect original cocktails and an intimate atmosphere. Although Hotel Maiyango is a true city centre hotel, the kitchen works hard to guarantee traceability and always sources as locally as possible. For instance, the majority of the fresh produce used in the restaurant is grown specially for Hotel Maiyango at a farm just seven miles away. This ethos is encapsulated by the hotel's mantra, 'Maiyango Loves Local', and extends not just to food but also to staff development, the community and supporting other local businesses.

Recommended in the area

Bradgate Park and deer sanctuary; Curve Theatre; Highcross Shopping Centre

Best Western Three Swans Hotel

★★★ 78% HOTEL

Address: 21 High Street, MARKET HARBOROUGH, LE16 7NJ
Tel: 01858 466644
Fax: 01858 433101
Email: sales@threeswans.co.uk
Website: www.bw-threeswanshotel.co.uk
Map ref: 3, SP78 Directions: M1 junct 20 take A304 to Market Harborough. A6 from Leicester, through town centre, hotel on right Rooms: 61 (20 GF) (8 fmly) S £71.50-£88.50 D £88-£110 (incl. bkfst) Facilities: STV Wi-fi Parking: 100

This 16th century coaching inn blends old-world charm with the comfort of a modern hotel. All 61 en suite bedrooms – some with four-poster beds – are individually designed. The refurbished Swans Restaurant serves traditional lunches on Sundays, and an a la carte dinner menu based around fresh, local ingredients. The Conservatory is a popular spot for coffee or an informal lunch or dinner. The hotel is licensed for weddings and has ample facilities for conferences and functions, plus a car park at the rear.

Recommended in the area

Market Harborough shopping; Rutland Water; Foxton Locks

Stapleford Park

★★★★ ◉◉ COUNTRY HOUSE HOTEL

Address: Stapleford, MELTON MOWBRAY,
LE14 2EF
Tel: 01572 787000
Fax: 01572 787651
Email: reservations@stapleford.co.uk
Website: www.staplefordpark.com
Map ref: 3, SK71 Directions: 1m SW of B676, 4m E of Melton Mowbray & 9m W of Colsterworth
Rooms: 55 (10 fmly) S £225-£275 D £295-£850 (incl. bkfst) Facilities: STV Wi-fi ☒ Tennis Spa Gym Sauna Parking: 120

Sitting in 500 acres of Capability Brown-designed parkland, Stapleford Park is one of England's finest stately homes. Despite the grandeur of the 17th century building, the hotel has a wonderfully homely feel. Eat in the Grinling Gibbons dining room or the more informal Pavilion restaurant. There's no shortage of things to do – from the Donald Steel-designed golf course, falconry school and clay pigeon shooting, to fishing, archery, tennis, swimming and a gym.

Recommended in the area

Rutland Water; Burghley House; Belvoir Castle; Rockingham Castle

Kilworth House Hotel

★★★★ 84% ◎◎ HOTEL

Address: Lutterworth Road, NORTH KILWORTH, LE17 6JE

Tel: 01858 880058

Fax: 01858 880349

Email: info@kilworthhouse.co.uk

Website: www.kilworthhouse.co.uk

Map ref: 3, SP68 **Directions:** A4304 towards Market Harborough, after Walcote, hotel 1.5m on right **Rooms:** 44 (13 GF) (2 fmly) S £140–£215 D £140–£215 **Facilities:** Wi-fi Gym **Parking:** 140 **Notes:** ⊗ Guide dogs only in bedrooms

This grand, grade II listed country house sits amid 38 acres of landscaped parkland. It's an enchanting place – a blend of Victorian opulence and contemporary luxury with a warm and welcoming atmosphere. There are 11 bedrooms on the first floor of the house, including two with four-poster beds, all furnished with a mixture of antiques, rich fabrics and the latest technology. Across the knot garden courtyard are a further 33 rooms, all individually designed in an elegant, country-house style. The two-Rosette Wordsworth Restaurant, with its double oak and stained glass doors, domed ceiling, glittering chandeliers, open fireplaces and views over the knot garden courtyard, is a gloriously ornate setting for some fine modern British cuisine. For a less formal alternative – or, perhaps, for morning coffee or afternoon tea – take a seat in the beautifully restored Victorian Orangery, which has a special ambience both day and night. With its modern conference facilities, private dining rooms, attentive staff, beauty therapy suite, mini-gym and vast grounds where muntjac deer dart across woodland trails, and the lake is well-stocked with fish, it's no wonder Kilworth House draws in business and leisure guests in equal measure.

Recommended in the area

Kilworth Springs Golf Club; Stanford Hall; Rutland Water

Saltfleet Haven

Best Western Bentley Hotel & Leisure Club

★★★ 85% HOTEL

Address: Newark Road, South Hykeham, LINCOLN, LN6 9NH
Tel: 01522 878000
Fax: 01522 878001
Email: infothebentleyhotel@btconnect.com
Website: www.thebentleyhotel.uk.com
Map ref: 8, SK97
Directions: From A1 take A46 E towards Lincoln for 10m. Over 1st rdbt on Lincoln Bypass to hotel 50yds on left **Rooms:** 80 (26 GF) (5 fmly) **S** £90-£115 **D** £105-£140 (incl. bkfst)
Facilities: STV Wi-fi ⊗ Spa Gym Sauna **Parking:** 170 **Notes:** ⊗ in bedrooms

In a lovely rural location, this fine modern hotel is only six miles south of the centre of Lincoln, making it ideal for visits to the historic city as well as the largely undiscovered, beautiful countryside around. The hotel has a very pleasing contemporary style and a range of bedrooms that includes some four-poster rooms and a spacious suite with a separate lounge area. All of the rooms have en suite bathrooms and include satellite TV, trouser presses, hairdryers, tea-and-coffee-making facilities and Wi-fi connection. The restaurant offers a good choice, from one-dish dining to fixed price and a full à la carte menu, and is particularly renowned for its carvery lunches. Snacks and lighter meals are available in the Martini Bar. This is Lincoln's only hotel with a leisure and health centre. It includes a superb indoor swimming pool, steam room, sauna and whirlpool, plus a gymnasium with qualified staff and a beauty salon offering various treatments and therapies – best to book in advance.

Recommended in the area

Lincoln; Doddington Hall and Gardens; Newark Aircraft Museum

Lincoln Cathedral

Brackenborough Hotel

★★★ 86% ⊛ HOTEL

Address: Cordeaux Corner, Brackenborough,
LOUTH, LN11 0SZ
Tel: 01507 609169
Fax: 01507 609413
Email: arlidgard@oakridgehotels.co.uk
Website: www.oakridgehotels.co.uk
Map ref: 8, TF38
Directions: Off A16 2m N of Louth

Rooms: 24 (6 GF) (2 fmly) **S** £82-£119 **D** £97-£154
(incl. bkfst) **Facilities:** Wi-fi **Parking:** 91 **Notes:** ⊗ in bedrooms

This 24-bedroom hotel sits in large, beautifully maintained gardens just outside the historic town of Louth, with lovely views over the surrounding countryside of the Lincolnshire Wolds. Every bedroom is contemporary but individual in design, and all come with Egyptian cotton bed linen and free internet access. The Bistro Bar is a popular, lively spot for breakfast, lunch and dinner, offering a modern European menu featuring plenty of top-notch regional ingredients, including fresh fish from Grimsby.
Recommended in the area
Lincoln Cathedral; Doddington Hall & Gardens; Lincolnshire Wolds Railway

Changing of the guard at the Horse Guards Parade

The Landmark London

★★★★★ ◉◉ HOTEL

Address: 222 Marylebone Road, LONDON,
NW1 6JQ
Tel: 020 7631 8000
Fax: 020 7631 8080
Email: reservations@thelandmark.co.uk
Website: www.landmarklondon.co.uk
Map ref: 4, TQ38
Directions: Adjacent to Marylebone Station
Rooms: 300 (60 fmly) S £239-£550 D £269-£580 Facilities:
STV Wi-fi ⓘ Spa Gym Sauna
Parking: 80 Notes: ⊗ in bedrooms

The Landmark London ranks among the finest of the capital's grand dame hotels. Built in 1899, it personifies classic Victorian opulence, and is perfectly located in one of London's most upmarket districts, close to all of the capital's main attractions. The guest rooms are some of the largest in London, averaging 55 sq metres. All 300 have beautiful Italian marble en suites, while room amenities include interactive television systems with email and internet access, laptop safes and air-conditioning. The Landmark's spectacular Winter Garden restaurant is situated beneath the soaring eight-storey glass atrium and offers international cuisine. For a more informal setting, the newly refurbished twotwentytwo bar and restaurant fits the bill, while for late-night drinks and cocktails, the Mirror Bar is the place to head for. The prestigious Landmark Spa and Health Club offers a complete wellbeing experience. It features a 15-metre semi-ozone swimming pool, whirlpool, a poolside sanarium, lavish treatment rooms and a state-of-the-art gymnasium. For pure luxury, try one of the ESPA beauty treatments or a stress-busting massage.

Recommended in the area

Marylebone High Street; Regent's Park; London Zoo; Wembley Stadium

Melia White House

★★★★ 80% HOTEL

Address: Albany Street, Regents Park, LONDON, NW1 3UP

Tel: 020 7391 3000

Fax: 020 7388 0091

Email: melia.white.house@solmelia.com

Website: www.melia-whitehouse.com

Map ref: 4, TQ38

Directions: Opposite Gt Portland St underground station **Rooms:** 581 (7 fmly) S £80-£280

D £80-£280 **Facilities:** STV Wi-fi Spa Gym Sauna **Parking:** 0 **Notes:** ⊗ in bedrooms

Managed by the Spanish Sol Melia company, this impressive art deco property is located just to the south of Regents Park, and only a few blocks north of Oxford Street. Spacious public areas offer a high degree of comfort and include an elegant cocktail bar. The en suite bedrooms come in a variety of sizes and are comfortable, stylish and well equipped with air-conditioning, hair dryer, magnifying mirror, tea and coffee tray, safe, trouser press, satellite TV, radio, direct-dial phone, and high-speed Wi-fi connection via laptop or TV. Room service is available 24 hours a day. Diners looking for somewhere fashionable to eat will approve of L'Albufera, an elegant, award-winning Spanish restaurant; for greater informality, The Place Brasserie offers buffet breakfast, lunch and dinner, with an emphasis on Mediterranean cuisine. Relax in comfortable Longfords Bar, while listening to live music (from Tuesdays to Saturdays). Among the hotel's other amenities are an air-conditioned gym with the latest cardiovascular equipment, and a modern therapy room full of treatments that 'alleviate and rejuvenate'. For those looking to stay longer in the capital, there are various apartments to choose from. The hotel also has a business centre.

Recommended in the area

Madame Tussaud's; Regent's Park; Oxford Street; Camden Town

London Bridge Hotel

★★★★ 77% HOTEL

Address: 8-18 London Bridge Street, LONDON, SE1 9SG
Tel: 020 7855 2200
Fax: 020 7855 2233
Email: sales@londonbridgehotel.com
Website: www.londonbridgehotel.com
Map ref: 4, TQ38
Directions: Access through London Bridge Station (bus/taxi yard), into London Bridge St (one-way). Hotel on left, 50yds from station
Rooms: 138 (12 fmly) **Facilities:** STV Wi-fi Gym Sauna
Notes: ⊗ in bedrooms

In the heart of vibrant Southwark, an area rich in architecture, museums, theatres and shopping opportunities, this is a tremendously chic, privately owned hotel with a stately entrance and a stunning interior that blends classical features with an ultra-modern interior. A calming blend of cream and earth tones combines with textures contrasting between smooth leather, polished wood, suede and coarse-weave fabrics. There's a touch of colour in the Londinium restaurant, named in recognition of the Roman artefacts unearthed during the building development, where red suede upholstery is set against polished walnut floors. Modern British cuisine is served in these elegant surroundings, with Malaysian food offered in the stylish Georgetown restaurant and more simple dishes available in the Borough Bar. The bedrooms are supremely relaxing and comfortable; fibre-optic reading lights, flat-screen TVs and complimentary Wi-fi among the in-room facilities. Deluxe rooms have a king-size bed, plus a sofa bed and walk-in closet, while the executive rooms and suites are designed with business guests in mind. The City, London's financial heart, is, after all, just a short walk away, across London Bridge.

Recommended in the area

Wembley Stadium and Arena; British Museum; National Portrait Gallery

Houses of Parliament

London Marriott Hotel County Hall

★★★★★ 88% 🏵 HOTEL

Address: County Hall, Westminster Bridge Road, LONDON, SE1 7PB

Tel: 020 7928 5200

Fax: 020 7928 5300

Email: sales.countyhall@marriott.com

Website: www.londonmarriottcountyhall.co.uk

Map ref: 4, TQ38 **Directions:** On South Bank, near Westminster Bridge **Rooms:** 200 (58 fmly)

S £165 D £165 **Facilities:** STV Wi-fi 🕃 Spa Gym Sauna **Parking:** 70 **Notes:** 🚫 in bedrooms

Occupying the former seat of the Greater London Council, this fine hotel has breathtaking views across the Thames to the Houses of Parliament. The conversion of the building to a hotel has retained many original features. Air-conditioned, spacious bedrooms are set up for work as well as relaxation and many have river views. The fine-dining County Hall Restaurant offers modern cuisine in a grand setting.

Recommended in the area

British Airways London Eye; London Aquarium; Houses of Parliament and Big Ben

The Halkin Hotel

★★★★★ ◉◉◉ TOWN HOUSE HOTEL
Address: Halkin Street, Belgravia, LONDON, SW1X 7DJ
Tel: 020 7333 1000
Fax: 020 7333 1100
Email: res@halkin.como.bz
Website: www.halkin.como.bz
Map ref: 4, TQ38
Directions: Between Belgrave Sq & Grosvenor Place. Via Chapel St into Headfort Place, left into Halkin St
Rooms: 41 S £250-£1500 D £250-£1500
Facilities: STV Wi-fi Gym **Notes:** ⊗ in bedrooms

Behind the Georgian-style facade is one of London's smartest hotels. Discreetly situated in a quiet street, The Halkin is surrounded by elegant buildings, smart shops, and is just a short stroll from Hyde Park Corner, Knightsbridge and Buckingham Palace. Inside, the style is contemporary Italian, much of the impact being derived from the use of luxury textiles in cool shades of taupe and cream. The bedrooms and suites are equipped to the highest standard with smart, all-marble bathrooms – among the largest in London – and many extras, including three dual-line phones with voice mail and modem connection, high-speed internet, fax, interactive cable television with CD and DVD services, air conditioning and personal bar. Each floor has been designed thematically – earth, wind, fire, water and the universe. Public areas include a lounge, an airy bar for light meals, drinks and cocktails, and then there's Nahm, David Thompson's award-winning Thai restaurant. Service from Armani-clad staff is attentive and friendly. Guests may use the new gym or enjoy the COMO Shambhala Health Club at The Halkin's sister hotel, The Metropolitan.

Recommended in the area

Green Park; Harrods; Science Museum

Jumeirah Carlton Tower

★★★★★ ◎◎ HOTEL

Address: Cadogan Place, LONDON, SW1X 9PY
Tel: 020 7235 1234
Fax: 020 7235 9129
Email: jctinfo@jumeirah.com
Website: www.jumeirahcarltontower.com
Map ref: 4, TQ38
Directions: A4 towards Knightsbridge, right onto Sloane St.
Hotel on left before Cadogan Place
Rooms: 220 (59 fmly) S £199-£7000
D £199-£7000 Facilities: STV Wi-fi ☺ Tennis Spa Gym Sauna
Parking: 170 Notes: ⊗ in bedrooms

The five-star Jumeirah Carlton Tower is situated in fashionable Knightsbridge, only moments away from Harrods, Harvey Nichols and the exclusive boutiques on Sloane Street. The hotel features 220 rooms, including 59 luxurious suites, with panoramic views over London's skyline and the private gardens of Cadogan Place. The Jumeirah Carlton Tower offers a wide choice of excellent dining options, including the Chinoiserie, popular for its traditional afternoon tea, and the renowned Rib Room, which has won many accolades over the years since opening in 1961. Alternatively, the GILT Champagne Lounge is the ultimate in sophistication and glamour. At The Peak Health Club & Spa, located on the ninth floor, guests and members can benefit from a fully equipped gym, state-of-the-art golf simulator, aerobics studio, sauna, steam room, 20-metre heated pool and a full range of beauty treatments, from detox wraps to body peels. The hotel also features nine private dining and meeting rooms, offering guests a choice of distinctive spaces for holding a wide range of functions, be it a cocktail reception, a dinner, a conference, wedding reception or marriage ceremony.

Recommended in the area

Hyde Park; Buckingham Palace; Science Museum

Jumeirah Lowndes Hotel

Address: 21 Lowndes Street, LONDON, SW1X 9ES
Tel: 020 7823 1234
Fax: 020 7235 1154
Email: jlhinfo@jumeirah.com
Website: www.jumeirahlowndeshotel.com
Map ref: 4, TQ38
Directions: M4 onto A4 into London. Left from Brompton Rd into Sloane St. Left into Pont St, Lowndes St next left. Hotel on right
Rooms: 87 **Facilities:** STV Wi-fi **Notes:** ⊗ in bedrooms

(As we went to press this hotel had not yet received its final inspection and rating following an extensive refurbishment.) The Jumeirah Lowndes Hotel is situated in the village of Belgravia, within walking distance of fashionable Knightsbridge with its designer boutiques and luxury department stores. This chic retreat overlooks a leafy London square and offers 87 sumptuous bedrooms, including 14 suites, enhanced by many special touches such as marble bathrooms with luxurious Temple Spa toiletries, plasma-screen TVs, Nespresso machines, internet access and i-Pod docks. Warm, personal service, a calming colour scheme and impressive use of space and light help to create an urban sanctuary, where guests really feel a sense of well-being and tranquillity despite being right in the heart of London. The lively, buzzing Mimosa Bar & Restaurant on the ground floor, with doors opening out onto the terrace, offers delectable modern European cuisine with a twist, based around the finest, freshest ingredients. For private dining or small business meetings, the exclusive and flexible Meeting Room is available. All guests have complimentary access to the facilities at sister hotel the Jumeirah Carlton Tower, including the exclusive Peak Health Club & Spa.

Recommended in the area

Hyde Park; Buckingham Palace; Science Museum

Mandarin Oriental Hyde Park

★★★★★ 90% ◎◎◎◎ HOTEL

Address: 66 Knightsbridge, LONDON, SW1X 7LA
Tel: 020 7235 2000
Fax: 020 7235 2001
Email: molon-reservations@mohg.com
Website: www.mandarinoriental.com/london
Map ref: 4, TQ38
Directions: Harrods on right, hotel 0.5m on left opp
Harvey Nichols **Rooms:** 198 **Facilities:** STV Wi-fi Spa
Gym Sauna **Notes:** ⊗ in bedrooms

Facing fashionable Knightsbridge and overlooking the royal acres of Hyde Park to the rear, this grand late-Victorian hotel was once a gentlemen's club. Today the frock-coated, top-hatted doormen greet highfliers, celebrities and the young and fashionable, for whom this is a popular destination. How many times, one wonders, have these liveried sentries watched the Household Cavalry clatter by on their way from Knightsbridge Barracks to Buckingham Palace? In keeping with the rest of the hotel, the bedrooms, many with park views, are unquestionably opulent, with antique furniture, plush carpets, marble bathrooms and the finest Irish linen and goose-down pillows. Guests have a choice of eating options, from the all-day-dining Park Restaurant, to the chic, award-winning Foliage, and the 'über trendy' Mandarin Bar which serves light snacks and cocktails and features live jazz nightly. In autumn 2010, the hotel will unveil two new fantastic dining experiences, including a collaboration between Mandarin Oriental Hyde Park and internationally renowned chef Heston Blumenthal of the famous Fat Duck in Bray, Berkshire. The hotel's stylish Spa is consistently voted one of the best in the country, and guests may find themselves easily seduced into unwinding in the steam room, vitality pool, sanarium or the calming Zen colour therapy relaxation area.

Recommended in the area

Victoria & Albert Museum; Royal Albert Hall; Harrods; Harvey Nichols

Sofitel London St James

★★★★★ 86% ● HOTEL

Address: 6 Waterloo Place, LONDON, SW1Y 4AN
Tel: 020 7747 2200
Fax: 020 7747 2210
Email: H3144@sofitel.com
Website: www.sofitestjames.com
Map ref: 4, TQ38
Directions: 3 mins walk from Piccadilly Circus and Trafalgar Square **Rooms:** 186 (98 fmly) **S** £180-£1400 **D** £180-£1400 **Facilities:** STV Wi-fi Spa Gym

A hidden gem in the centre of London, Sofitel London St James lies discreetly at the heart of the prestigious area of St James, moments away from Piccadilly Circus, Trafalgar Square and theatreland. Created in a magnificent grade II listed building, the hotel's 186 contemporary and luxurious bedrooms and suites are equipped to the highest standard, with world-class Mybed beds, interactive high definition TVs, media hubs, laptop safes, hairdryers, ironing boards and tea-and-coffee-making facilities. On the ground floor is the renowned Brasserie Roux, a lively and elegant 100-seater brasserie inspired by the famous French chef Albert Roux. The St James bar, with its wide range of champagnes and cocktails, provides the ideal meeting place before dinner, after a show or just for a nightcap. The unique and exceptional Rose Lounge is feminine, warm and cosy with its cream and pink colour scheme – the perfect setting to enjoy a traditional afternoon tea to a backdrop of music from the hotel's resident harpist. Should you wish to unwind some more, head to the newly opened So SPA by Sofitel, with its five contemporary treatment rooms as well as a hamam. The hotel also offers advanced fitness and wellness equipment in the gym, So FIT by Sofitel. For business and functions there are 11 dining and meeting rooms featuring state-of-the-art technology.

Recommended in the area

St James's Park; Buckingham Palace; Trafalgar Square

The Stafford

★★★★★ ◉◉ HOTEL

Address: 16-18 St James's Place, LONDON, SW1A 1NJ
Tel: 020 7493 0111
Fax: 020 7493 7121
Email: information@thestaffordhotel.co.uk
Website: www.thestaffordhotel.co.uk
Map ref: 4, TQ38
Directions: Off Pall Mall into St James's St. 2nd left into St James's Place
Rooms: 105 (8 GF)
Facilities: STV Wi-fi Gym **Notes:** ⊗ in bedrooms

Buckingham Palace is just a stone's throw away from this imposing hotel in the heart of genteel St James's. Every guest room and suite in the Main House is individually furnished and decorated with striking fabrics and wallpapers, and period furnishings and antiques. Twelve beautifully restored suites and bedrooms in the 17th-century stable courtyard all feature timbers thought to have been reclaimed from old sailing ships in the 1750s. The two-storey Guv'nor's Suite contains a lounge, library/dining room, minstrels' gallery, king-size bedroom, two bathrooms and fully fitted kitchen. The recently added 26 suites in the Stafford Mews are timelessly elegant and feature spacious living areas and marble bathrooms. Great food and wines play a large part in any stay at The Stafford, where the award-winning kitchen team offers modern British and classical dishes. The American Bar, famed for serving 'the best martini in London', and where every single artefact and memento adorning its walls and ceiling has been donated by a Stafford client over 40 years, is ideal for a light lunch and pre- or post-theatre supper. In summer the balconies are filled with flowers, and in the winter the sight of decorated Christmas trees outside each door is magical.

Recommended in the area

Buckingham Palace; Bond Street; Piccadilly

St James's Hotel and Club

★★★★★ 85% ⊛⊛⊛ TOWN HOUSE HOTEL
Address: 7-8 Park Place, LONDON, SW1A 1LP
Tel: 020 7316 1600
Fax: 020 7316 1603
Email: info@stjameshotelandclub.com
Website: www.stjameshotelandclub.com
Map ref: 4, TQ38
Directions: Off St James's St
Rooms: 60 (15 GF) (8 fmly) S £215-£345
D £215-£650 Facilities: Wi-fi Notes: ⊗ in bedrooms

Located in a quiet cul-de-sac only moments from the shops
and galleries of St James's and Mayfair, the St James's Hotel
and Club boasts 50 bedrooms and 10 suites of elegant and contemporary design, some with private
balconies or terraces. The Victorian building was completely refurbished in 2008, and the designer's
use of natural fabrics including walls of sumptuous leather, cashmere and silk, creates a sophisticated
yet relaxed atmosphere. All rooms are equipped with complimentary high speed wireless internet, air
conditioning, ISDN phones, plasma screens, i-Pod docking stations and a VDA multi-media system
including digital television. In 2009 executive chef William Drabble joined the St James's Hotel and
Club from Aubergine in Chelsea, where he held a Michelin star for a decade. In 'Seven Park Place' he
offers a menu inspired by his love of French cuisine but using top quality, seasonal British ingredients,
while more informal classic dishes are served in 'William's Bar and Bistro'. The St James's has been
providing the highest standards of hospitality and service since first opening its doors as a gentleman's
chamber for the English aristocracy in 1892. Today it maintains the same high standards as its
predecessor, but with all the luxury and comfort you'd expect from a 21st century five-star hotel.
Recommended in the area
The Royal Academy; Buckingham Palace; Piccadilly Circus

The Capital

★★★★★ TOWN HOUSE HOTEL

Address: Basil Street, Knightsbridge, LONDON,
SW3 1AT
Tel: 020 7589 5171
Fax: 020 7225 0011
Email: reservations@capitalhotel.co.uk
Website: www.capitalhotel.co.uk
Map ref: 4, TQ38
Directions: 20yds from Harrods
Rooms: 49 S £200-£230 D £280-£455
Facilities: STV Wi-fi **Parking:** 21 **Notes:** ⊗ in bedrooms

Just yards from Harrods, Harvey Nichols and Sloane Street, and within easy reach of the West End, The Capital Hotel and Apartments offers luxury accommodation and personal service in the heart of one of London's most prestigious neighbourhoods. Created in 1969 by David Levin, it is to this day privately owned and run by the Levin family. Muted tones characterise the chic decor, which combines contemporary and antique furniture. The Capital's 49 bedrooms and suites come in a variety of styles, but each has a luxurious marble bathroom and an interactive television system with satellite TV, email and movies on demand. All the suites and double rooms have super-king-size beds with handmade mattresses and Egyptian cotton bedding. The Capital Restaurant has long held a reputation for being one of the finest in the country, and that looks set to continue with the appointment in 2009 of award-winning French chef Jerome Ponchelle (The Capital's Rosette award was not confirmed at the time of going to press). Afternoon tea is served in The Capital's elegant lounge, and cocktails are a speciality in the stylish bar.

Recommended in the area

Harrods; Buckingham Palace; Hyde Park

The Draycott Hotel

★★★★★ 78% TOWN HOUSE HOTEL
Address: 26 Cadogan Gardens, LONDON, SW3 2RP
Tel: 020 7730 6466
Fax: 020 7730 0236
Email: reservations@draycotthotel.com
Website: www.draycotthotel.com
Map ref: 4, TQ38
Directions: From Sloane Sq station towards Peter Jones, keep
to left. At Kings Rd take 1st right into Cadogan Gdns, 2nd right,
hotel on left Rooms: 35 (2 GF) (9 fmly) S £155.25-£178.25
D £253-£362.25 Facilities: STV Wi-fi

Combining Edwardian grandeur with the feel of a private
residence, albeit a luxurious one, the hotel is a skilful conversion of three elegant town houses. It is
part of the Cadogan estate, built by the eponymous peer around Sloane Square, the hub of this ever-
fashionable district. The bedrooms all have high ceilings, fireplaces and carefully selected antiques.
Each is named after a theatrical personality and decorated around a print, poster or other memento
associated with that character. More practical considerations include a well-proportioned en suite
bathroom, air conditioning, satellite TV and CD music system, and Sea Island sheets covering the
specially made large beds with some rooms looking out over the garden. Start the day in the Breakfast
Room, adorned with masks of famous artistes, such as Dame Kiri Te Kanawa, and framed programmes
of plays performed at the nearby Royal Court Theatre. Although there is no formal restaurant, a 24-hour
room service menu offers a selection of seasonal meals and snacks. There is also a private dining room
that combines the decadence of The Draycott Hotel with the cosiness of a private home. The fully air-
conditioned, oak-panelled Donald Wolfit Suite is a conference room with its own private garden square.
Recommended in the area
Harrods; Hyde Park; Kensington Gardens Serpentine Gallery; Natural History Museum; V&A Museum

The Levin

★ ★ ★ ★ TOWN HOUSE HOTEL

Address: 28 Basil Street, Knightsbridge, LONDON,
SW3 1AS
Tel: 020 7589 6286
Fax: 020 7823 7826
Email: reservations@thelevin.co.uk
Website: www.thelevinhotel.co.uk
Map ref: 4, TQ38
Directions: 20yds from Harrods
Rooms: 12 D £205-£485 (incl. bkfst)
Facilities: STV Wi-fi **Parking:** 11 **Notes:** ⊗ in bedrooms

It would be hard to beat The Levin's location, tucked away in quiet Basil Street yet literally a stone's throw from Harrods. This sophisticated boutique hotel offers all the comforts of home to discerning travellers who crave a central London hotel with personality and charm. That it has in spades, thanks to owner and operator David Levin and his team of highly experienced, professional and friendly staff. The Levin's 12 contemporary bedrooms are designed to please customers with an eye for detail and love of beautiful things. Each has a luxurious marble bathroom and, for the ultimate in glamour, they even come with their own in-room champagne and cocktail bar. In the public areas the hotel's design takes its lead from the 1930s – think pistachio-coloured love seats, Tibetan silk rugs and baby-blue chandeliers. Breakfast, lunch, afternoon tea and dinner are served in the warm and buzzy Le Metro Bar & Brasserie which, like the hotel itself, is one of Knightsbridge's best-kept secrets. Long treasured by the locals and recently given a fresh new look, it serves an all-day menu of brasserie classics, complemented by an eclectic and impressive selection of wines by the glass.

Recommended in the area

Harrods; Hyde Park; South Kensington museums

Hyde Park

The Cranley

★★★★ 79% TOWN HOUSE HOTEL

Address: 10 Bina Gardens, South Kensington,
LONDON, SW5 0LA
Tel: 020 7373 0123
Fax: 020 7373 9497
Email: info@thecranley.com
Website: www.thecranley.com
Map ref: 4, TQ38
Directions: Gloucester Rd towards Old Brompton Rd.
3rd right after station into Hereford Sq, then 3rd left
into Bina Gardens **Rooms:** 38 (5 GF) **Facilities:** STV Wi-fi **Notes:** ⊗ in bedrooms

In a quiet Chelsea street, this charming 19th-century town house hotel appeals to both business and leisure guests alike. The interior is characterised by original floor tiles, Chinese blue, mustard and plum walls, and antique furniture. Some bedrooms have king-size four-posters, although most have canopied half-testers; all have a writing desk, Wi-fi and electronic safe. Start the day with continental breakfast, take a light luncheon (or supper) in your room, and enjoy an apéritif and canapés before dinner.

Recommended in the area

Harrods; Science Museum; Hyde Park

Millennium & Copthorne Hotels

★★★★ 76% HOTEL

Address: Stamford Bridge, Fulham Road, LONDON,
SW6 1HS
Tel: 020 7565 1400
Fax: 020 7565 1450
Email: reservations@chelseafc.com
Website: www.millenniumhotels.co.uk
Map ref: 4, TQ38 **Directions:** 4 mins walk from
Fulham Broadway tube station
Rooms: 275 (64 fmly) **S** £74.75-£247
D £74.75-£247 **Facilities:** STV Wi-fi ☜ Spa Gym Sauna **Parking:** 180 **Notes:** ⊗ in bedrooms

Millennium & Copthorne Hotels at Chelsea Football Club are nestled in the heart of one of London's most upmarket districts, with the famous Kings Road just a stone's throw away. The two hotels, which are immediately next-door to each other, sit at the centre of the Chelsea FC Stamford Bridge complex and have recently undergone a stylish, multi-million-pound makeover. Guests can enjoy special residential and dining matchday packages, plus access to the exclusive Chelsea Health Club & Spa which offers a state-of-the-art gym, 25-metre pool and a fantastic range of luxury treatments. Thanks to Millennium & Copthorne Hotels' partnership with Chelsea Football Club, the stadium's 21 function rooms and 60 syndicate rooms are available to complement the hotels' own meetings and events facilities, meaning any event can be catered for, no matter how big or small. The Millennium Hotel features an exclusive Club Lounge, where guests can enjoy a continental breakfast, all-day hot drinks and light bites, evening cocktails and canapés, as well as complimentary Wi-fi. A secured underground car park can be accessed from both hotels, and when it comes to dining and socialising, there's a choice of chic restaurants and bars, including 55 restaurant & Bar, Marco Pierre White's and Frankie's.

Recommended in the area

Chelsea Football Club; Knightsbridge and Kensington shopping; Earls Court and Olympia exhibitions

The Bentley Hotel

★★★★★ 83% HOTEL

Address: 27-33 Harrington Gardens, LONDON,
SW7 4JX
Tel: 020 7244 5555
Fax: 020 7244 5566
Email: info@thebentley-hotel.com
Website: www.thebentley-hotel.com
Map ref: 4, TQ38
Directions: S of A4 into Knightsbridge at junct with
Gloucester Rd, right, 2nd right turn, hotel on left just
after mini-rdbt
Rooms: 64 **Facilities:** Wi-fi Spa Gym Sauna **Notes:** ⊗ in bedrooms

The Bentley London, part of the Waldorf Astoria Collection, captures the lavish grandeur of a bygone era. The 64 beautifully designed rooms and suites are graced with rich fabrics and hand-crafted furniture, and each comes with five-star amenities such as personal safes, internet access, fully stocked mini-bars and the latest audio-visual entertainment systems. The stunning marble-clad en suite bathrooms are all fitted with whirlpool Jacuzzi baths and separate walk-in showers. The hotel's elegant Peridot restaurant, looking out over neighbouring gardens, serves breakfast and afternoon tea, and a brasserie-style menu for lunch and dinner. Classic cocktails, signature martinis and premium spirits can be enjoyed in the Malachite cocktail lounge while listening to the soothing sounds of a live jazz pianist. For leisure and relaxation, there's a fully equipped gym and the Le Kalon Spa, offering an enticing range of superior spa and beauty treatments. The Bentley London is one of only a few hotels in the capital to offer its guests the pure indulgence of a hammam (Turkish steam bath).

Recommended in the area

Knightsbridge and Chelsea shopping; Victoria & Albert and Natural History Museums; Kensington Palace and Gardens

Cavendish London

★★★★ 81% ⊚ HOTEL

Address: 81 Jermyn Street, LONDON, SW1Y 6JF
Tel: 020 7930 2111
Fax: 020 7839 2125
Email: info@thecavendishlondon.com
Website: www.thecavendishlondon.com
Map ref: 4, TQ38
Directions: From Piccadilly, (pass The Ritz), right into Duke St before Fortnum & Mason
Rooms: 230 (12 fmly) **Facilities:** STV Wi-fi
Parking: 50 **Notes:** ⊗ in bedrooms

Situated on the prestigious Jermyn Street, in the heart of Piccadilly, the smart Cavendish Hotel offers guests the ultimate in luxury. Although the location makes it ideal for sampling the thrill of both London's theatres and its renowned shopping opportunities, it also provides a chance to escape the hustle and bustle of the city. It was run in Edwardian times by Rosa Lewis, the 'Duchess of Duke St', famous for her hospitality and cooking, and the tradition continues to this day. Inside, however, the hotel now features cutting-edge design, carried through from the public areas to the bedrooms, which have some of the best views in London. All 230 en suite rooms – including spacious executive rooms and suites – boast elegant furnishings, subtle lighting and clean, uncluttered lines, complemented by Villeroy and Boch bathrooms. Each comes fully equipped with the latest technology, including flatscreen LCD TV with over 600 channels and high-speed broadband. The AA Rosette-awarded David Britton at The Cavendish Restaurant serves an indulgent breakfast, as well as informal lunches and dinners, and the emphasis is on British cuisine using sustainably sourced ingredients. The monthly changing menus feature the best of seasonal and regional produce.

Recommended in the area

Fortnum & Mason; Buckingham Palace; Piccadilly Circus

Cannizaro House

★★★★ 79% ⊛⊛ COUNTRY HOUSE HOTEL

Address: West Side, Wimbledon Common,
          LONDON, SW19 4UE
Tel: 020 8879 1464
Fax: 020 8879 7338
Email: info@cannizarohouse.com
Website: www.cannizarohouse.com
Map ref: 4, TQ38 **Directions:** From A3 follow A219
signed Wimbledon into Parkside, right onto Cannizaro
Rd, sharp right onto Westside Common **Rooms:** 46
(5 GF) (10 fmly) **S** £99-£395 **D** £99-£395 (incl. bkfst) **Facilities:** STV Wi-fi **Parking:** 95

Cannizaro House is a true little gem tucked away in an idyllic location in SW19. The hotel sits just on the edge of Cannizaro Park and Wimbledon Common, and has 46 beautifully designed bedrooms and six meeting rooms, two with their own terrace, making it a perfect destination for business and pleasure. The two-Rosette restaurant serves imaginative modern European food, while the bar offers an extensive cocktail selection and drinks list.

Recommended in the area

Wimbledon Common; Wimbledon Village; Wimbledon Lawn Tennis Museum

Athenaeum Hotel & Apartments

★★★★★ ⊛ HOTEL

Address: 116 Piccadilly, LONDON, W1J 7BJ
Tel: 020 7499 3464
Fax: 020 7493 1860
Email: info@athenaeumhotel.com
Website: www.athenaeumhotel.com
Map ref: 4, TQ38 **Directions:** On Piccadilly, overlooking Green
Park **Rooms:** 157 **D** £150-£710 **Facilities:** STV Wi-fi Spa Gym
Sauna **Notes:** ⊗ in bedrooms

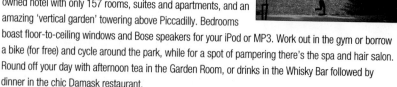

The luxurious Athenaeum, overlooking Green Park, is a family-owned hotel with only 157 rooms, suites and apartments, and an amazing 'vertical garden' towering above Piccadilly. Bedrooms boast floor-to-ceiling windows and Bose speakers for your iPod or MP3. Work out in the gym or borrow a bike (for free) and cycle around the park, while for a spot of pampering there's the spa and hair salon. Round off your day with afternoon tea in the Garden Room, or drinks in the Whisky Bar followed by dinner in the chic Damask restaurant.

Recommended in the area

Green Park; Mayfair boutiques; Buckingham Palace

Brown's Hotel

★★★★★ 88% ◉◉◉ HOTEL

Address: Albemarle Street, Mayfair, LONDON,
W1S 4BP
Tel: 020 7493 6020
Fax: 020 7493 9381
Email: reservations.browns@roccofortecollection.com
Website: www.roccofortecollection.com
Map ref: 4, TQ38 **Directions:** A short walk from Green Park,
Bond St & Piccadilly **Rooms:** 117 D £275-£3200
Facilities: STV Wi-fi Spa Gym **Notes:** ⊗ Civil Weddings 70

Situated in Albemarle Street in the heart of Mayfair, Rocco
Forte's Brown's Hotel must surely have one of the best
addresses in London. Sarah Brown, Lady Byron's maid, opened Brown's with her husband in 1837 as
London's first hotel. It was here that Rudyard Kipling wrote The Jungle Book, Agatha Christie penned At
Bertram's Hotel, and Alexander Graham Bell made the first ever European telephone call. Following a
£24 million renovation, this legendary hotel blends a traditional English style with a contemporary twist
to create a chic and sophisticated atmosphere. Brown's Hotel boasts 117 luxurious rooms and suites,
elegantly designed and equipped with the latest technology. The Albemarle restaurant specialises in
fine British cooking, using top-notch seasonal ingredients in such classic dishes as potted Morecambe
Bay shrimps, roasts from the carving trolley, and spotted dick with custard. The English Tea Room
provides a haven to return to after a day's shopping, while The Donovan Bar is one of London's hottest
meeting places. The Spa at Brown's offers a wide range of luxurious treatments, plus a 24-hour gym.
For business guests and functions, Brown's Hotel has six private dining and meeting rooms, all with an
abundance of natural daylight, high ceilings and beautiful antique furniture.

Recommended in the area

Bond Street shopping; the West End; Green Park

The Dorchester

★★★★★ ⊛⊛⊛ HOTEL

Address: Park Lane, LONDON, W1K 1QA
Tel: 020 7629 8888
Fax: 020 7629 8080
Email: info@thedorchester.com
Website: www.thedorchester.com
Map ref: 4, TQ38
Directions: Halfway along Park Ln between Hyde Park Corner & Marble Arch
Rooms: 250 **Facilities:** STV Wi-fi Spa Gym Sauna
Notes: ⊗ in bedrooms

From the day it opened in 1931, this legendary hotel has witnessed the comings and goings of many a limousine. Pass by at any time and there'll be a Rolls-Royce, Bentley or Porsche dropping off a world statesman, film star or industry magnate. Standing on the edge of Mayfair, it is minutes away from the exclusive shops of Bond Street and Knightsbridge. The spacious bedrooms and suites, beautifully decorated in English country house style, all overlook Hyde Park or the hotel's landscaped terraces. Their capacious, Italian-marble bathrooms are believed to have the deepest baths in London. The Dorchester is celebrated for its food, but first head for the bar where the Martini, Manhattan and White Lady cocktails were created. Alain Ducasse offers fine French cuisine, while the Grill Room specialises in British cooking and China Tang serves highly rated Cantonese food. Afternoon tea to live piano music in The Promenade is an institution among many Londoners. The Spa is a calm and peaceful retreat with steam rooms, spa baths, a fully equipped gymnasium and an extensive range of beauty and therapeutic treatments. At the front is a huge plane tree – one of the 'Great Trees of London' – it is stunning at Christmas time.

Recommended in the area

Buckingham Palace; Royal Academy of Arts; Piccadilly Circus

Buckingham Palace

Hyatt Regency London – The Churchill

★★★★★ 82% ◉◉◉ HOTEL

Address: 30 Portman Square, LONDON, W1H 7BH
Tel: 020 7486 5800
Fax: 020 7486 1255
Email: london.churchill@hyatt.com
Website: www.london.churchill.hyatt.com
Map ref: 4, TQ38
Directions: From Marble Arch rdbt, follow signs for Oxford Circus onto Oxford St. Left turn after 2nd lights onto Portman St. Hotel on left **Rooms:** 444 **S** £213-£437 **D** £213-£437
Facilities: STV Wi-fi Tennis Gym Sauna **Parking:** 48 **Notes:** ⊗ in bedrooms

In the heart of the West End, this hotel is perfectly placed for London's main attractions. Elegant bedrooms and suites offer extreme comfort and many thoughtful extras. Dining experiences include The Montagu and top-notch Italian cuisine in the Locanda Locatelli restaurant.

Recommended in the area

Buckingham Palace; Hyde Park; Theatreland

The Langham, London

★★★★★ 84%  HOTEL

Address: Portland Place, LONDON,
W1B 1JA

Tel: 020 7636 1000

Fax: 020 7323 2340

Email: lon.info@langhamhotels.com

Website: www.langhamlondon.com

Map ref: 4, TQ38 **Directions:** N of Regent St,
left opposite All Soul's Church

Rooms: 380 (5 fmly) **S** £199-£500 **D** £199-£5000

Facilities: STV Wi-fi ⊗ Spa Gym Sauna **Notes:** ⊗ in bedrooms

The Langham, London has been enchanting guests since it opened as Europe's first 'grand hotel' in 1865. In 2009 the hotel was reborn following a multi-million pound renovation, bringing it fully into the 21st century while retaining the grace and elegance of a bygone era. From the grandeur of its new entrance to the timeless style of its public rooms and bedrooms, The Langham certainly ranks among London's top luxury hotels. All 380 exquisitely appointed guest rooms evoke a warm, residential feel. Choose from the modern and elegant Grand rooms or the traditionally styled Classic rooms. The Landau offers a blend of contemporary European cuisine and British classics, all based around the finest seasonal ingredients. The chic and glamorous bar Artesian offers imaginative cocktails and houses a selection of over 70 rums. Palm Court is said to be where the tradition of afternoon tea was born over 140 years ago. Today, choose from either the Wonderland traditional afternoon tea or the unique Bijoux Tea, inspired by the collections of top jewellery designers. The Langham Health & Fitness Club features a state-of-the-art gym, 16-metre pool, men and women's saunas, steam rooms and solarium. A luxury new spa is planned to open soon.

Recommended in the area

The Wallace Collection; Hyde Park; Trafalgar Square

Millennium Hotel London Mayfair

★★★★ 80% ◉◉ HOTEL

Address: Grosvenor Square, LONDON, W1K 2HP
Tel: 020 7629 9400
Fax: 020 7629 7736
Email: reservations@millenniumhotels.co.uk
Website: www.millenniumhotels.co.uk
Map ref: 4, TQ38 **Directions:** S side of Grosvenor Square
Rooms: 336 **S** £145-£520 **D** £145-£520 **Facilities:** STV Wi-fi
Gym **Notes:** ⊗ in bedrooms

Built as a magnificent townhouse in the 18th century, this hotel, in the heart of London's most exclusive and fashionable shopping district, still exudes an ambience of cultured luxury. The air-conditioned bedrooms, never less than 26 square metres in size, all have seating areas and king-size or twin beds. Most have fine views over Grosvenor Square. Facilities include internet access (there's also Wi-fi throughout the hotel), mini-bar and tea-and-coffee-making supplies, and a rollaway bed can be provided in some of the rooms for a child at a supplement. The main restaurant at the hotel is Avista, a 75-seat Italian restaurant with a private dining room for 12 and featuring its own street entrance at 39 Grosvenor Square. Michele Granziera, Head Chef of Avista, combines a variety of both rustic and contemporary Italian dishes with a personal touch. The Shogun Restaurant has a wide menu of authentic Japanese dishes, including hand-rolled sushi. Bars include the trendy, contemporary Avista Bar and the ultra-stylish Pine Bar. Business guests have the use of a 24-hour Business Centre with computer stations and office equipment, plus mobile phone and pager rentals. The hotel also has a wedding licence, and ten function rooms provide facilities for events with up to 700 guests.

Recommended in the area

West End shopping; West End theatres; Hyde Park

The Washington Mayfair Hotel

★★★★ 77% HOTEL

Address: 5-7 Curzon Street, Mayfair, LONDON,
W1J 5HE
Tel: 020 7499 7000
Fax: 020 7495 6172
Email: sales@washington-mayfair.co.uk
Website: www.washington-mayfair.co.uk
Map ref: 4, TQ38 **Directions:** From Green Park station take
Piccadilly exit & turn right. 4th street on right into Curzon Street
Rooms: 171 S £150-£700 D £150-£700 **Facilities:** Wi-fi Gym
Notes: ⊗ in bedrooms

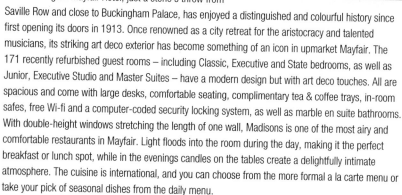

The Washington Mayfair Hotel, just a stone's throw from
Saville Row and close to Buckingham Palace, has enjoyed a distinguished and colourful history since
first opening its doors in 1913. Once renowned as a city retreat for the aristocracy and talented
musicians, its striking art deco exterior has become something of an icon in upmarket Mayfair. The
171 recently refurbished guest rooms – including Classic, Executive and State bedrooms, as well as
Junior, Executive Studio and Master Suites – have a modern design but with art deco touches. All are
spacious and come with large desks, comfortable seating, complimentary tea & coffee trays, in-room
safes, free Wi-fi and a computer-coded security locking system, as well as marble en suite bathrooms.
With double-height windows stretching the length of one wall, Madisons is one of the most airy and
comfortable restaurants in Mayfair. Light floods into the room during the day, making it the perfect
breakfast or lunch spot, while in the evenings candles on the tables create a delightfully intimate
atmosphere. The cuisine is international, and you can choose from the more formal a la carte menu or
take your pick of seasonal dishes from the daily menu.

Recommended in the area

Mayfair shopping; Buckingham Palace; Piccadilly

Lancaster London

★★★★ 81% @ HOTEL

Address: Lancaster Terrace, LONDON, W2 2TY
Tel: 020 7262 6737
Fax: 020 7724 3191
Email: book@royallancaster.com
Website: www.royallancaster.com
Map ref: 4, TQ38
Directions: Adjacent to Lancaster Gate underground station
Rooms: 416 (11 fmly) **S** £113.85–£356.50
D £113.85–£356.50 **Facilities:** STV Wi-fi **Parking:** 65 **Notes:** ⊗ in bedrooms

There's one thing guests at Lancaster London must surely always agree on – the views are breathtaking. With Hyde Park directly to the south, and vistas east to the City of London, the hotel has arguably the best outlook in the capital. And those stunning views can be enjoyed from on high in the superior bedrooms or from the hotel's restaurants. Of course, you needn't just see the heart of the city from behind glass – from here you can easily venture out and explore, with Marble Arch and the plethora of Oxford Street shops just an easy stroll from the hotel, and Harrods and the rest of Knightsbridge only 10 minutes by taxi. Even Heathrow Airport is a mere 20-minute ride on the Heathrow Express from nearby Paddington Railway Station. Alongside world-class guest service and a strong environmental ethos, the hotel boasts an elegant Lounge Bar, two award-winning restaurants and some of London's largest, most flexible banqueting and event facilities. Designed to be the perfect base for both business and leisure visits to the city, the 416 guest rooms offer every luxury, with beautiful oak furniture, deep-pile carpets and exquisite marble bathrooms. Modern facilities include flat-screen TVs, high-speed wireless internet access and multi-lingual voicemail.

Recommended in the area

Kensington Gardens and Hyde Park; Marble Arch; Royal Albert Hall

Milestone Hotel

★★★★★ ❀ HOTEL

Address: 1 Kensington Court, LONDON, W8 5DL
Tel: 020 7917 1000
Fax: 020 7917 1010
Email: bookms@rchmail.com
Website: www.milestonehotel.com
Map ref: 4, TQ38
Directions: From Warwick Rd right into Kensington High St. Hotel 400yds past Kensington underground
Rooms: 63 (2 GF) (3 fmly) S £275-£311
Facilities: STV Wi-fi ⊗ Spa Gym Sauna Parking: 1

The Milestone's combination of country-house ambience and chic city elegance is something of a mirror to its surroundings, with Hyde Park and Kensington Gardens across the road and some of London's most fashionable shopping just around the corner. The dedication to personal attention (the hotel has won awards for service) includes a welcome with champagne, sherry or tea, a turndown service and limousine shopping trips, and that's just the beginning. Take a luxury suite and you'll also get 24-hour butler service and canapés each evening. The bedrooms are all individually decorated, featuring exquisite fabrics, soft furnishings and antique and hand-painted furniture. The stunning Mistinguett Suite, for instance, is a tribute to the 1920s 'Queen of the Paris Music Halls'. The suite is richly furnished with silvery greys and scarlet and boasts a spacious private terrace with table and chairs. The public areas are equally sumptuous: the intimate Cheneston's serving the finest British cuisine; the informal Conservatory; and the cosy Park Lounge, perfect for afternoon tea. The health club is for residents only and includes a resistance pool, fully-equipped gym and resident beauty therapist.

Recommended in the area

Kensington Palace; Royal Albert Hall; South Kensington Museums

Royal Garden Hotel

★★★★★ ◉◉◉ HOTEL

Address: 2-24 Kensington High Street, LONDON,
W8 4PT
Tel: 020 7937 8000
Fax: 020 7361 1991
Email: sales@royalgardenhotel.co.uk
Website: www.royalgardenhotel.co.uk
Map ref: 4, TQ38
Directions: Next to Kensington Palace
Rooms: 396 (19 fmly) S £171.35-£240.35
D £205.85-£274.85 **Facilities:** STV Wi-fi Spa Gym Sauna **Notes:** ⊗ in bedrooms

In the heart of Kensington, the Royal Garden Hotel is the perfect place to stay whether on business or exploring London. There are 396 beautifully appointed bedrooms to choose from, including 37 suites, plus two restaurants, three bars, a 24-hour business centre and 24-hour room service. The hotel also has a choice of 10 conference and banqueting rooms, all of which have been recently refurbished and can accommodate up to 550 delegates. The Soma centre is the hotel's holistic health centre and spa, offering a gym, sauna and steam room, plus a wide range of beauty treatments and classes in yoga, Pilates and kick boxing. Head to the award-winning Min Jiang restaurant on the 10th floor for an authentic Chinese experience in an elegant setting looking out over Kensington Gardens, Hyde Park and the London skyline beyond. Enjoy superb dim sum and be sure not to miss the famous Beijing duck roasted in a special wood-burning oven. Alternatively, the newly appointed Park Terrace restaurant, lounge and bar on the ground floor is open for breakfast, lunch, afternoon tea, dinner and all-day snacks. Here, the setting is relaxed and informal, the focus is on fresh British produce, and there are large windows through which to enjoy the vista of Kensington Gardens and Palace.

Recommended in the area

Harrods; Hyde Park; Kensington Gardens Serpentine Gallery; Natural History Museum; V&A Museum

The mid 20th-century Roman Catholic Cathedral of Christ the King, Liverpool

River Mersey, Birkenhead

RiverHill Hotel

★★★ 80% HOTEL

Address: Talbot Road, Prenton, BIRKENHEAD,
CH43 2HJ
Tel: 0151 653 3773
Fax: 0151 653 7162
Email: reception@theriverhill.co.uk
Website: www.theriverhill.co.uk
Map ref: 5, SJ38
Directions: M53 junct 3, A552. Left onto B5151 at
lights, hotel 0.5m on right

Rooms: 15 (1 fmly) **Facilities:** STV Wi-fi **Parking:** 32 **Notes:** ⊗ in bedrooms

The RiverHill stands in its own beautiful grounds in Oxton, a quiet residential neighbourhood near Birkenhead. It is run by Nick and Michelle Burn, who also run the Grove House Hotel in Wallasey. The attractively furnished en suite bedrooms have many thoughtful extras. There are 2 bridal suites, each with four-poster bed. The Bay Tree Restaurant offers carte and fixed price menus and quality wines.

Recommended in the area

Speke Hall (NT); Bidston Observatory; Ness Botanic Gardens

Grove House Hotel

★★★ 79% HOTEL

Address: Grove Road, WALLASEY, CH45 3HF
Tel: 0151 639 3947 & 0151 630 4558
Fax: 0151 639 0028
Email: reception@thegrovehouse.co.uk
Website: www.thegrovehouse.co.uk
Map ref: 7, SJ29
Directions: M53 junct 1, A554 (Wallasey New Brighton), right after church onto Harrison Drive, left after Windsors Garage onto Grove Rd

Rooms: 14 (7 fmly) **S** £69.50 **D** £79.50-£135 **Facilities:** Wi-fi **Parking:** 28 **Notes:** ⊗ in bedrooms

Located on the Wirral peninsula, Grove House Hotel has miles of coastal walks, water-based activities and first-class golf courses right on its doorstep. It's also a convenient base for exploring the city of Liverpool, with its World Heritage listed waterfront and excellent museums and entertainment venues. The hotel boasts a pretty garden and is peacefully situated in a residential area of the town, yet it's only a short distance from the seafront promenade and the underground station for Liverpool, and just a mile away from the M53. The bedrooms are beautifully furnished and equipped with facilities for making hot drinks, a trouser press and direct-dial telephone, and each has a luxurious bathroom. One of the rooms is large enough to accommodate a family, and there is also a bridal suite with four-poster bed, which can be booked to include a champagne breakfast. The bar-lounge is a great place to relax at the end of the day before enjoying a meal in the newly refurbished, oak-panelled restaurant, which overlooks the garden. Here, service is impeccable and the excellent choice of dishes on both the carte and set menus is complemented by a wide-ranging wine list. All in all, this is a friendly place offering high standards and good value.

Recommended in the area

Heritage Centre of Port Sunlight; Williamson Art Gallery and Museum; Ellesmere Port Boat Museum

NORFOLK

Boats stranded by the out-going tide at Wells-Next-the-Sea

Blakeney

The Blakeney Hotel

★★★ 82% ◉ HOTEL

Address: The Quay, BLAKENEY, Holt, NR25 7NE
Tel: 01263 740797
Fax: 01263 740795
Email: reception@blakeney-hotel.co.uk
Website: www.blakeney-hotel.co.uk
Map ref: 4, TG04
Directions: Off A149 (coast road) 8m W of Sheringham
Rooms: 64 (18 GF) (20 fmly) S £82-£138
D £164-£300 (incl. bkfst & dinner) **Facilities:** Wi-fi ◉ Gym Sauna **Parking:** 60

A traditional, privately owned hotel right on the quayside, overlooking the estuary and salt marshes. Many of the rooms, some with balconies, look out over the impressive landscape to Blakeney Point, now part of the North Norfolk Heritage Coast. Terraces lead from others to the south-facing gardens. There are two comfortable lounges, one with an open fire. The restaurant and bar share the same panorama as a backdrop to hearty English breakfasts, light lunches and seasonal cuisine.
Recommended in the area
Holkham Hall; Sandringham; North Norfolk Railway

Hoste Arms Hotel

★★★ 87% ◉◉ HOTEL

Address: The Green, BURNHAM MARKET,
King's Lynn, PE31 8HD
Tel: 01328 738777
Fax: 01328 730103
Email: reception@hostearms.co.uk
Website: www.hostearms.co.uk
Map ref: 4, TF84
Directions: Signed on B1155, 5m W of
Wells-next-the-Sea
Rooms: 35 (7 GF) **S** £104-£190 **D** £128-£225 (incl. bkfst) **Facilities:** STV Wi-fi **Parking:** 45

This 17th-century former coaching inn overlooks the village green in an Area of Outstanding Natural Beauty, close to north Norfolk's unspoilt beaches. Admiral Nelson, who was born in the next village, used to meet his companions here, and today it is still very much the hub of the community. Its well-travelled hosts, Paul and Jeanne Whittome, pride themselves on providing a relaxed atmosphere, but not at the expense of the highest standards of service, dining and accommodation. The standard doubles, family bedrooms, four-posters, junior suites and penthouse, all designed by Jeanne, are provided with pure Egyptian cotton bedlinen and plasma TVs. Some rooms are in the exotic Zulu wing, which reflects her South African heritage. Drop in for a simple lunch in the buzzy front bar, warmed when necessary by a log fire, head for a sunny table in the Moroccan garden, or take afternoon tea in the conservatory. Book a romantic dinner in the panelled restaurant, where the Hoste's chefs create dishes that owe much to locally sourced produce, not least a great selection of local seafood from the nearby coast. The imaginative menu is complemented by a 200-bin wine list that includes some keenly priced classics.

Recommended in the area

Norfolk Coast Path; Wells & Walsingham Light Railway; Blakeney Point

Sea Marge Hotel

★★★ 82% ◉◉ HOTEL

Address: 16 High Street, Overstrand, CROMER,
NR27 0AB
Tel: 01263 579579
Fax: 01263 579524
Email: info@mackenziehotels.com
Website: www.mackenziehotels.com
Map ref: 4, TG24
Directions: A140 from Norwich then A149 to
Cromer, B1159 to Overstrand. Hotel in village centre
Rooms: 25 (2 GF) (6 fmly) S £91 D £142 (incl. bkfst)
Facilities: Wi-fi **Parking:** 50

Perched high on a clifftop on the beautiful North Norfolk coast, with five acres of terraced gardens sweeping down to the cliff edge, is this elegant privately-run hotel. The fine Edwardian building is grade II listed and steeped in history. It was commissioned in 1908 as a seaside country gentleman's residence. At the time Overstrand and the surrounding 'Poppyland' was a fashionable holiday destination for the rich and powerful, and Winston Churchill was a frequent visitor. After years of neglect, the building was restored to its former glory and opened as a hotel in 1996. The bedrooms are sympathetically designed to retain the ambience of the house, and contain all the modern comforts you'd expect. Frazer's Restaurant combines the elegance of a bygone era with 21st century style, offering a modern British menu inspired by the best local and seasonal produce. Add to this attentive but unobtrusive service, and you can look forward to a memorable stay. The Sea Marge Hotel is within easy reach of all the coastal and countryside delights North Norfolk has to offer.

Recommended in the area

Blickling Hall; Bure Valley Railway; Bewilderwood Tree House Adventure

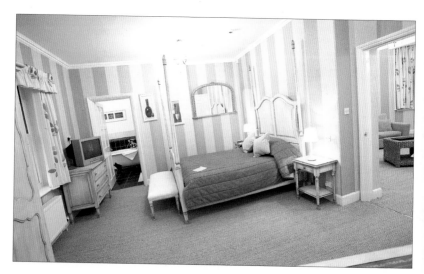

The Kings Head Hotel

★★★ 86% ◉ HOTEL

Address: GREAT BIRCHAM, King's Lynn, PE31 6RJ
Tel: 01485 578265
Fax: 01485 578635
Email: welcome@the-kings-head-bircham.co.uk
Website: www.the-kings-head-bircham.co.uk
Map ref: 4, TF73
Directions: From King's Lynn take A149 towards Fakenham. After Hillington, turn left onto B1153, to Great Bircham
Rooms: 12 (2 fmly) **Facilities:** Wi-fi **Parking:** 25

A historic, traditional inn exterior gives way to what is now a contemporary hotel that has been refurbished using fine, colour co-ordinated fabrics and chic furniture. The bedrooms are spacious and each has an individual style and decor, a king-size bed, a luxurious and spacious bathroom and many thoughtful touches that include fresh flowers, a decanter of port and home-made biscuits. The restaurant is also in contemporary style, and, together with the bar, overlooks the sheltered courtyard from where a garden leads off, giving unprecedented views across the fields to Bircham Windmill. The bar stocks the finest local real ales among other beverages, and the food here and in the restaurant is highly regarded. The head chef produces dishes that are innovative but not overcomplicated. Starters might range from Thornham oysters with vodka chilli granita to Caesar salad with Norfolk smoked trout; main courses from pan-seared fillet of grey mullet with marinated artichoke, sunblushed tomatoes, chargrilled chicory and pesto dressing, to a Kings Head burger with gruyère, crispy bacon, home-cut chips and mustard mayonnaise. Meals are served both in the bar and the restaurant, with roaring log fires in winter and alfresco dining – including barbecues – in summer.

Recommended in the area

Sandringham; Bircham Windmill; Norfolk Lavender

Holkham Bay Beach

The Lawns

★ ★ ★ ★ ◉ RESTAURANT WITH ROOMS

Address: 26 Station Road, HOLT, NR25 6BS
Tel: 01263 713390
Email: mail@lawnsatholt.co.uk
Website: www.lawnsatholt.co.uk
Map ref: 4, TG03
Directions: A148 (Cromer Rd). 0.25m from
Holt rdbt, turn left, 400yds along Station Rd
Rooms: 8 D £85–£110 (incl. bkfst)
Facilities: Wi-fi Parking: 14 Notes: ⊗ in bedrooms

The Lawns is a three-minute walk from the centre of the Georgian town of Holt, and close to the wonderful North Norfolk coast. A fully licensed wine bar and restaurant, with plenty of space to sit and enjoy a meal and a glass of wine or locally brewed beer, it's open to both residents and non-residents. The menu reflects the seasons and features plenty of local produce, including fresh fish. The eight light and airy bedrooms, all with baths and double beds, are on the upper floor of the Georgian building and mostly look out over the large south-facing garden.

Recommended in the area

Norfolk Coast Path; Blickling Hall; North Norfolk Railway

Caley Hall Hotel

★★★ 82% HOTEL

Address: Old Hunstanton Road, HUNSTANTON,
PE36 6HH
Tel: 01485 533486
Fax: 01485 533348
Email: mail@caleyhallhotel.co.uk
Website: www.caleyhallhotel.co.uk
Map ref: 4, TF64
Directions: (1m from Hunstanton, on A149)
Rooms: 40 (30 GF) (20 fmly) S £50–£200
D £70–£200 (incl. bkfst) **Facilities:** STV Wi-fi **Parking:** 50

Located where the north Norfolk coast curves southwest into The Wash, this is a good base for long walks along wide beaches and exploring unspoilt countryside dotted with sleepy villages. Caley Hall is a lovely 17th-century brick-and-flint house which, from the front, presents a fairly modest farmhouse appearance, but former barns, stables and extensions tucked away at the back have been beautifully converted to provide additional accommodation. Most of the rooms, all with en suite bathrooms, are at ground level, grouped around several sheltered patio areas, and have satellite TV, DVD and CD players, a refrigerator and tea-and-coffee-making facilities. There's individual heating in each room, so guests can adjust the temperature. The deluxe rooms are more spacious – one has a four-poster bed – and there's a suite with a whirlpool bath, plus some rooms for mobility-impaired guests. The restaurant is housed in the old stables, but the decor is chic rather than rustic, with high-back leather chairs and modern light-wood tables. Breakfast, lunch and dinner are served, with an evening menu that might include grilled seabass, braised local beef, a traditional roast and vegetarian options. There's also a bright, spacious bar, open all day, with lots of cosy, soft leather sofas.

Recommended in the area

Sandringham; Titchwell RSPB Reserve; Holkham Hall

St Giles House Hotel

★★★★ 81% ◉◉ HOTEL

Address: 41-45 St Giles Street, NORWICH, NR2 1JR
Tel: 01603 275180
Fax: 0845 299 1905
Email: reception@stgileshousehotel.com
Website: www.stgileshousehotel.com
Map ref: 4, TG20
Directions: A11 into central Norwich. Left at rdbt (Chapelfield Shopping Centre). 3rd exit at next rdbt. Left onto St Giles St. Hotel on left
Rooms: 24 S £120-£210 D £130-£220 (incl. bkfst)
Facilities: Wi-fi Parking: 23 Notes: ⊗ in bedrooms

In the centre of historic Norwich, a baroque-style, Grade II listed building and an adjacent Georgian building have been stunningly restored and transformed into this luxurious boutique hotel. Exceptionally chic throughout, several features are outstanding, including the spectacular glass dome and crystal chandelier in the main lounge of the Walnut Suite – one of the three function and conference suites – and the delightful Parisian-style terrace. Many original features have been retained throughout the building, including fabulous wood panelling, ornamental plasterwork and marble floors. All of the bedrooms and suites are spacious, luxurious and have been individually designed. They are equipped with flat-screen TVs and DVD players, mini-bars and tea-and-coffee-making equipment, free Wi-fi access and complimentary L'Occitane beauty products. The stylish, open-plan lounge bar and restaurant offers contemporary dining in a relaxing atmosphere, and the menus focus on local ingredients, with a commitment to providing top quality as well as good value.

Recommended in the area

Norwich Cathedral; Norwich Castle; Theatre Royal

Dales Country House Hotel

★★★★ 83% ◎◎ HOTEL

Address: Lodge Hill, Upper Sheringham,
SHERINGHAM, NR26 8TJ
Tel: 01263 824555
Fax: 01263 822647
Email: dales@mackenziehotels.com
Website: www.mackenziehotels.com
Map ref: 4, TG14
Directions: on B1157 1m S of Sheringham, from
A148 take turn at entrance to Sheringham Park,
0.5m, hotel on left
Rooms: 21 (5 GF) **S** £95-£194 **D** £142-£204 (incl. bkfst & dinner)
Facilities: Wi-fi Tennis Croquet Petanque **Parking:** 50 **Notes:** ⊗ in bedrooms 🚼 under 14 yrs

Nestled in National Trust parkland, yet close to the North Norfolk coast, is this quintessentially English grade II listed country-house hotel. Thanks to sympathetic restoration and attention to detail, many original features remain for guests to enjoy today, including a splendid oak staircase, mullioned and stained-glass windows and original fireplaces. Outside, the tennis court, croquet lawn and a pond in the shape of Norfolk have all been restored, too. Each of the luxurious en suite bedrooms is refreshingly different: some have traditional oak furniture and beautiful old English fabrics, while others have a contemporary feel that blends well with the rest of the house. All are fine examples of timeless style combined with every modern comfort. The intimate Upcher's Restaurant, with two AA Rosettes, specialises in contemporary English cuisine prepared from the finest local ingredients. Whether you choose fish from the North Norfolk coast, or game from local estates, you can't go far wrong.

Recommended in the area

Felbrigg Hall; Sheringham Park; Hillside Shire Horse Sanctuary

Norfolk lavender, West Newton

Titchwell Manor Hotel

★★★ 86% ◉◉ HOTEL

Address: TITCHWELL, Brancaster, PE31 8BB
Tel: 01485 210221
Fax: 01485 210104
Email: margaret@titchwellmanor.com
Website: www.titchwellmanor.com
Map ref: 4, TF74 **Directions:** On A149 (coast road)
between Brancaster & Thornham **Rooms:** 26 (16 GF)
(4 fmly) **D** £110-£250 (incl. bkfst) **Parking:** 50

Golfers come for the two championship courses nearby; nature lovers come for the rich birdlife of the marshes; foodies come for the cuisine of head chef Eric Snaith, and others come just for the relaxing atmosphere and stylish accommodation. The rooms are split between the main hotel – a brick-and-flint Victorian farmhouse – and a converted barn, a cottage and around a herb-filled courtyard. All boast chic, contemporary furnishings and some have sea views. There are some family rooms and even dog-friendly rooms complete with bowls and biscuits. The restaurant offers a selection of innovative, beautifully presented dishes, while simpler, but equally accomplished, cooking is available in the bar.

Recommended in the area

RSPB Titchwell Marsh Reserve; Peddars Way and Norfolk Coast Path; Norfolk Lavender

Through the gardens of Cottesbrooke Hall

Rushton Hall Hotel and Spa

★★★★ 80% ◉◉ COUNTRY HOUSE HOTEL

Address: KETTERING, NN14 1RR
Tel: 01536 713001
Fax: 01536 713010
Email: enquiries@rushtonhall.com
Website: www.rushtonhall.com
Map ref: 3, SP87
Directions: A14 junct 7. A43 to Corby then A6003 to Rushton turn after bridge
Rooms: 45 (3 GF) (5 fmly) S £150-£350
D £150-£350 (incl. bkfst) **Facilities:** Wi-fi ⊗ Tennis Spa Gym Sauna Steam Room Sun Shower
Treatment Rooms **Parking:** 140 **Notes:** ⊗ in bedrooms

Rushton Hall is a magnificent Grade I listed Elizabethan country house, surrounded by beautiful, tranquil countryside where a wide range of activities and country pursuits are available. The east Midlands road network makes it easy to get to, which makes it a popular conference and wedding venue. The grandeur of the building is balanced by an ambience of comfort, where guests can relax by one of the big open fireplaces and enjoy the attentive hospitality. Bedrooms are richly decorated in individual style, from elegant superior rooms to wood-panelled rooms with magnificent four-poster beds. All have Wi-fi and flat-screen TVs, and some of the en suite bathrooms have a large bath and separate shower. The restaurant occupies the grand oak-panelled dining room and as much attention is paid to the sourcing of ingredients as to the creation of the menus. There is also a brasserie, and afternoon tea is served in the Great Hall or in the courtyard when the weather is good. Guests have the use of a fitness suite, outdoor tennis court, billiard table, swimming pool, indoor and outdoor spa, steam room, sauna and sun shower. Beauty treatments are also available.

Recommended in the area

Triangular Lodge; Boughton House; Rockingham Speedway; Rockingham Castle; Rutland Water

Upper Coquetdale, Northumberland National Park

Langley Castle Hotel

★★★★ 82% ◉◉ HOTEL

Address: Langley on Tyne, HEXHAM, NE47 5LU
Tel: 01434 688888
Fax: 01434 684019
Email: manager@langleycastle.com
Website: www.langleycastle.com
Map ref: 6, NY96
Directions: From A69 S on A686 for 2m.
Hotel on right
Rooms: 27 (9 GF) (8 fmly) S £112.50-£199.50
D £139-£269 (incl. bkfst) **Facilities:** STV Wi-fi **Parking:** 70
Notes: ⊗ in bedrooms

A genuine 14th-century castle, restored and transformed into a magnificent and comfortable hotel, set in its own 12-acre woodland estate. All nine guest bedchambers have private facilities, and some boast window seats set into 7ft-thick walls, four-poster beds, and even a sauna and spa bath. CastleView and CastleView Lodge, converted Grade I listed buildings within the grounds, offer additional guest rooms. All the bedrooms have draped canopies over the beds, satellite TV and stunning views up to the main castle. The splendid drawing room, with blazing log fire, traceries and stained glass, together with the oak-panelled cocktail bar, complement the intimate atmosphere of the Josephine Restaurant. The food served here is of the highest order, making the most of fresh, local produce, with fish and game a speciality. The exclusive nature of the castle makes Langley the perfect destination to be pampered in unique surroundings, and it's ideally located for discovering the delights of Hadrian's Wall, Bamburgh Castle, Holy Island and the Scottish Borders. The Castle is only 30 minutes from Newcastle city centre and 40 minutes form Newcastle Airport.

Recommended in the area

Hadrian's Wall; Bamburgh Castle; Hexham Abbey

Newstead Abbey formal gardens

Langar Hall

★★★ 81% ◉◉ HOTEL

Address: LANGAR, NG13 9HG
Tel: 01949 860559
Fax: 01949 861045
Email: info@langarhall.co.uk
Website: www.langarhall.com
Map ref: 6, SK73
Directions: Via Bingham from A52 or Cropwell Bishop from A46, both signed. Hotel behind church
Rooms: 12 (1 GF) (1 fmly) S £85-£125
D £95-£210 (incl. bkfst) Facilities: Wi-fi Parking: 20

Langar Hall was built in 1837 on the site of a great historic house, the home of Admiral Lord Howe. It stands in peaceful seclusion overlooking lovely gardens, beyond which sheep graze among ancient trees. There's a croquet lawn in the grounds and a network of medieval fishponds stocked with carp. This charming hotel is the family home of Imogen Skirving, who, in running Langar Hall manages to combine high standards of hotel-keeping with the hospitality of an informal country house where children are welcome. Most of the bedrooms enjoy delightful views, and every one is quiet, comfortable and well-equipped, particularly for guests who have business to attend to in Nottingham. Downstairs, the study is reserved as a quiet room for reading and meetings, while the white sitting room is the perfect spot for afternoon tea and drinks before dinner, and the Indian room makes a good setting for private parties and conferences. The dining room is an elegant pillared hall renowned locally for its fresh, seasonal food with an emphasis on game in winter and fish in summer. Langar Hall lends itself superbly to exclusive house parties.

Recommended in the area

Belvoir Castle; Trent Bridge Cricket Ground; Newark International Antiques and Collectors Fair

Hart's Hotel

★★★★ 82% ◉◉ HOTEL

Address: Standard Hill, Park Row, NOTTINGHAM, NG1 6GN
Tel: 0115 988 1900
Fax: 0115 947 7600
Email: reception@hartshotel.co.uk
Website: www.hartsnottingham.co.uk
Map ref: 6, SK53
Directions: At junct of Park Row & Ropewalk, close to city centre
Rooms: 32 (7 GF) (1 fmly) **Facilities:** STV Wi-fi Gym **Parking:** 19

A privately owned boutique hotel built to an award-winning design in 2002 on the former ramparts of Nottingham's medieval castle, close to the bustling city centre. Light, contemporary rooms feature top quality beds with goose-down pillows and duvets, and Egyptian cotton bed linen. Mini-bars are stocked with wines, beers and fresh milk for your cafetière coffee, while other standard features include CD, radio, TV with satellite channels, internet access, DDI lines and voicemail. Some rooms have French doors leading out into the pretty garden – a perfect spot for a relaxing gin and tonic before dinner in Hart's Restaurant. Dine on modern British cooking in one of the newly installed intimate booths and choose from owner Tim Hart's wine list, which has a generous selection from smaller producers. An alternative to the restaurant is the more casual Park Bar, with original artwork on display, high-backed sofas, red leather armchairs, and courtyard seating. Hart's Upstairs is a popular venue for private parties, weddings and business meetings. From the hotel's garden there are extensive views across the city and beyond. A nightly charge is made for the secure, barrier-controlled car park.

Recommended in the area

City of Caves; Nottingham Royal Centre; Nottingham Playhouse

The Grange Hotel

★★★ 82% ◉ HOTEL

Address: 73 London Road, NEWARK, NG24 1RZ
Tel: 01636 703399
Fax: 01636 702328
Email: info@grangenewark.co.uk
Website: www.grangenewark.co.uk
Map ref: 8, SK75
Directions: From A1 follow signs to Balderton, hotel opposite Polish War Graves
Rooms: 19 (1 fmly) S £79-£110
D £110-£155 (incl. bkfst) **Facilities:** Wi-fi **Parking:** 17 **Notes:** ⊗ in bedrooms

A family-run, Victorian-era hotel in a conservation area, just a short walk from the town centre. Skilfully renovated, Newark Civic Trust gave it an award for the way original features, such as a beautiful tiled floor in one of the entrance areas, have been retained. Public rooms include a bar called Potters, with framed illustrations of old crockery, and a residents' lounge. Beyond Potters is a stone-flagged patio shaded by tall yews and the immaculate landscaped garden, winner of a Newark in Bloom award. The bedrooms, some with four-posters, all feature newly-designed bathrooms with bath and shower, co-ordinated soft furnishings, desk space with phone and computer access point, TV, radio alarm, beverage-making and ironing facilities, hairdryer, trouser press and, last but not least, a rubber duck for the very young. High-ceilinged Cutlers restaurant, named after the antique cutlery on display, offers a frequently changing, à la carte menu, with main courses such as braised blade of beef; baked herb-crusted sea bass; and broccoli, cheese and potato bake. That it attracts non-residents as well as hotel guests says much about the restaurant's local reputation. Weddings and business functions are expertly catered for.

Recommended in the area

Newark Castle and Gardens; Newark International Antiques Fair; Newark Air Museum

Oxford's Radcliffe Observatory

The Bay Tree Hotel

★★★ 79% ⚜ HOTEL

Address: Sheep Street, BURFORD, OX18 4LW
Tel: 01993 822791
Fax: 01993 823008
Email: info@baytreehotel.info
Website: www.cotswold-inns-hotels.co.uk/bay-tree
Map ref: 3, SP21
Directions: A40 or A361 to Burford. From High St turn into Sheep St, next to old market square. Hotel on right
Rooms: 21 (2 fmly) Facilities: Wi-fi Parking: 50

Much of this delightful old inn's character comes from the flagstone floors, tapestries, high-raftered hall, galleried stairs and tastefully furnished oak-panelled bedrooms, some with four-poster or half-tester beds. Public areas consist of the country-style Woolsack Bar, a sophisticated airy restaurant with original leaded windows, a selection of meeting rooms and an attractive walled garden. An alternative to the restaurant's candle-lit atmosphere is the Woolsack's extensive menu of lighter meals.

Recommended in the area

Cotswold Wildlife Park; Blenheim Palace; City of Oxford

The Lamb Inn

★★★ 83% ⚜⚜ SMALL HOTEL

Address: Sheep Street, BURFORD, OX18 4LR
Tel: 01993 823155
Fax: 01993 822228
Email: info@lambinn-burford.co.uk
Website: www.cotswold-inns-hotels.co.uk/lamb
Map ref: 3, SP21
Directions: A40 into Burford, downhill, 1st left into Sheep St, hotel last on right
Rooms: 17 (4 GF) (1 fmly)
Facilities: Wi-fi

To quote the owners, "The phrase 'charming old inn' is used much too freely, but the Lamb has a genuine right to it", with stone-flagged floors, log fires and many other time-worn features. The cosy lounges, with deep armchairs, are tranquillity itself. The en suite bedrooms contain fine furniture, much of it antique, in addition to the usual amenities, including home-made cookies. All overlook leafy side streets, or the hotel courtyard. The airy restaurant serves traditional English food with a modern twist.

Recommended in the area

Cotswold Wildlife Park; Blenheim Palace; City of Oxford

Miller of Mansfield

★ ★ ★ ★ ★ ❀ RESTAURANT WITH ROOMS

Address: High St, GORING,
RG8 9AW
Tel: 01491 872829
Fax: 01491 873100
Email: reservations@millerofmansfield.com
Website: www.millerofmansfield.com
Map ref: 3, SU67
Rooms: 13 (2 fmly) S £100-£125 D £125-225
Facilities: Wi-fi Parking: 2

The recently renovated Miller of Mansfield is a haven of laid back calm in a quiet village setting in Goring on Thames, overlooking the beautiful Chiltern Hills. The 13 eclectically designed rooms and suites offer all of the comforts one would expect, including flat-screen digital TVs, marble bathrooms with stone resin freestanding baths and/or luxury rain showers, and amazing organic latex mattresses. Further pampering comes in the form of natural REN toiletries, Egyptian cotton linens and thick bathrobes. Culinary treats of the modern British kind await you in the acclaimed restaurant and bar. Menus change regularly to reflect the seasons and the kitchen uses the best of local and British produce. You're bound to find something to excite on the wine list and there's also a fine selection of local real ales. The Miller is the perfect destination for a relaxing break away, either over the weekend or for a quiet midweek escape. For business users, free hi-speed internet access through the Wi-fi HotSpot, great meeting facilities and exemplary levels of service and hospitality make the Miller the ideal home away from home when you need to stay in the Thames Valley.

Recommended in the area

Basildon Park (NT); Beale Park Wildlife Park & Gardens; Henley on Thames

Blenheim Palace

RUTLAND

Rutland Water

Normanton Church, Rutland Water

Barnsdale Lodge Hotel

★★★ 78% ⚙ HOTEL

Address: The Avenue, Rutland Water, North Shore,
OAKHAM, LE15 8AH
Tel: 01572 724678
Fax: 01572 724961
Email: enquiries@barnsdalelodge.co.uk
Website: www.barnsdalelodge.co.uk
Map ref: 3, SK80
Directions: Off A1 onto A606. Hotel 5m on right,
2m E of Oakham

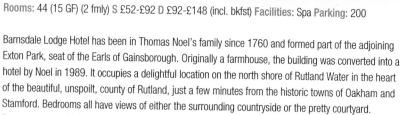

Rooms: 44 (15 GF) (2 fmly) **S** £52-£92 **D** £92-£148 (incl. bkfst) **Facilities:** Spa **Parking:** 200

Barnsdale Lodge Hotel has been in Thomas Noel's family since 1760 and formed part of the adjoining Exton Park, seat of the Earls of Gainsborough. Originally a farmhouse, the building was converted into a hotel by Noel in 1989. It occupies a delightful location on the north shore of Rutland Water in the heart of the beautiful, unspoilt, county of Rutland, just a few minutes from the historic towns of Oakham and Stamford. Bedrooms all have views of either the surrounding countryside or the pretty courtyard.

Recommended in the area

Rutland Water; Barnsdale Gardens; Burghley House

Hambleton Hall

★★★★ ◉◉◉◉ COUNTRY HOUSE HOTEL

Address: Hambleton, OAKHAM, LE15 8TH
Tel: 01572 756991
Fax: 01572 724721
Email: hotel@hambletonhall.com
Website: www.hambletonhall.com
Map ref: 3, SK80
Directions: 3m E off A606
Rooms: 17 S £175-£205 D £205-£600 (incl. bkfst)
Facilities: STV ⚛ Tennis Parking: 40

This family-run hotel is a magnificent Victorian house, standing in its own beautiful gardens and enjoying fine views over Rutland Water, the largest man-made lake in western Europe. Its rooms are highly individual in character, furnished with fine fabrics and sumptuous furniture. The Master rooms are the largest, and many of them have wonderful views overlooking the lake, while the smaller Standard rooms overlook the hotel's lawn and handsome cedar trees. The most luxurious rooms are in the two-bedroom Croquet Pavilion, a folly 50 yards from the main building. In the public areas there are open fireplaces in the cosy bar and sumptuous drawing-room. The restaurant serves outstanding cuisine, using local produce as far as possible. The food incorporates fresh and seasonal ingredients, and menus change frequently. Three private dining rooms are available. Each month there is a Wine Dinner. Adventurous residents can participate in rock-climbing, windsurfing or canoeing in the local area. The hotel is a popular venue for business meetings, held in the ground floor of the main house. Full business support is available, including secretarial, fax, OHP, email and other services. The hotel is popular for prestigious private functions of all kinds, including wedding parties.

Recommended in the area

Burghley House; Rutland Water; Grimsthorpe Castle; Kelmarsh Hall Gardens

The Lord Nelson House Hotel

★★★★ ◎◎ HOTEL

Address: 11 Market Place, OAKHAM, LE15 6HR
Tel: 01572 723199
Email: simon@nicksrestaurant.co.uk
Website: www.nicksrestaurant.co.uk
Map ref: 3, SK80
Directions: A1(M) onto A606, after 2nd rdbt, Market Place on right
Rooms: 4 S £55-£85 D £85-£115
Facilities Wi-fi Parking 3

Nestled in the corner of the square in the charming market town of Oakham, this restaurant with rooms makes the perfect weekend retreat. The quaint and cosy period dining room is a welcoming setting for some fine modern European cooking based around seasonal, high quality local produce. Dinner might begin with red mullet and roast pepper tart au fin with aubergine caviar and tempura of tiger prawn, followed by roast pork belly with champ potato cake, black pudding and red onion souffle, crackling, braised Savoy cabbage and a cider jus. Dessert could be blueberry creme brulee with blueberry compote and sorbet, or you could go for a selection of local cheeses with fig and walnut bread and damson chutney. The small but carefully chosen wine list offers a good selection by the glass. The four en suite guest bedrooms are individually designed, with plenty of period features and antiques along with modern comforts like flat-screen TVs mini-bars and free Wi-fi. Take your pick from the nautical-themed Lord Horatio Nelson Room, the romantic Lady Emma Hamilton Room, the contemporary Lady Fanny Nelson Room, or the colonial style Sir Thomas Hardy Room.

Recommended in the area

Oakham Castle; Rutland Water; Rutland Railway Museum

Ludlow Castle and Dinham Bridge on the River Teme

Wynnstay Hotel

★★★★ 80% ◉◉ HOTEL

Address:	Church Street, OSWESTRY, SY11 2SZ
Tel:	01691 655261
Fax:	01691 670606
Email:	info@wynnstayhotel.com
Website:	www.wynnstayhotel.com
Map ref:	5, SJ22

Directions: B4083 to town, fork left at Honda Garage, right at lights. Hotel opposite church
Rooms: 34 (5 fmly) S £65-£85 D £95-£111
Facilities: Wi-fi ⊗ Spa Gym Sauna **Parking:** 80 **Notes:** ⊗ in bedrooms

Once a coaching inn and posting house on the London – Holyhead and Liverpool – Cardiff routes, this largely Georgian property is entered from the street through an imposing four-columned portico. Elegant public areas include the former Coach House, now a health, leisure and beauty centre with gym, Finnish sauna, aromatic steam room, 10-person jet spa, pool, spray tan booth, sun shower and three purpose-built beauty therapy rooms offering an extensive range of spa treatments. The rooms are complete with private facilities including welcome tray, digital TVs , modem points, Wi-fi, trouser press and hairdryer. There are family rooms and eight executive rooms which have various individual features, including four poster and king size beds, whirlpool baths and sitting room. The Four Seasons Restaurant which prides itself on its use of fresh and local ingredients, offers an eclectic mix of dishes created and developed by the head chef, ranging from the traditional roast to a balance of lighter more creative dishes of an international appeal. The Pavilion Lounge Bar also offers excellent bar meals both at lunch and dinner, seven days a week. Wilson's Wine Bar is the ideal location for pre-dinner drinks or to spend an enjoyable evening with friends.

Recommended in the area

Chirk Castle; Shrewsbury; Chester

Prince Rupert Hotel

★★★ 83% HOTEL

Address: Butcher Row, SHREWSBURY, SY1 1UQ
Tel: 01743 499955
Fax: 01743 357306
Email: reservations@prince-rupert-hotel.co.uk
Website: www.prince-rupert-hotel.co.uk
Map ref: 2, SJ41
Directions: Follow town centre signs, over English Bridge & Wyle Cop Hill. Right into Fish St, 200yds
Rooms: 70 (4 fmly) S £69 D £99-£175 (incl. bkfst)
Facilities: Wi-fi Spa Gym Sauna **Parking:** 70 **Notes:** ⊗ in bedrooms

Situated in the heart of medieval Shrewsbury, this privately owned hotel is the former home of Prince Rupert, grandson of James I. Surrounded by cobblestone streets and Tudor buildings, it stands cheek-by-jowl with the town's main attractions. Many bedrooms, including the 12th-century Mansion House Suites (some with four-poster canopy bed) and 15th-century Tudor Suites, retain exposed beams and other original features. All are tastefully furnished with pocket-sprung beds, fluffy towels, velvet-textured blankets, hairdryer and welcome tray. The rooms at the front have views of the historic and famous St Alkmunds Square, while many at the rear overlook the Mansion House courtyard garden. Wi-fi extends to all, as well as to public areas and conference suites. For dining, head for the Royalist Restaurant, featuring an a la carte menu which focuses on fresh seasonal produce; the oak-panelled Chambers Brasserie serves typical British food, and the oak beamed La Trattoria – just three minutes' walk away – is, of course, Italian. Camellias Tea Rooms offers relaxation to the sound of a grand piano. The health suite includes a fully equipped Nautilus weights room, jacuzzi, sauna and steam shower. Guests may also try to snooker each other on a full-size table.

Recommended in the area

Shrewsbury Abbey and Castle; Ironbridge Gorge; Stokesay Castle

Rowton Castle Hotel

★★★ 88% ◉ HOTEL

Address: Halfway House, SHREWSBURY, SY5 9EP
Tel: 01743 884044
Fax: 01743 884949
Email: post@rowtoncastle.com
Website: www.rowtoncastle.com
Map ref: 2, SJ41
Directions: from A5 near Shrewsbury take A458 to Welshpool. Hotel 4m on right
Rooms: 19 (3 fmly) **Facilities:** Wi-fi
Parking: 100 **Notes:** ⊗ in bedrooms

A castle has stood in the grounds at Rowton for nearly 800 years. The building has seen many changes and alterations over the centuries but has remained primarily a family home. It has now been transformed into a luxury country hotel, retaining the spendour of yesteryear whilst providing the facilities anticipated by the most discerning of guests. Rowton Castle is a beautiful 17th-century, Grade II listed building, set in 17 acres of tranquil grounds, six miles west of the historic town of Shrewsbury. The castle boasts 19 charming, individually designed bedrooms, seven with period four-poster beds. Each beautifully appointed room has a fully equipped bathroom, TV, direct-dial telephone, Wi-fi and excellent beverage-making facilities. Personal service and attention to detail are hallmarks of Rowton Castle's excellent reputation and this is ably demonstrated in the hotel's award-winning Cedar Restaurant. Oak panelling with 17th-century carving, velvet armchairs and intimate lighting are a perfect backdrop to this fine-dining experience. An extensive fixed price menu offers a mouthwatering selection for all tastes, complemented by an interesting choice of wines from around the world. Rowton Castle is a fairytale venue for weddings and has excellent conference facilities.

Recommended in the area

The Long Mynd; Welshpool and Llanfair Light Railway; Offa's Dyke Path

SOMERSET

A view of Exmoor National Park from Dunkery Beacon, the highest point on Exmoor, National Trust

The Royal Crescent, Bath

Best Western The Cliffe Hotel

★★★ 84% ✿ HOTEL

Address: Cliffe Drive, Crowe Hill, Limpley Stoke,
BATH, BA2 7FY

Tel: 01225 723226

Fax: 01225 723871

Email: cliffe@bestwestern.co.uk

Website: www.bw-cliffehotel.co.uk

Map ref: 2, ST76 **Directions:** A36 S from Bath onto
B3108, left towards Bradford-on-Avon, 0.5m. Right
before bridge through village, hotel on right

Rooms: 11 (4 GF) (2 fmly) S £85-£120 D £130-£200 (incl. bkfst) **Facilities:** Wi-fi ॽ **Parking:** 20

The peace and tranquillity here is not surprising, given its setting in over three acres of woodland, with spectacular views over the Avon Valley. Individually styled bedrooms include two with four-posters and one with whirlpool bath, and after a fine meal in the restaurant, you can relax in the comfortable lounge. A small meeting room is available. A heated outdoor pool is open from June to September, weather permitting, and canal day boats and bikes can be hired locally.

Recommended in the area

World Heritage City of Bath; Lacock Abbey and Village (NT); Westwood Manor (NT)

Dukes Hotel

★★★ 82% ◉◉ SMALL HOTEL

Address: Great Pulteney Street, BATH, BA2 4DN
Tel: 01225 787960
Fax: 01225 787961
Email: info@dukesbath.co.uk
Website: www.dukesbath.co.uk
Map ref: 2, ST76
Directions: A46 to Bath, at rdbt right on A4.
4th set of lights turn left (A36), then right onto Great Pulteney St.
Hotel on left **Rooms:** 17 (2 GF) (5 fmly) **S** £99-£140
D £131-£232 (incl. bkfst) **Facilities:** Wi-fi

An expertly restored, bow-fronted, Grade I listed Georgian townhouse where the rooms are decorated with period furniture, fine fabrics, prints and portraits. Surviving original plasterwork includes delicate features such as Adams-style urns and floral swags. In winter a blazing log fire in the lounge gives a warm welcome, while in summer the peaceful courtyard terrace, with a sparkling fountain, is perfect for a relaxing meal or drink. The en suite bedrooms and six suites (two with four-posters) have been restored to their original spacious dimensions. Many have enormous sash windows and splendid views over Great Pulteney Street, the Bath skyline or the surrounding countryside. Each differs in size and design, some Georgian themed, others more contemporary. All have bath and/or power shower, large fluffy towels and bathrobes, digital TV, Wi-fi access and hairdryer. The Cavendish Restaurant and Bar offers modern British seasonal cooking, using carefully sourced, locally grown and reared organic and free-range produce. A fixed-price lunch menu offers two or three courses and the dinner menu is à la carte. There are two smaller, more intimate, dining rooms which can be reserved for private receptions.

Recommended in the area

Thermae Bath Spa; Roman Baths; Royal Crescent and Circus

Glastonbury Tor

The Queensberry Hotel

★★★ ◎◎ HOTEL

Address: Russel Street, BATH, BA1 2QF
Tel: 01225 447928
Fax: 01225 446065
Email: reservations@thequeensberry.co.uk
Website: www.thequeensberry.co.uk
Map ref: 2, ST76
Directions: 100mtrs from the Assembly Rooms
Rooms: 29 (2 GF) (2 fmly) S £115-£170
D £120-£425 **Facilities:** Wi-fi
Parking: 9 **Notes:** ⊗ in bedrooms

Four Georgian town houses form this charming hotel, located in a quiet residential street close to the city centre. There is a choice of sumptuously furnished drawing rooms, an inviting bar and secluded terraced gardens. The spacious bedrooms are individually designed, combining up-to-date comfort with original features. Expect marble bathrooms, flat-screen televisions and White Company toiletries. The stylish Olive Tree restaurant specialises in modern British cuisine with Mediterranean influences.

Recommended in the area

Thermae Bath Spa; Beckford's Tower; Claverton Pumping Station

Channel House Hotel

★★ 85% SMALL HOTEL

Address: Church Path, MINEHEAD, TA24 5QG
Tel: 01643 703229
Fax: 01643 708925
Email: channelhouse@btconnect.com
Website: www.channelhouse.co.uk
Map ref: 2, SS94
Directions: From A39 right at rdbt to seafront, then left onto promenade. 1st right, 1st left to Blenheim Gdns and 1st right into Northfield Rd

Rooms: 8 S £66-£80 D £102-£130 (incl. bkfst) **Parking:** 10
Notes: ⊗ in bedrooms ⟨⟩ under 15 yrs

Channel House was originally built as a gentleman's residence in 1902 and began life as a hotel in 1958. The hotel nestles on the lower slopes of North Hill in the ancient fishing town of Minehead (originally spelt Myned, meaning 'hill' in old English) and has far reaching views stretching over the Bristol Channel and Exmoor. Standing as it does in over an acre of beautifully maintained gardens, the feeling of peace and tranquillity is with you from the moment you arrive at Channel House. Inside, the staff are friendly and welcoming and the hotel is elegantly furnished, with comfortable lounges to relax in and tastefully appointed bedrooms with superb en suite bathrooms. Head to the cocktail bar for a pre-dinner drink before sitting down to eat in the attractive dining room, where the food and service are of the highest order. The menu changes daily, with vegetarian options always included, and all dishes are prepared on the premises using fresh, local produce. Channel House is the perfect base for exploring beautiful Exmoor National Park, Dunster with its castle, Porlock and Lynmouth, but there are other gems nearby such as North Hill and the villages of Selworthy, Bossington and Allerford.

Recommended in the area

Exmoor National Park; West Somerset Railway; Dunster Castle

The Oaks Hotel

★★★ 83% ⊛ HOTEL

Address: PORLOCK, TA24 8ES
Tel: 01643 862265 Fax: 01643 863131
Email: info@oakshotel.co.uk
Website: www.oakshotel.co.uk
Map ref: 2, SS84
Directions: From E of A39, enter village, then follow hotel sign Rooms: 8 S £127.50 D £195 (incl. dinner)
Facilities: Wi-fi Parking: 12
Notes: ⊗ in bedrooms ⚹ under 8 yrs

Tim and Anne Riley have excelled in restoring this Edwardian country house setamong the majestic trees that gave it its name. From its lofty location, it has wonderful views of Exmoor and the Bristol Channel from bedrooms and the dining room. The lounge, with log fires in winter, is the place for afternoon tea and after-dinner coffee, or just to relax after a walk. Bedrooms have en suite baths and showers, fresh flowers, Egyptian cotton linen, TV and tea-making facilities. The dining room has a four-course, largely traditional menu, on which everything, from marmalade to after-dinner chocolates, is home made.

Recommended in the area South West Coast Path; Watersmeet House (NT); Exmoor Bird Gardens

Holbrook House

★★★ 79% ⊛⊛ COUNTRY HOUSE HOTEL

Address: Holbrook, WINCANTON, BA9 8BS
Tel: 01963 824466 & 828844
Fax: 01963 32681
Email: enquiries@holbrookhouse.co.uk
Website: www.holbrookhouse.co.uk
Map ref: 2, ST72
Directions: From A303 at Wincanton left onto A371 towards Castle Cary & Shepton Mallet
Rooms: 21 (5 GF) (2 fmly) D £140-£250 (incl. bkfst)
Facilities: Wi-fi ⊗ Tennis Spa Gym Sauna Parking: 200

This privately owned Georgian country-house hotel is surrounded by 20 acres of unspoiled woodland and rolling pastures. There are 21 luxurious, characterful bedrooms, split between the main house and the walled garden. The Cedar Restaurant is an elegant setting for some superb Anglo-French cuisine, while more informal dining can be enjoyed in the Stables Bar, part of the health club and spa. A third dining option is the Morning Room, serving afternoon tea, lighter dishes and Sunday roast lunches.

Recommended in the area

Fleet Air Museum; Montacute House (NT); Wells Cathedral

Fairoak Pools, sunset

Three Queens Hotel

★★★ 81% 🏵 HOTEL

Address: One Bridge Street, BURTON UPON TRENT, DE14 1SY
Tel: 01283 523800 & 0845 230 1332
Fax: 01283 523823
Email: hotel@threequeenshotel.co.uk
Website: www.threequeenshotel.co.uk
Map ref: 6, SK22 **Directions:** On A511 in Burton upon Trent
at junct of Bridge St & High St. Town side of Old River Bridge
Rooms: 38 S £55-£90 D £65-£130 (incl. bkfst)
Facilities: STV Wi-fi **Parking:** 40 **Notes:** ⊗ in bedrooms

The privately owned Three Queens Hotel is a special venue for
both business and pleasure, set in the heart of the brewery
town of Burton Upon Trent, minutes away from scenic walks, cultural sights and family attractions. The
hotel's abiding philosophy is, "find the things that the group hotels can't do – and do it!", thus you can
expect excellent service from the moment you arrive. Forget the usual laborious registration procedure
– here it's a simple question of whether you'd like breakfast and a complimentary newspaper, then a
helping hand with your luggage, assistance to ensure the key card works, and a car wash if you stay
midweek. The hotel's 38 en suite bedrooms are newly-equipped with the latest Genesis flat-screen
in-room entertainment system, with high-speed internet access either on-screen or through your
own laptop. A selection of function rooms provides perfect spaces for intimate meetings or larger
conferences, while the dining facilities cater for all business and social occasions. Snacks are served in
the Princes bar, and breakfast in the Kings Room is the ideal way to start the day. In the evening treat
yourself to a three-course dinner in the Rosette-awarded Grill Room. Wine tastings, gourmet evenings
and champagne breakfasts are held throughout the year.

Recommended in the area

Alton Towers; Donnington Park; Calke Abbey (NT)

The Roaches and Hen Cloud, Peak District National Park

B W Stoke-on-Trent Moat House

★★★★ 74% HOTEL

Address: Etruria Hall, Festival Way, Etruria,
STOKE-ON-TRENT, ST1 5BQ
Tel: 0870 225 4601 & 01782 206101
Fax: 01782 206101
Email: reservations.stoke@qmh-hotels.com
Website: www.bestwestern.co.uk/content/
hotel-details-leisure.aspx/hotel/83862
Map ref: 7, SJ84
Directions: M6/A500. A53 Festival Park. Keep in left
lane exit, take first slip road on left. Left at island, hotel opposite at next island
Rooms: 147 (63 fmly) S £49-£129 D £59-£129
Facilities: Wi-fi ☯ Spa Gym Sauna Parking: 350 Notes: ⊗ in bedrooms

Not only is this hotel perfectly placed for visiting the Potteries, it is actually built within the grounds of Etruria Hall, the former home of Josiah Wedgwood, now a conference centre. The hotel has a range of leisure facilities and the Viva Bar and Brasserie. The bedrooms are decorated in contemporary style.
Recommended in the area
Etruria Industrial Museum; Wedgwood Visitor Centre; Gladstone Pottery Museum; Trentham Gardens

SUFFOLK

Orford Castle

Wentworth Hotel

★★★ 88% ◉◉ HOTEL

Address: Wentworth Road, ALDEBURGH, IP15 5BD
Tel: 01728 452312
Fax: 01728 454343
Email: stay@wentworth-aldeburgh.co.uk
Website: www.wentworth-aldeburgh.com
Map ref: 4, TM45
Directions: Off A12 onto A1094, 6m to Aldeburgh, with church on left, left at bottom of hill
Rooms: 35 (5 GF) S £58-£100 D £98-£232 (incl. bkfst) **Facilities:** Wi-fi **Parking:** 30

This triple-gabled hotel has been managed by the Pritt family since 1920, and this continuous thread is responsible for the fact that the Wentworth is everything a seaside hotel should be. The attractive and well-maintained public rooms include three lounges furnished with comfortable chairs and sofas, which are sunny spots in summer and cosy places to relax by an open fire in winter. Outside are two sea-facing gardens in which to soak up the sun with a morning coffee, light lunch or cream tea. Many of the regularly refurbished en suite bedrooms have good views of the North Sea, for which the hotel thoughtfully provides binoculars. Seven rooms in Darfield House, just opposite the main building, are particularly spacious and well appointed. For those who find stairs difficult (there's no lift) there are five ground floor rooms. Room sizes and outlook do vary, and these differences are reflected in the tariff. You can start the day here with a locally smoked kipper, as part of your 'full-house' cooked breakfast. At lunchtime, the terrace bar menu offers a wide choice, from a fresh crab sandwich to traditional cod and chips, and the elegant candlelit restaurant has a daily changing dinner menu based on fresh local produce.

Recommended in the area

Minsmere (RSPB) Reserve; Snape Maltings (Aldeburgh Festival); Suffolk Heritage Coast

The Bildeston Crown

★★★ ◉◉◉ HOTEL

Address: 104 High Street, BILDESTON, Ipswich, IP7 7EB
Tel: 01449 740510
Fax: 01449 741843
Email: hayley@thebildestoncrown.co.uk
Website: www.thebildestoncrown.co.uk
Map ref: 4, TL94

Directions: A12 junct 31, turn right onto B1070 & follow signs to Hadleigh. At T-junct turn left onto A1141, then immediately right onto B1115. Hotel 0.5m
Rooms: 13 S £80-£150 D £150-£250 (incl. bkfst) **Facilities:** STV Wi-fi **Parking:** 30

In a village deep in picturesque countryside, stands this 15th-century, heavily timbered coaching inn. Although completely refurbished, original features, including log fires, oak beams and period furniture ensure that you'll remain conscious of its ancestry. Much thought has gone into the bedrooms, each of which includes flat-screen TV, an extensive library of music available via an in-wall control panel, concealed speakers in the en suite bathroom and shower area, and internet access. The luxurious Black Fuschia room, with dramatic black decor and a super king-sized bed, is apparently 'not for the faint-hearted'. At the centre of the Crown lies the restaurant, where paintings line the walls and locally sourced seasonal cuisine ranges from the classic to interpretations of the traditional. A typical dinner might be pan-seared fillet of mackerel with leek tart, followed by breast of Suffolk chicken with confit leg and poached lobster, and set-milk cream with balsamic figs to finish. Red Poll beef from the hotel's own herd is always a possibility, and there's also an eight-course tasting menu. On a fine day, eat or drink in the central courtyard, or try one of the two bars where the full restaurant menu is also available.

Recommended in the area

Lavenham; Colne Valley Railway; Constable Country

Timber work on the 14th century Little Hall at Lavenham

Best Western Priory Hotel

★★★ 82% ◉◉ HOTEL

Address: Mildenhall Road, BURY ST EDMUNDS, IP32 6EH

Tel: 01284 766181

Fax: 01284 767604

Email: reservations@prioryhotel.co.uk

Website: www.prioryhotel.co.uk

Map ref: 4, TL86

Directions: From A14 take Bury St Edmunds W slip road. Follow signs to Brandon. At mini-rdbt turn right. Hotel 0.5m on left

Rooms: 38 (30 GF) (1 fmly) **Facilities:** Free Wi-fi **Parking:** 60

In a delightful town surrounded by pretty countryside and landscaped gardens, this is a charming hotel with spacious, individually designed bedrooms. All include a 10-channel TV and high speed Wi-fi. The food is exceptional, with British and European influences. Hazelnut crusted Denham Castle lamb rump, marjoram pomme puree, tomatoes and feve beans is an example of the fare.

Recommended in the area

St Edmundsbury Cathedral and Abbey Gardens; Greene King Visitors Centre; Ickworth House

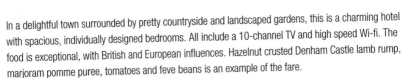

Hintlesham Hall Hotel

★★★★ ◉◉ HOTEL

Address: George Street, HINTLESHAM, Ipswich,
IP8 3NS

Tel: 01473 652334

Fax: 01473 652463

Email: reservations@hintleshamhall.com

Website: www.hintleshamhall.com

Map ref: 4, TM04

Directions: 4m W of Ipswich on A1071 to
Hadleigh & Sudbury

Rooms: 33 (10 GF) S £120-£165 D £150-£450 Facilities: ⤳ Tennis Gym Parking: 60

Hospitality and service are absolute priorities at this imposing 16th-century, Grade I listed country house hotel in 175 acres of landscaped gardens and grounds. The building is distinguished by its Georgian additions, most notably the façade, as well as by earlier Stuart interior embellishments. Works of art and antiques abound throughout, particularly in the spacious public rooms and restaurants. Individually decorated bedrooms and suites come in varying shapes, sizes and styles, but consistently applied are their high degree of comfort, tasteful furnishings and thoughtful extras. Wander around the grounds before heading for the grand Salon, largest of the three dining rooms, and Head Chef Alan Ford's well-balanced carte, from which examples include grilled fillet of haddock served in a mussel and clam chowder, and tournedos of beef with braised oxtail and horseradish. Many of the dishes encompass fresh herbs from the famous garden, designed by the late Robert Carrier, who bought the then derelict Hall in 1972. The award-winning 350-bin wine list includes a generous selection of half-bottles. Health and beauty and specialist treatments, and a newly equipped gym with instructors, now complement the seasonal pool. A championship PGA golf course is adjacent to the Hall.

Recommended in the area

Constable Country; Aldeburgh; Newmarket Racecourse

milsoms Kesgrave Hall

★★★ 85% ● HOTEL

Address: Hall Road, KESGRAVE, IP5 2PU
Tel: 01473 333741
Fax: 01473 617614
Email: reception@kesgravehall.com
Website: www.kesgravehall.com
Map ref: 4, TM46
Directions: A12 N of Ipswich, left at Ipswich/
Woodbridge rdbt onto B1214. Right after 0.5m into
Hall Rd. Hotel 200yds on left
Rooms: 23 (8 GF) (4 fmly) **S** £90-£165 **D** £110-£195 **Facilities:** STV Wi-fi **Parking:** 100

A grade II listed mansion transformed in 2008 into a contemporary brasserie with private dining, meeting spaces and bedrooms, situated in over 38 acres of park and woodland. The 23 bedrooms are all different in style and range from standard to super deluxe with huge walk-in showers. In the open plan restaurant, head chef Stuart Oliver champions all that is great about Suffolk produce, with food served all day and dining on the terrace under a huge architectural sail.

Recommended in the area

Suffolk Heritage Coast; Aldeburgh and Snape; Sutton Hoo (NT)

The Angel

★★★★ ● RESTAURANT WITH ROOMS

Address: Market Place, LAVENHAM, CO10 9QZ
Tel: 01787 247388
Fax: 01787 248344
Email: angel@maypolehotels.com
Website: www.maypolehotels.com
Map ref: 4, TL94 **Directions:** From A14 take Bury
E & Sudbury turn onto A143. After 4m take A1141
to Lavenham. Off High Street **Rooms** 8 (1 fmly) **S**
£85-£105 **D** £105-£135 **Facilities:** Wi-fi **Parking** 5

The Angel was first licensed in 1420 and is believed to be the oldest inn in the medieval town of Lavenham. Although much altered over the centuries, the building retains plenty of old-world character, including exposed beams and a large inglenook fireplace. There are eight smart, comfortable bedrooms with TV, telephone, tea-and-coffee-making facilities and hairdryer. The Angel has held an AA Rosette consistently since 1995 and everything is prepared on the premises from mostly local ingredients. The same menu is served in the restaurant, bar, snug or out on the terrace or in the garden.

Recommended in the area

Lavenham town; Bury St Edmunds; Orford

The Swan

★★★★ 82% ◉◉ HOTEL

Address: High Street, LAVENHAM, CO10 9QA

Tel: 01787 247477

Fax: 01787 248286

Email: info@theswanatlavenham.co.uk

Website: www.theswanatlavenham.co.uk

Map ref: 4, TL94

Directions: From Bury St Edmunds take A134 (S), then A1141 to Lavenham

Rooms: 45 (13 GF) (11 fmly) **S** £85-£95

D £170-£290 (incl. bkfst) **Facilities:** STV Wi-fi **Parking:** 62

This iconic hotel dates back to the 15th century and is located in a village famous for the similarly ancient buildings that line its streets. Many people visit Lavenham just to marvel at its historic charms, but a stay at The Swan truly completes the experience. Ancient oak beams, inglenook fireplaces and original medieval wall paintings, together with a beautiful decor of rich fabrics, provide a perfect ambience. History oozes from every fibre of the building. The Old Bar is particularly interesting for its World War II memorabilia and a wall signed by British and American airmen who were stationed at Lavenham Airfield. The bedrooms are equally historic, but with contemporary furnishings sympathetically incorporated. Expect modern bathrooms, plasma-screen TVs and facilities for making tea and coffee. As well as standard double rooms there are mezzanine suites, and some have four-poster beds. The Swan offers several dining options, including the informal Garden Bar Restaurant, the Old Bar, outdoors in the garden in summer, or the elegant Gallery Restaurant. Executive chef David Ryan's modern British cuisine has won the hotel an enviable reputation for fine dining. The sumptuous traditional afternoon teas are as good as they get.

Recommended in the area

Lavenham Guildhall; Kentwell Hall; Ickworth House

The Olde Bull Inn

★★★ 80% ❀ HOTEL

Address: The Street, Barton Mills, MILDENHALL,
Bury St Edmunds, IP28 6AA
Tel: 01638 711001
Fax: 01638 712003
Email: bookings@bullinn-bartonmills.com
Website: www.bullinn-bartonmills.com
Map ref: 4, TL77 Directions: Off A11 between
Newmarket & Mildenhall, signed Barton Mills. Hotel
nr Five Ways rdbt Rooms: 14 (2 GF) (2 fmly)
S £75-£95 D £85-£115 (incl. bkfst) Facilities: STV Wi-fi Parking: 60 Notes: ⊗

This 16th century coaching inn in the lovely village of Barton Mills was rescued from dereliction and reopened as a hotel in the year 2000. In 2007 its current owners took over and embarked on a total refurbishment, transforming the hotel's 14 bedrooms into charming boutique accommodation with a mixture of period details, designer fabrics and wallpapers and contemporary furniture. Every bedroom is individually designed and has a new en suite bathroom along with flat-screen TV with Freeview, direct-dial telephone, beverage tray and hairdryer. Food is one of the biggest draws at The Olde Bull Inn, with everything made in-house using the best, freshest ingredients from local suppliers. The charming Oak Room Restaurant has an AA Rosette and serves modern British food, including the signature 'fillet steak tower' – best local beef covered in a creamy pepper sauce, layered with onions and resting on a parsnip and potato rosti. The daily specials board always offers something seasonal to supplement the main menu, such as Brancaster mussels or Thornham oysters. Less formal meals and snacks – along with local real ales – are served in the cosy bar with its log fire, and in the summer you can dine al fresco in the courtyard.

Recommended in the area

Shopping and punting in Cambridge; Center Parcs spa at Elveden Forest; Go Ape! at Thetford Forest

The Crown & Castle

★★★ 85% ◎◎ HOTEL
Address: ORFORD, IP12 2LJ
Tel: 01394 450205
Email: info@crownandcastle.co.uk
Website: www.crownandcastle.co.uk
Map ref: 4, TM45
Directions: Turn right from B1084 on entering
village, towards castle Rooms: 19 (11 GF) (1 fmly)
S £92-£164 D £115-£205 (incl. bkfst)
Facilities: Wi-fi Parking: 20 Notes: 👶 under 4 yrs

Ruth and David Watson have created a delightful inn that brings together good food, a genial atmosphere, and stylishly simple, well designed accommodation. The location, next to Orford's old castle keep, is peaceful and perfect for exploring the Suffolk Heritage Coast. Bedrooms are bright and airy, with contemporary decor and furnishings. Garden rooms are the most spacious, and have a semi-private terrace overlooking the castle. Food is a highlight – hardly surprising, since Ruth is an award-winning food writer – with interesting dishes featuring the finest locally sourced ingredients.
Recommended in the area
Snape Maltings; Orford Ness (NT); Sutton Hoo

The Crown

★★ 85% ◎ HOTEL
Address: 90 High Street, SOUTHWOLD, IP18 6DP
Tel: 01502 722275
Fax: 01502 727263
Email: crown.hotel@adnams.co.uk
Website: www.adnams.co.uk
Map ref: 4, TM57
Directions: A12 onto A1095 to Southwold.
Hotel on left in High Street
Rooms: 14 (2 fmly) Parking: 23
Notes: ⊗ in bedrooms

Southwold is famous for its lighthouse right in the town, and that Adnams has brewed beer here for six centuries. The lighthouse is round the corner, and Adnams owns this intimate small hotel, wine bar, pub and restaurant. Bedrooms are reached through twisting corridors, and once you see the beds and contemporary furniture you'll realise why booking ahead is advisable. The Crown is renowned too as a place to eat good, locally sourced food and drink.
Recommended in the area
Suffolk Heritage Coast; Minsmere; Snape Maltings

The Scrape at Minsmere

Swan Hotel

★★★ 83% ◉◉ HOTEL

Address: Market Place, SOUTHWOLD, IP18 6EG
Tel: 01502 722186
Fax: 01502 724800
Email: swan.hotel@adnams.co.uk
Website: www.adnams.co.uk
Map ref: 4, TM57
Directions: A1095 to Southwold. Hotel in town centre. Parking via archway to left of building
Rooms: 42 (17 GF) S £50–£98 D £80–£220 (incl. bkfst)
Parking: 35

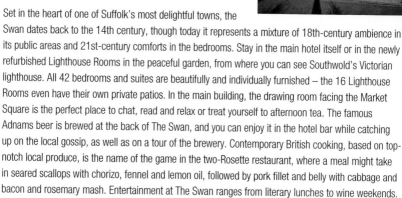

Set in the heart of one of Suffolk's most delightful towns, the Swan dates back to the 14th century, though today it represents a mixture of 18th-century ambience in its public areas and 21st-century comforts in the bedrooms. Stay in the main hotel itself or in the newly refurbished Lighthouse Rooms in the peaceful garden, from where you can see Southwold's Victorian lighthouse. All 42 bedrooms and suites are beautifully and individually furnished – the 16 Lighthouse Rooms even have their own private patios. In the main building, the drawing room facing the Market Square is the perfect place to chat, read and relax or treat yourself to afternoon tea. The famous Adnams beer is brewed at the back of The Swan, and you can enjoy it in the hotel bar while catching up on the local gossip, as well as on a tour of the brewery. Contemporary British cooking, based on top-notch local produce, is the name of the game in the two-Rosette restaurant, where a meal might take in seared scallops with chorizo, fennel and lemon oil, followed by pork fillet and belly with cabbage and bacon and rosemary mash. Entertainment at The Swan ranges from literary lunches to wine weekends. Dogs are welcome to stay in selected rooms by prior arrangement.

Recommended in the area

Adnams Brewery; Southwold town; Minsmere RSPB reserve

The Westleton Crown

★★★ 78% ◉◉ HOTEL

Address: The Street, WESTLETON, Nr Southwold, IP17 3AD
Tel: 01728 648777
Fax: 01728 648239
Email: reception@westletoncrown.co.uk
Website: www.westletoncrown.co.uk
Map ref: 4, TM46
Directions: A12 N, turn right for Westleton just after Yoxford. Hotel opposite on entering Westleton
Rooms: 25 (8 GF) (3 fmly) S £95-£115 D £115-£180 (incl. bkfst) **Facilities:** Wi-fi **Parking:** 45

Whether you want to get away from it all on a short break or need somewhere to stay on business, the Westleton Crown has it all. Dating back to the 12th century, this traditional coaching inn retains the character and rustic charm of its heritage, but with all the comforts the 21st century traveller could hope for. The bar has the feel of a genuine local, with a warm welcome and plenty of Suffolk ales to enjoy. Meals may be taken in the elegant dining room, cosy parlour or stylish conservatory, as well as in the charming terraced gardens during warmer weather. Food is taken extremely seriously at the Westleton Crown, with everything – from bread to soups, pates and ice cream – made in-house from the finest, freshest ingredients. Menus are imaginative and varied and complemented by an extensive wine list. The 25 bedrooms are individually designed and exceptionally comfortable. Those in the main inn are more traditional in style, while more contemporary rooms can be found in the newly converted stables and cottages. Whichever you choose, expect flat-screen TVs, tea-and-coffee-making facilities, beautiful bathrooms and luxuriously large beds with fully sprung mattresses, goose down duvets and crisp white Egyptian cotton linen.

Recommended in the area

RSPB Minsmere reserve; Dunwich; Snape Maltings

Beach huts, Southwold

Satis House Hotel

★★★ 88% ◉◉ COUNTRY HOUSE HOTEL
Address: YOXFORD, IP17 3EX
Tel: 01728 668418
Fax: 01728 668640
Email: enquiries@satishouse.co.uk
Website: www.satishouse.co.uk
Map ref: 4, TM36 Directions: Off A12 between
Ipswich & Lowestoft. 9m E Aldeburgh & Snape
Rooms: 9 (2 GF) (1 fmly) Facilities: STV Parking: 30

Charles Dickens is said to have written Great Expectations while staying at this 18th-century residence as a friend of the owners. Today it remains the elegant house it was during Dickens' visit in 1860, but it's been completely refurbished in recent years and offers a variety of en suite rooms ranging from antique chic to contemporary, some with feature beds and one with a large balcony. All have Egyptian cotton sheets, tea-and-coffee-making facilities, flat-screen TV and DVD player. The restaurant serves modern British cuisine based around seasonal and local ingredients.

Recommended in the area

Southwold; Aldeburgh; Framlingham Castle

SURREY

Arch widow at the ruins of Waverley Abbey

Runnymede Hotel & Spa

★★★★ 78% HOTEL

Address: Windsor Road, EGHAM, TW20 0AG
Tel: 01784 436171
Fax: 01784 436340
Email: info@runnymedehotel.com
Website: www.runnymedehotel.com
Map ref: 3, TQ07
Directions: M25 junct 13, onto A308
towards Windsor
Rooms: 180 (19 fmly) S £98-£258 D £155-£345
Facilities: STV Wi-fi ⊗ Tennis Spa Gym Sauna **Parking:** 280 **Notes:** ⊗ in bedrooms

From its peaceful location beside the River Thames, this large modern hotel offers an excellent range of leisure and corporate facilities. Guest rooms are comfortably furnished and offer many delights, from cosy duvets to fast broadband access, while a good few have views of the river. In the Leftbank Restaurant, produce is carefully sourced: organic salmon from the Shetlands, fish and shellfish delivered daily from Brixham, free range eggs from North Devon and Aberdeen Angus beef from Scotland. Local market gardener, Mario, supplies salads, spinach, tomatoes and rocket, and also imports fruit and vegetables from his extended family in Sicily. The result is 'an eclectic fusion' of Mediterranean and British food. An extensive wine list includes some imaginative bins. Informal Charlie Bell's restaurant, named after a 19th-century local lock-keeper, provides everything from a rib-eye steak to a Caesar salad, all prepared in an open kitchen. With its riverside terrace and gardens, The Conservatory is the place for a pot of Earl Grey or a classic cocktail or two. In the health spa, swim in the 18-metre pool, relax in the whirlpool bath, saunas or eucalyptus steam room, or work up a sweat in the dance studio, gym or playing tennis.

Recommended in the area

Windsor Castle; Legoland; Magna Carta Memorial

Lythe Hill Hotel & Spa

★★★★ 76% ◉ HOTEL

Address: Petworth Road, HASLEMERE, GU27 3BQ

Tel: 01428 651251

Fax: 01428 644131

Email: lythe@lythehill.co.uk

Website: www.lythehill.co.uk

Map ref: 3, SU93

Directions: Left from High St onto B2131.
Hotel 1.25m on right

Rooms: 41 (18 GF) (8 fmly)

Facilities: Wi-fi ⊗ Tennis Spa Gym Sauna **Parking:** 200

A haven of comfort and elegance in the heart of the English countryside and set in 22 acres of tranquil Surrey countryside, the small, luxury Lythe Hill Hotel & Spa offers the perfect retreat for the discerning guest. From luxury suites and antique four-poster beds to double rooms and garden suites, each of the 41 bedrooms is individually designed to reflect its unique character. The bedrooms in the historic listed buildings are gracious and stately, while those in the newer buildings are modern and stylish. For an unforgettable dining experience, choose The Restaurant at Lythe Hill Hotel & Spa and sit in the oak panelled dining room or the New Room overlooking the lake and parkland. Amarna Spa is inspired by the life of Queen Nefertiti, whose name means 'the beautiful one has arrived'. Aptly set in the Surrey Hills Area of Outstanding Natural Beauty, Amarna Spa has been designed to reflect Nefertiti's desire for tranquillity underpinned by her passion for pampering.

Recommended in the area

Haslemere; Petworth House (NT); Goodwood horse and motor racing; Lurgashall Winery

View out to sea from the white cliffs of Beachy Head

Thistle Brighton

★★★★ 78% HOTEL

Address: King's Road, BRIGHTON, BN1 2GS
Tel: 01273 206700
Fax: 0870 333 9229
Email: Brighton@Thistle.co.uk
Website: www.thistlehotels.com/brighton
Map ref: 3, TQ30
Directions: A23 to seafront. At rdbt turn right, hotel 200yds on right **Rooms:** 210 (29 fmly)
Facilities: Wi-fi ⓢ Spa **Parking:** 68

A relaxed and easy-going hotel – just like the city itself. Across the road is the beach, to the left is Brighton Pier, and round the corner is The Lanes, a labyrinth of narrow streets crammed with boutiques, antique shops, bars and restaurants. In the bedrooms, many looking over the Channel, everything from bed linen to toiletries has been carefully chosen. The lounge and bar offer light refreshments, while the Promenade restaurant offers a choice of menus. Tap into Wi-fi anywhere in the hotel.

Recommended in the area

The Royal Pavilion; Devil's Dyke; South Downs Way

The Devonshire Park Hotel

★★★ 78% HOTEL

Address: 27-29 Carlisle Road, EASTBOURNE, BN21 4JR
Tel: 01323 728144
Fax: 01323 419734
Email: info@devonshire-park-hotel.co.uk
Website: www.devonshire-park-hotel.co.uk
Map ref: 4, TV69 **Directions:** Follow signs to seafront, exit at Wish Tower. Hotel opposite Congress Theatre **Rooms:** 35 (8 GF) **S** £45-£75 **D** £80-£150 (incl. bkfst) **Facilities:** STV Wi-fi **Parking:** 25 **Notes:** ⊗ in bedrooms ⊀ under 12 yrs

This elegant Victorian hotel boasts one of the finest locations in Eastbourne, opposite Devonshire Park and The Congress Theatre. It's just a short stroll to the shops from here too, and only 150 metres to the main promenade. The 29 rooms are spacious, comfortable and contemporary in style, and all enjoy good views. Two suites have private patios and one has its own sun terrace. The restaurant offers a traditional English menu, while light lunches are served in the bar.

Recommended in the area

Devonshire Park International Tennis Centre; Eastbourne promenade; South Downs National Park

The Grand Hotel

★★★★★ 83% ◉◉ HOTEL

Address: King Edward's Parade, EASTBOURNE,
BN21 4EQ
Tel: 01323 412345
Fax: 01323 412233
Email: reservations@grandeastbourne.com
Website: www.grandeastbourne.com
Map ref: 4, TV69
Directions: On seafront W of Eastbourne, 1m from
railway station **Rooms:** 152 (4 GF) (20 fmly)
D £195–£540 (incl. bkfst) **Facilities:** STV ⓢ ⚲ Spa Gym Sauna **Parking:** 80 **Notes:** ⊶ on request

Standing majestically along the Eastbourne seafront and affectionately known as 'The White Palace',
the 19th century Grand Hotel is a truly impressive venue. The view of the great hall on arrival leaves
you in no doubt of this, an impression that continues throughout the hotel, which has played host in
the past to such renowned figures as Winston Churchill and Charlie Chaplin. Each of the bedrooms
and suites is individually decorated and beautifully presented. Many of the rooms enjoy panoramic
views over the English Channel and have their own private balcony. The Grand Hotel boasts 12 private
function rooms available for intimate private meetings, large wedding ceremonies and receptions
and lavish events. Children are well catered for, with a playroom supervised by qualified carers and
a welcome pack on arrival. There is a choice of fine dining in the Mirabelle Restaurant or the equally
superb Garden Restaurant. For something lighter, perhaps after a bracing walk along the seafront on
the hotel's doorstep, the Grand's afternoon teas, served in the great hall, are not to be missed. Leisure
facilities include indoor and outdoor heated pools, a gym and a range of spa treatments.

Recommended in the area

Beachy Head; Glyndebourne Opera House; Drusillas Zoo; Sovereign Harbour

Ashdown Park Hotel and Country Club

★★★★ ◎◎ HOTEL

Address: Wych Cross, FOREST ROW, RH18 5JR
Tel: 01342 824988
Fax: 01342 826206
Email: reservations@ashdownpark.com
Website: www.ashdownpark.com
Map ref: 3, TQ43
Directions: A264 to East Grinstead, then A22 to Eastbourne. 2m S of Forest Row at Wych Cross lights. Left to Hartfield, hotel on right 0.75m **Rooms:** 106 (16 GF) **D** £195-£455 (incl. bkfst)
Facilities: STV Wi-fi ⊕ Tennis Spa Gym Sauna **Parking:** 200 **Notes:** ✦ on request

Set within 186 acres of lakes, secret gardens, manicured lawns, woodland trails and unspoilt countryside, Ashdown Park sits proudly at the heart of Ashdown Forest. Evolving from a 19th century listed mansion house, the hotel provides today's guests with the perfect setting to relax, unwind and indulge. The sense of grandeur carries through to the lavishly decorated bedrooms, which overlook the beautiful grounds. All differ in shape, style and décor, and come with thoughtful extras such as bathrobes, mineral water and Molton Brown toiletries. Facilities include palatial lounges, the Richard Towneley Suite (a sympathetically restored former chapel ideal for exclusive meetings and wedding parties) and the critically acclaimed, fine-dining Anderida Restaurant. Lighter lunches are served in the drawing rooms and Fairways Lounge of the Country Club. The extensive indoor and outdoor leisure facilities include an indoor pool, gymnasium, tennis courts, 18-hole golf course and spa with a range of treatments available.

Recommended in the area

Bluebell Railway; Sheffield Park Gardens; Royal Tunbridge Wells

The Lanes, Brighton

Newick Park Hotel & Country Estate

★★★ ◉◉◉ HOTEL

Address: NEWICK, BN8 4SB
Tel: 01825 723633
Fax: 01825 723969
Email: bookings@newickpark.co.uk
Website: www.newickpark.co.uk
Map ref: 3, TQ42
Directions: Exit A272 at Newick Green, 1m, pass church & pub. Turn left, hotel 0.25m on right
Rooms: 16 (1 GF) (5 fmly) **S** £125 **D** £165-£285 (incl. bkfst)
Facilities: Wi-fi ⚡ Tennis Fishing **Parking:** 52

Newick Park is a beautiful Grade II listed Georgian country-house hotel set in over 200 acres of landscaped gardens and parkland with stunning views across rural Sussex towards the South Downs. Being both privately owned and run, guests enjoy an outstanding level of service along with complete peace and privacy. The spacious bedrooms are all beautifully furnished, with wonderfully comfortable beds and fine antique furniture. The award-winning restaurant makes fine use of organic fruit and vegetables from the walled garden, and game from the estate. Newick Park is the perfect place for a relaxing, luxurious break, but for those who can't leave the office behind, complimentary Wi-fi is available throughout the hotel. If you are looking for a more adventurous trip away, quad biking, tank driving and clay pigeon shooting are also on offer, to name but a few pre-bookable activities.

Recommended in the area

Glyndebourne Opera; Sheffield Park Gardens; Brighton's Lanes

Dale Hill Hotel & Golf Club

★★★★ 82% ⦿ HOTEL

Address: TICEHURST, TN5 7DQ
Tel: 01580 200112
Fax: 01580 201249
Email: info@dalehill.co.uk
Website: www.dalehill.co.uk
Map ref: 4, TQ63
Directions: M25 junct 5/A21. 5m after Lamberhurst turn right at lights onto B2087 to Flimwell. Hotel 1m on left
Rooms: 35 (23 GF) (8 fmly) S £80-£90 D £90-£130 (incl. bkfst)
Facilities: STV Wi-fi ⓧ Gym Sauna Parking: 220 Notes: ⊗ in bedrooms

Set in magnificent countryside, with views across the High Weald, this modern hotel is only a short drive from the village. Extensive public rooms include a lounge bar, conservatory brasserie, formal restaurant and the lively Spike Bar, which is where golfers, fresh from playing one of the two 18-hole courses, like to congregate (and commiserate). Dale Hill also has an indoor heated swimming pool and gym. Spacious en suite bedrooms feature radio, TV, direct-dial phones, modem access, hairdryer, tea and coffee facilities, safe and trouser press. Those on the south side of the hotel overlook the golf course, the executive rooms having the extra advantage of balconies. The modern European menu in the elegant AA Rosette-winning Wealden View Restaurant is complemented by an international wine list. For simpler dishes, head for The Eighteenth Restaurant, to the Lounge for a traditional Sussex afternoon tea, or the Club House Bar to catch up on the latest sports scores. The new conference and banqueting suite can accommodate up to 200 delegates. Ian Woosnam, 1991 Masters winner, designed the championship standard, 6,500-yard golf course; the Old Course attracts the high handicappers.

Recommended in the area

Groombridge Place; Bodiam Castle; Kent & East Sussex Railway

WEST SUSSEX

Boats on River Arun and Arundel Castle

Bailiffscourt Hotel & Spa

★★★ 85% ◉◉ HOTEL

Address: Climping Street, CLIMPING, BN17 5RW
Tel: 01903 723511
Fax: 01903 723107
Email: bailiffscourt@hshotels.co.uk
Website: www.hshotels.co.uk
Map ref: 3, SU90
Directions: A259, follow Climping Beach signs.
Hotel 0.5m on right **Rooms:** 39 (16 GF) (25 fmly) **S** £200-£485
D £215-£545 (incl. bkfst) **Facilities:** STV Wi-fi ③ ⊰ Tennis Spa
Gym Sauna **Parking:** 100

Appearances can be deceptive. From the outside, Bailiffscourt is a classic, part-thatched, part-tiled manor house, reached down a quiet lane behind unspoilt Climping beach. But actually, it dates from only the 1920s, when Sir Walter Guinness gathered stone and wood from all over England to create the buildings that are Bailiffscourt as a family retreat. Gothic mullioned windows overlook the rose-clad courtyard, whilst narrow passageways lead through a series of intimate lounges and sitting rooms. Many of the public rooms feature open log fires and fine antiques, tapestries and fresh flowers. Located in the grounds, bedrooms vary from the atmospheric, with log fires, oak beams and four-poster beds, to the spacious and contemporary. Baylies, the master suite, with its huge vaulted ceiling, open fire and vast bathroom with walk-in shower and twin baths is for that special occasion. Classic European cooking is the mainstay of The Tapestry Restaurant, and during the summer lunch and afternoon tea may be enjoyed in the courtyard. The award-winning spa has heated indoor and outdoor pools, sauna, steam room, hot tub, gym and treatment rooms. Take a walk through the 30-acre grounds to the beach, counting peacocks along the way.

Recommended in the area

Walk through hotel grounds to beach; Goodwood; South Downs National Park; Arundel Castle

Ockenden Manor

★★★ ◉◉◉ HOTEL

Address: Ockenden Lane, CUCKFIELD, RH17 5LD
Tel: 01444 416111
Fax: 01444 415549
Email: reservations@ockenden-manor.com
Website: www.hshotels.co.uk
Map ref: 3, TQ32
Directions: A23 towards Brighton. 4.5m left onto B2115 towards Haywards Heath. Cuckfield 3m. Ockenden Lane off High St. Hotel at end
Rooms: 22 (4 GF) (4 fmly) **S** £108-£199 **D** £183-£376 (incl. bkfst)
Facilities: STV Wi-fi **Parking:** 43

Tucked away down a little country lane lies this charming Elizabethan manor house. With open views across nine acres of beautifully maintained grounds to the South Downs, the hotel is within easy reach of some of the region's great houses and gardens, as well as raffish Brighton and rather genteel Eastbourne. The public rooms, including an elegant sitting room, retain much of their original character. En suite bedrooms are all individually furnished and provided with satellite TV, direct-dial phone, trouser press, hairdryer and hospitality tray. All are named after members of the two families who have owned the hotel since 1520. Merrick, for example, has its own dining room, while Elizabeth is reached by a private staircase and is apparently home to a 'friendly but sad' ghost. In the wood-panelled restaurant, with its ornately painted ceiling and stained glass windows, you can expect some seriously good French-oriented food. The seven-course tasting menu is worth starving yourself for. A small dining room is suitable for semi-private dining, while in summer light meals can be taken on the terrace or in the gardens. Ockenden has a huge wine cellar, sourced from all over the world.

Recommended in the area

Wakehurst Place; Hever Castle; Glyndebourne Opera House

The Felbridge Hotel & Spa

★★★★ 86% ◉◉ HOTEL

Address: London Road, EAST GRINSTEAD,
RH19 2BH
Tel: 01342 337700
Fax: 01342 337715
Email: sales@felbridgehotel.co.uk
Website: www.felbridgehotel.co.uk
Map ref: 3, TQ33
Directions: From W exit M23 junct 10, follow signs
to A22. From N, exit M25 junct 6. Hotel on A22 at
Felbridge **Rooms:** 120 (53 GF) (16 fmly) **S** £79-£290 **D** £79-£290
Facilities: STV Wi-fi ⊗ Spa Gym Sauna **Parking:** 300 **Notes:** ⊗ in bedroom

Conveniently located on the edge of town, with Gatwick Airport about 15 minutes' away, this hotel has recently undergone a complete refurbishment. Fashionably designed bedrooms are finished to a high standard, with ultra-comfortable beds, power showers, flat-screen TVs, Wi-fi, irons and ironing boards, hairdryers, safes and hot beverage facilities. Most of the suites have double washbasins and separate showers, while robes, slippers, a complimentary basket of fresh fruit and a bottle of wine await guests in the luxury studios and junior suites. The two-AA Rosette Anise restaurant, with its subtle lighting and sophisticated colour scheme of grey, cream and black, serves modern British cuisine along the lines of south coast skate wing poached in butter with pickled samphire, pancetta, golden raisin and chicory salad, and South Downs lamb served three ways with pea, broad bean, mint, girolle and lamb broth flavours. The kitchen sources produce from Sussex, Surrey and Kent wherever possible. The less formal Bay Tree restaurant is open for breakfast, lunch and dinner, while a range of food and drinks is also available in the contemporary QUBE Bar, lounge and library.

Recommended in the area

Chartwell; Bluebell Railway; Wakehurst Place

Looking over surrounding countryside from the Fulking Escarpment

Langshott Manor

★★★★ ◉◉ COUNTRY HOUSE HOTEL

Address: Langshott Lane, HORLEY, RH6 9LN
Tel: 01293 786680
Fax: 01293 783905
Email: admin@langshottmanor.com
Website: www.langshottmanor.com
Map ref: 3, TQ24
Directions: From A23 take Ladbroke Rd, off Chequers rdbt to Langshott, after 0.75m hotel on right
Rooms: 22 (8 GF) (2 fmly) S £130-£150 D £150-£320 (incl. bkfst)
Facilities: STV Wi-fi **Parking:** 25 **Notes:** ⊗ in bedrooms

A brick and timber-framed Tudor manor house, with roses around the door, pretty gardens and even a section of moat, Langshott Manor exudes the grandeur of a former age. This, of course, makes it a perfect place to recuperate after a long-haul flight or to spend the night before the honeymoon flight. In fact, you can exclusively hire the entire hotel for a house-party style wedding. Bedrooms are either in the main house or the mews, and all are sumptuous, some with four-poster beds, open fireplaces and perhaps a private deck. There's even a four-poster bath in one of the bathrooms, all of which are individually styled and absolutely stunning. Dining in the Mulberry restaurant is always an occasion, with innovative dishes served in elegant surroundings. Less formal dining is offered in the lounge. Surrounded by beautiful countryside, Langshott Manor is less than 25 miles from London and in very close proximity (8 minutes) to Gatwick Airport. It is an ideal place to relax on your first and last stop in the country.

Recommended in the area

Wakehurst Place Gardens; Chartwell; Denbies Vineyard

Stanhill Court Hotel

★★★ 85% ◉◉ HOTEL

Address: Stanhill Road, Charlwood, HORLEY, RH6 0EP
Tel: 01293 862166
Fax: 01293 862773
Email: enquiries@stanhillcourthotel.co.uk
Website: www.stanhillcourthotel.co.uk
Map ref: 3, TQ24
Directions: N of Charlwood towards Newdigate
Rooms: 34 (1 GF) (3 fmly) **Parking:** 110

Named after the hill on which it stands, and surrounded by rolling downland, Stanhill Court was built in 1881 as a family home. It stands amid 35 acres of ancient woodland and though it is only four miles from Gatwick Airport, it is not on a flight path, so peace and tranquillity are assured. The first owners were clearly not short of money, and original features that remain include warm, elaborately carved wood panelling, a minstrels' gallery, a barrel roof and fine stained glass windows. In keeping with all of this, many of the bedrooms have four-poster beds and all are individually decorated to complement the character of the house. Two sympathetically constructed wings provide additional accommodation and function suites. Restaurant 1881 provides a wonderful setting for a meal, with rich wood panelling and enhanced by an open fire in winter. International cuisine is produced by the kitchen team, and might include dishes such as confit duck leg with dauphinoise potatoes and truffled green beans, finished with a thyme jus; or parmesan-glazed poached smoked haddock with wholegrain mustard mash and wilted spinach. An international wine list of 200 bins is offered. Personal, attentive service is one of the hallmarks of this fine hotel.

Recommended in the area

North Downs Way; Bluebell Railway; Wakehurst Place

Sofitel London Gatwick

★★★★ 80% ⊛ HOTEL

Address: North Terminal, GATWICK AIRPORT, RH6 0PH
Tel: 01293 567070 & 555000
Fax: 01293 567739
Email: h6204-re@accor.com
Website: www.sofitel.com
Map ref: 3, TQ24
Directions: M23 junct 9, follow to 2nd rdbt. Hotel large white building straight ahead
Rooms: 518 (19 fmly) **Facilities:** Wi-fi Gym Sauna **Parking:** 200 **Notes:** ⊗ in bedrooms

Who would have thought that staying overnight at the airport before or after a flight could be so desirable? The Sofitel offers handy 'Park & Fly' packages to those on the outward journey, and is the only hotel directly linked to Gatwick's North Terminal (with a monorail link to the South Terminal). The air-conditioned bedrooms are modern and stylish, and some boast runway views. There are three restaurants on site, including the AA Rosetted La Brasserie. Here, the kitchen uses high quality, locally-sourced ingredients in accurately cooked French and British dishes, such as rillettes of pork, duck and foie gras with Calvados jelly, crisp apple salad and onion toast, and free-range Rusper lamb (cutlets and sweetbreads) with caramelised shallots, potato drop scone and port wine jus. Alternatively, Le Café, with its al fresco feel, offers all-day dining, while Gatwick Oriental specialises in Chinese cuisine. There's also 24-hour room service and two bars to choose from. The Sofitel Airline Lounge is ideal for passengers arriving on an early flight who may need to freshen up for a meeting or onward journey, and offers light snacks, fully equipped individual shower rooms, pressing service, internet and relaxation areas. The hotel also has a range of meeting rooms suitable for between three and 300 delegates.

Recommended in the area

Lingfield Park Racecourse; Hever Castle; Worth Abbey

Bluebell Railway

Spread Eagle Hotel and Spa

★★★ 80% ◉◉ HOTEL

Address: South Street, MIDHURST, GU29 9NH
Tel: 01730 816911
Fax: 01730 815668
Email: spreadeagle@hshotels.co.uk
Website: www.hshotels.co.uk/spread/
spreadeagle-main.htm
Map ref: 3, SU82 **Directions:** M25 junct 10, A3
to Milford, take A286 to Midhurst. Hotel adjacent to
market square **Rooms:** 34 (8 GF) **S** £90-£495
D £100-£495 (incl. bkfst) **Facilities:** STV Wi-fi ⊛ Spa Gym Sauna **Parking:** 75

This ancient coaching inn has been offering accommodation to travellers since 1430, and was
described by Hilaire Belloc as, "that oldest and most revered of all the prime inns of this world". The
building is brimful of original features, including sloping floors, huge inglenook fireplaces and Tudor
bread ovens, while the individually styled bedrooms – oak-panelled in the main house – provide up-to-
the-minute comforts. The Tapestry Restaurant serves modern British cuisine.

Recommended in the area

Goodwood Estate; Petworth House; Cowdray Park

TYNE & WEAR

Millennium Bridge in Newcastle upon Tyne

Vermont Hotel

★★★★ 81% ◉ HOTEL

Address: Castle Garth, NEWCASTLE UPON TYNE, NE1 1RQ
Tel: 0191 233 1010
Fax: 0191 233 1234
Email: info@vermont-hotel.co.uk
Website: www.vermont-hotel.com
Map ref: 7, NZ26
Directions: City centre by high level bridge & castle keep
Rooms: 101 (12 fmly) S £100-£190 D £100-£190
Facilities: STV Wi-fi Gym **Parking:** 100

Adjacent to the castle and close to the buzzing Quayside area, this imposing, 12-storey, independently owned hotel enjoys fine views of the Tyne and Millennium Bridges. With an exterior style described as '1930s Manhattan tower', its plush interior is both traditional and contemporary. All bedrooms, including the grand suites, are equipped with three telephones, computer modem fax port, work desk, fully stocked mini-bar, satellite TV, and complimentary tea and coffee facilities. The elegant reception lounge encourages relaxation, while the Bridge Restaurant is open for breakfast, lunch and dinner. Through its windows, the Tyne Bridge looks close enough to reach out and pluck the suspension cables. The Blue Room provides the perfect setting for private dining in luxurious surroundings for up to 80 guests. The informal Redwood Bar is an intimate meeting place serving a large selection of wines and light meals until the early hours. Martha's Bar and Courtyard is popular too, particularly with the 20-somethings. Seven meeting and conference rooms cater as effortlessly for 300 people at a cocktail function as they do for a one-to-one meeting. A Health and Fitness Centre is also available.

Recommended in the area

Newcastle Cathedral; Baltic Centre for Contemporary Art; Sage Centre, Gateshead

WARWICKSHIRE

View towards the ruins of Kenilworth Castle

The sun sets and gleams in the background of Warwick Castle mill seen from Mill Gardens

Lea Marston Hotel

★★★★ 76% ◉ HOTEL

Address: Haunch Lane, LEA MARSTON, Sutton
Coldfield, B76 0BY
Tel: 01675 470468 & 471305
Fax: 01675 470871
Email: info@leamarstonhotel.co.uk
Website: www.leamarstonhotel.co.uk
Map ref: 3, SP29
Directions: M42 junct 9, A4097 to Kingsbury. Hotel
signed 1.5m on right
Rooms: 88 (49 GF) (4 fmly) **Facilities:** STV Wi-fi ⊗ Tennis Spa Gym Sauna
Parking: 220 **Notes:** ⊗ in bedrooms

The Lea Marston is a modern hotel within easy reach of motorway, rail and air links. Lounges are spacious, airy and comfortable, while all bedrooms and the larger suites come with all the expected facilities. Enjoy fine dining in the Adderley Restaurant or pub classics in Hathaways bar. The hotel offers facilities for conferences, wedding receptions and civil ceremonies.

Recommended in the area

Drayton Manor Theme Park; Lichfield Cathedral; Staffordshire Regimental Museum; Twycross Zoo

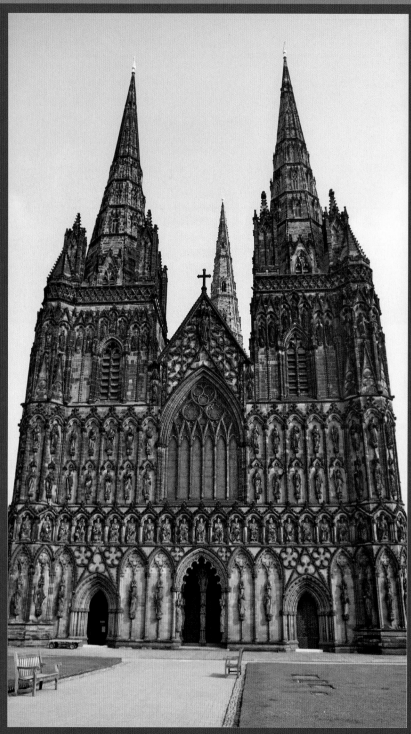

Lichfield Cathedral

Fairlawns Hotel & Spa

★★★ 85% ⊛⊛ HOTEL

Address: 178 Little Aston Road, WALSALL,
WS9 0NU
Tel: 01922 455122
Fax: 01922 743148
Email: reception@fairlawns.co.uk
Website: www.fairlawns.co.uk
Map ref: 3, SP09
Directions: Off A452 towards Aldridge at x-roads
with A454. Hotel 600yds on right
Rooms: 59 (1 GF) (8 fmly) **S** £75-£165 **D** £85-£245 (incl. bkfst)
Facilities: STV Wi-fi ⓢ Tennis Spa Gym Sauna **Parking:** 150

Owned and run by the Pette family since 1984, Fairlawns Hotel and Spa lies in open countryside yet is close to Walsall, Sutton Coldfield and Lichfield and has good motorway access. Standing in nine acres of landscaped grounds, the hotel also boasts an adult health club and spa, and guests have complimentary use of all the facilities, including a 20-metre indoor pool, two gyms and an impressive hydrotherapy suite. Beauty treatments and special spa days can also be arranged. The hotel's comfortable bedrooms, some modern, some more traditional, include family rooms and suites. All have modern facilities such as free high-speed Wi-fi access, digital flat-screen TV with Sky Sports channels, hairdryer, ironing facilities and good-quality toiletries (note that some smoking rooms are available). Quieter rooms and suites are located in a separate wing, away from normal hotel activities. Presided over by the Midlands Chef of the Year, Neil Atkins, the AA Rosette-winning Fairlawns Restaurant offers lunch and dinner in comfortable, elegant surroundings, with attentive service and imaginative food, especially seafood, and it is little wonder that this is a popular local dining venue.

Recommended in the area

Walsall Art Gallery; Lichfield Cathedral; Cannock Chase Area of Outstanding Natural Beauty

WILTSHIRE

Stonehenge

Lucknam Park Hotel & Spa

★★★★★ ⊛⊛⊛ COUNTRY HOUSE HOTEL
& SPA

Address: COLERNE, SN14 8AZ
Tel: 01225 742777
Fax: 01225 743536
Email: reservations@lucknampark.co.uk
Website: www.lucknampark.co.uk
Map ref: 2, ST87
Directions: M4 junct 17, A350 towards
Chippenham, then A420 towards Bristol for 3m. At
Ford left to Colerne, 3m, right at x-rds, entrance on right
Rooms: 42 (16 GF) **S** £280-£950 **D** £280-£950
Facilities: STV Wi-fi ⊗ Tennis Spa Gym Sauna **Parking:** 70 **Notes:** ⊗ in bedrooms

Lucknam Park Hotel & Spa is a magnificent listed Palladian mansion which sits proudly at the end of a glorious mile-long drive lined with beech and lime trees. The hotel's 42 individually designed bedrooms, including 13 impressive suites, are truly luxurious. For a spot of pampering, head to the stunning spa, with its 20-metre pool, nine state-of-the-art treatment rooms, five thermal cabins, indoor and outdoor hydrotherapy pool, saltwater plunge pool and innovative skin and bodycare experiences. Within The Spa, The Brasserie, with its open kitchen and wood-fired oven, offers contemporary and stylish dining, including a healthy option menu. For fine-dining at its best, the elegant three-Rosette The Park restaurant, serving accomplished modern British cuisine, is not to be missed. After all that wining and dining, you might feel like a bit of exercise, in which case Lucknam Park has it all: two floodlit tennis courts, a five-a-side football pitch, bicycles, walking and jogging trails, croquet and an extensive equestrian centre are all within the beautiful grounds.

Recommended in the area
Bath; Lacock Village (NT); Wells Cathedral

King Alfred's Tower on the Stourhead Estate

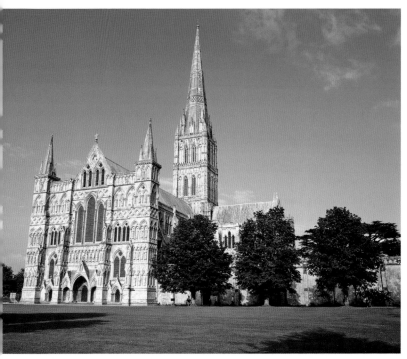

Sailisbury Cathedral

Whatley Manor

★★★★★ ❀❀❀❀ HOTEL

Address: Easton Grey, MALMESBURY, SN16 0RB
Tel: 01666 822888
Fax: 01666 826120
Email: reservations@whatleymanor.com
Website: www.whatleymanor.com
Map ref: 2, ST98
Directions: M4 junct 17, follow signs to Malmesbury, continue over 2 rdbts. Follow B4040 & signs for Sherston, hotel 2m on left

Rooms: 23 (4 GF) **D** £295-£855 (incl. bkfst) **Facilities:** STV Wi-fi Spa Gym Sauna **Parking:** 100

This privately-owned hotel sits within 12 acres of pretty Wiltshire countryside. The 23 bedrooms and suites are individually furnished in a sophisticated and contemporary style. With Martin Burge, one of the UK's most talented chefs, at the helm, dinner in the elegant Dining Room is not to be missed. Alternatively, Le Mazot is an informal Swiss-style brasserie, open daily for lunch and dinner. The Aquarias spa boasts one of the largest hydrotherapy pools in Britain.
Recommended in the area
Bath; Cheltenham; Westonbirt Aboretum

The Manor

★★★★ RESTAURANT WITH ROOMS
Address: SP3 4HF
Tel: 01980 620216
Email: info@rollestonemanor.com
Website: www.rollestonemanor.com
Map ref: 3, SU04
Rooms: 7 D £80-£130 Facilities: Wi-fi

This Grade II listed manor near Stonehenge has been the home of the Smith family for more than 60 years. When the previous Mrs Smith's children fled the nest she opened The Manor as a traditional B&B, but recently the house, still owned by the family, has undergone an extensive renovation to transform it into a luxury restaurant with rooms. The seven bedrooms now come with all the 21st century comforts you'd expect - such as DVD players, wireless internet and iPod docks - while retaining much of their period charm and appeal. Each en suite bedroom is named after a past owner of the house and is individually designed, with antiques, beautiful soft furnishings and features such as free-standing roll-top baths and four-poster beds. Some may be used as family rooms and there's a bedroom on the ground floor for those who are unable to manage the stairs. The restaurant at The Manor serves plenty of fine Wiltshire produce from a seasonally changing menu of mainly British and European classics. Steeped in history, The Manor is a charming and peaceful place to stay with a genuinely warm and friendly atmosphere.

Recommended in the area

Stonehenge; Salisbury Cathedral and city; Longleat Safari Park

View to North Hill from Worcestershire Beacon in the Malvern Hills in Great Malvern

Malvern Hills

Barcelo The Lygon Arms

★★★★ 80% @@ HOTEL

Address: High Street, BROADWAY, WR12 7DU
Tel: 01386 852255
Fax: 01386 854470
Email: thelygonarms@barcelo-hotels.co.uk
Website: www.barcelo-hotels.co.uk
Map ref: 3, SP03
Directions: From Evesham take A44 signed Oxford,
5m. Follow Broadway signs. Hotel on left
Rooms: 78 (9 GF) **S** £115-£245
Facilities: STV Wi-fi ⏱ Tennis Spa Gym Sauna **Parking:** 200

This charming hotel at the heart of the picture-postcard village of Broadway has been welcoming travellers since the 16th century. Its honey-coloured stone walls, antiques, flagstone floors, wood panelling, stone mullions and antiques exude a sense of history, while modern features have been sympathetically introduced, including a superb spa complex with a retractable glass roof over the swimming pool. The Great Hall Restaurant serves modern European cuisine.

Recommended in the area

The Cotswold Way; Hidcote Manor (NT); Sudeley Castle

Brockencote Hall Country House Hotel

★★★ ◉◉ HOTEL

Address: CHADDESLEY CORBETT, DY10 4PY
Tel: 01562 777876
Fax: 01562 777872
Email: info@brockencotehall.com
Website: www.brockencotehall.com
Map ref: 2, SO87
Directions: 0.5m W, off A448, opposite St Cassians Church
Rooms: 17 (5 GF) (2 fmly) S £96-£140 D £120-£190 (incl. bkfst)
Facilities: Wi-fi Tennis **Parking:** 45 **Notes:** ⊗ in bedrooms

This fine mansion stands in 70 acres of landscaped grounds featuring a lake and splendid trees, beyond which the Worcestershire countryside extends to the Malvern Hills. Sheep graze within sight of residents taking tea in the conservatory. The high-ceilinged rooms have many period features and elegant fabrics and furnishings. Some rooms have a four-poster bed and a whirlpool bath, while all have en suite facilities, a restful view, satellite television, a telephone and wireless internet access. There are two conference rooms, able to accommodate 10 and 20 delegates respectively. The public rooms are light and airy, and warmed by log fires in the winter. In the elegant chandelier-lit restaurant, the outstanding cuisine bears the stamp of the owner's and the head chef's French training. The menu also offers a choice of lighter dishes and is supported by an extensive wine cellar. The hotel is licensed for civil wedding ceremonies and is well equipped to host wedding receptions. Brockencote Hall is only 30 minutes from Birmingham, with its international airport.

Recommended in the area

Ironbridge Gorge; Severn Valley Steam Railway; West Midlands Safari Park

Gainsborough House Hotel

★★★ 80% HOTEL

Address: Bewdley Hill, KIDDERMINSTER, DY11 6BS
Tel: 01562 820041
Fax: 01562 66179
Email: reservations@gainsboroughhousehotel.com
Website: www.gainsboroughhousehotel.com
Map ref: 2, SO87 **Directions:** Follow A456 to Kidderminster (West Midlands Safari Park), pass hospital, hotel 500yds on left **Rooms:** 42 (12 GF) (16 fmly) S £55-£75 D £75-£95 (incl. bkfst) **Facilities:** STV Wi-fi **Parking:** 90 **Notes:** ⊗ in bedrooms

The Gainsborough House Hotel occupies a handsome listed building close to the centre of Kidderminster. There are 42 modern, comfortable bedrooms, all with air-conditioning, flat-screen TV, free broadband and refreshments. A team of professional, courteous and friendly staff are on hand to see to the needs of every guest. The restaurant at the Gainsborough House Hotel is spacious and contemporary and serves modern British cuisine prepared from the freshest local ingredients.

Recommended in the area

West Midlands Safari Park; Severn Valley Railway; Worcester

The Granary Hotel & Restaurant

★★★ 78% ◉◉ HOTEL

Address: Heath Lane, Shenstone, KIDDERMINSTER, DY10 4BS
Tel: 01562 777535
Fax: 01562 777722
Email: info@granary-hotel.co.uk
Website: www.granary-hotel.co.uk
Map ref: 2, SO87
Directions: On A450 between Stourbridge & Worcester, 1m from Kidderminster
Rooms: 18 (18 GF) (1 fmly) S £75-£90 D £90-£140 (incl. bkfst) **Facilities:** Wi-fi **Parking:** 96

Amid lovely Worcestershire countryside, with views of the Abberley Hills, this bright and modern hotel is a rural hideaway handy for exploring the Midlands' industrial heritage. Recent investment has given the place a chic contemporary decor, and refurbished the bedrooms and bathrooms (the power showers are terrific). The restaurant, renowned for carvery lunches, supports local produce wherever possible, and the à la carte dinner menu offers such dishes as local pheasant with Madeira and chestnut sauce.

Recommended in the area

Black Country Museum; Severn Valley Railway; West Midlands Safari Park

Views from the top of the tower of Worcester Cathedral over the River Severn

The Cotford Hotel

★★★ 79% @ HOTEL

Address: 51 Graham Road, MALVERN, WR14 2HU
Tel: 01684 572427
Fax: 01684 572952
Email: reservations@cotfordhotel.co.uk
Website: www.cotfordhotel.co.uk
Map ref: 2, SO74
Directions: From Worcester follow signs to Malvern on A449. Left into Graham Rd signed town centre, hotel on right
Rooms: 15 (1 GF) (3 fmly) **S** £65-£79 **D** £99-£115 (incl. bkfst) **Facilities:** STV Wi-fi **Parking:** 15

This Victorian gothic hotel, nestled at the foot of the beautiful Malvern Hills, was built in 1851 as a summer residence for the Bishop of Worcester. Many original details have been beautifully preserved, not least the bishop's private chapel which is now home to the L'amuse Bouche restaurant. Before or after a meal, relax in front of an open fire in the piano lounge or the bar, or perhaps enjoy a drink on the terrace during the summer months. The hotel's landscaped gardens, are a joy to explore.
Recommended in the area
The Malvern Hills (AONB); Great Malvern Priory; Little Malvern Court

Worcester Cathedral

Severn Valley Railway

Abbey Hotel Golf & Country Club

★★★★ 78% HOTEL

Address:	Hither Green Lane, Dagnell End Road, Bordesley, REDDITCH, B98 9BE
Tel:	01527 406600
Fax:	01527 406514
Email:	info@theabbeyhotel.co.uk
Website:	www.theabbeyhotel.co.uk
Map ref:	3, SP06

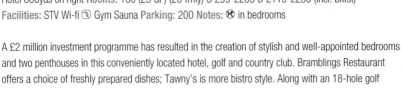

Directions: M42 junct 2, A441 to Redditch. End of carriageway turn left (A441), Dagnell End Rd on left. Hotel 600yds on right **Rooms:** 100 (23 GF) (20 fmly) **S** £99-£205 **D** £110-£255 (incl. bkfst) **Facilities:** STV Wi-fi ⊗ Gym Sauna **Parking:** 200 **Notes:** ⊗ in bedrooms

A £2 million investment programme has resulted in the creation of stylish and well-appointed bedrooms and two penthouses in this conveniently located hotel, golf and country club. Bramblings Restaurant offers a choice of freshly prepared dishes; Tawny's is more bistro style. Along with an 18-hole golf course with pro shop, there's a large indoor pool, beauty salon and health club.

Recommended in the area

Coughton Court (NT); Severn Valley Railway; Anne Hathaway's Cottage

Old stone gatepost south of the peak of Roseberry Topping hill, North York Moors National Park

The Boar's Head Hotel

★★★ 83% ◉◉ HOTEL

Address: Ripley Castle Estate, HARROGATE, HG3 3AY
Tel: 01423 771888
Fax: 01423 771509
Email: reservations@boarsheadripley.co.uk
Website: www.boarsheadripley.co.uk
Map ref: 6, SE35
Directions: On A61 (Harrogate to Ripon road). Hotel in town centre
Rooms: 25 (2 fmly) S £105-£125 D £125-£150 (incl. bkfst) **Facilities:** Wi-fi Tennis **Parking:** 50

Part of the Ripley Castle Estate, this former coaching inn has plenty of old-world charm. Both the public areas and bedrooms are furnished in a traditional country-house style, with fabrics and fittings chosen by Ripley Castle's own Lady Ingilby. Relax in front of a roaring log fire in one of the comfortable lounges before making your choice between the two dining areas. The Bistro offers more straightforward dishes, while the formal two-Rosette Restaurant offers refined modern British cooking.

Recommended in the area
Ripley Castle & Gardens; Harrogate; York

Rudding Park Hotel & Golf

★★★★ ◉◉ HOTEL

Address: Rudding Park, Follifoot, HARROGATE, HG3 1JH
Tel: 01423 871350
Fax: 01423 872286
Email: reservations@ruddingpark.com
Website: www.ruddingpark.co.uk
Map ref: 6, SE35
Directions: From A61 at rdbt with A658 take York exit, follow signs to Rudding Park
Rooms: 49 (19 GF) S £122.50-£175 D £144-£420 (incl. bkfst) **Facilities:** STV Wi-fi **Parking:** 150

Rudding Park is a luxurious retreat sitting in 300 acres of mature parkland just south of the beautiful spa town of Harrogate. The open fireplace and fresh flowers in reception reflect the warm welcome for which the hotel is renowned. The Clocktower Bar and Restaurant overlooks the gardens and offers modern British cuisine, including a Yorkshire menu. An 18-hole golf course and six-hole short course run through the existing parkland.

Recommended in the area
Harewood House; Castle Howard; Jorvik Viking Centre

Feversham Arms Hotel & Verbena Spa

★★★★ 80% ◉◉ HOTEL

Address: HELMSLEY, YO62 5AG
Tel: 01439 770766
Fax: 01439 770346
Email: info@fevershamarmshotel.com
Website: www.fevershamarmshotel.com
Map ref: 6, SE68 **Directions:** A168 (signed

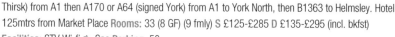

Thirsk) from A1 then A170 or A64 (signed York) from A1 to York North, then B1363 to Helmsley. Hotel 125mtrs from Market Place **Rooms:** 33 (8 GF) (9 fmly) **S** £125-£285 **D** £135-£295 (incl. bkfst) **Facilities:** STV Wi-fi ↘ Spa **Parking:** 50

What a difference a few years, a sizeable investment and a lot of vision makes. When experienced hotelier Simon Rhatigan took over The Feversham Arms in the quaint market town of Helmsley in 2003, it was little more than a pub with rooms. But ever since, Rhatigan has been gradually transforming the old inn into a luxurious hideaway – and the result is a stunning small hotel eminently worthy of the title 'AA Hotel of the Year 2009-2010'. The Feversham Arms now has 33 rooms, including 22 suites, ranging from the more traditional-style doubles in the original pub to the beautiful Spa Suites above the Verbena Spa. All are individually designed and come with Bang & Olufsen TVs with DVD/CD players, L'Occitaine toiletries and Egyptian cotton bedding. The Spa Suites boast balconies overlooking the outdoor heated pool (open all year – so you can even swim outside on Christmas Day!). For pure relaxation, head to the Verbena Spa, with its heat experience, treatment range, and outdoor hot tub. The conservatory-style restaurant makes a romantic setting for some superb modern British cuisine.

Recommended in the area

North Yorkshire Moors National Park; Whitby; Castle Howard; Rievaulx Abbey

Lastingham Grange Hotel

★★★ 80% HOTEL

Address: LASTINGHAM, York, YO62 6TH
Tel: 01751 417345 & 417402
Fax: 01751 417358
Email: reservations@lastinghamgrange.com
Website: www.lastinghamgrange.com
Map ref: 8, SE79
Directions: From A170 follow signs for Appleton-le-Moors, continue into Lastingham, pass church on left & turn right then left up hill. Hotel on right
Rooms: 12 (2 fmly) S £100-£125 D £180-£210 (incl. bkfst) Facilities: Wi-fi Parking: 30

A stone-walled, 17th-century farmhouse built around a courtyard, and now standing in ten acres of well-kept gardens and fields on the edge of the moors. Since the mid-50s it has been run by the Woods, whose family home it still is. The tastefully furnished and decorated bedrooms are very well equipped, and the spacious lounge and beautiful dining room look on to the terrace and rose garden. Seasonal menus might include beef and venison goulash, and baked salmon with leek and cider sauce.

Recommended in the area

City of York; North Yorks Moors National Park; Rievaulx Abbey

Hob Green Hotel

★★★ 82% COUNTRY HOUSE HOTEL

Address: MARKINGTON, HG3 3PJ
Tel: 01423 770031
Fax: 01423 771589
Email: info@hobgreen.com
Website: www.hobgreen.com
Map ref: 6, SE26 Directions: From A61, 4m N of Harrogate, left at Wormald Green, follow hotel signs
Rooms: 12 (1 fmly) S £95-£115
D £115-£135 (incl. bkfst) Parking: 40

Hob Green is a late 18th-century property standing in beautiful gardens, surrounded by rolling countryside. The 12 en suite bedrooms are well equipped and individually furnished in a traditional English style. The building retains much of its period character; public rooms are furnished with antiques and offer lovely views over the valley below. A sun room, with an Oriental theme, leads out onto a delightful terrace. The restaurant makes much use of seasonal local produce, including fruit and vegetables from the hotel's own Victorian kitchen garden.

Recommended in the area

Ripon racecourse; Harrogate; Fountains Abbey; Studley Royal Water Garden

Three Tuns

★★★★ ➠ RESTAURANT WITH ROOMS

Address: 9 South End, Osmotherley
NORTHALLERTON DL6 3BN
Tel: 01609 883301
Fax: 01609 883988
Email: enquiries@threetunsrestaurant.co.uk
Website: www.threetunsrestaurant.co.uk
Map ref: 8, SE39
Directions: NE of Northallerton. Off A19 into Osmotherley village
Rooms: 7 (en suite) (1 GF) S £55 D £85

This family-run establishment, situated in the picturesque village of Osmotherley in the North Yorkshire Moors, is full of character. With its friendly, informal atmosphere and great food, it is a popular destination for business travellers, tourists and locals alike – 'Delicious food in a beautiful restaurant' was how Paddy Burt described it in The Telegraph. The Charles Rennie Mackintosh-inspired decor sets it apart, and the bedrooms – some situated above the bar, some located in an adjoining annexe – vary in size but are stylishly furnished in pine throughout. All rooms are en suite, including one family room and one on the ground floor, and have colour TV, large beds, fluffy pillows and tea and coffee-making facilities; some rooms enjoy stunning views of the Cleveland Hills. The homely lounge contains a video and CD player, and there's a film and music collection available for guests to browse through and enjoy. The restaurant is a real draw, offering an imaginative range of wholesome, modern British dishes with the emphasis on fine local produce and with fine wines and traditional cask conditioned ales to wash it all down. A hearty breakfast, lunch, afternoon tea and dinner are all on offer. There is also a beautifully peaceful secret garden to enjoy.

Recommended in the area

The Forbidden Corner; Wensleydale Railway; Mount Grace Priory

Best Western Ox Pasture Hall Country Hotel

★★★ 80% ❀ HOTEL

Address: Lady Edith's Drive, Raincliffe Woods, SCARBOROUGH, YO12 5TD

Tel: 01723 365295

Fax: 01723 355156

Email: oxpasture.hall@btconnect.com

Website: www.oxpasturehall.com

Map ref: 6, TA08 **Directions:** A171, left onto Lady Edith's Drive, 1.5m, hotel on right **Rooms:** 22 (14 GF) (1 fmly) S £70-£110 D £90-£180 (incl. bkfst) **Facilities:** Wi-fi **Parking:** 100

Ox Pasture Hall is one of today's new breed of luxury country-house hotel – fresh, unstuffy and full of rustic style and charm. The setting is gorgeous, within 17 acres of landscaped gardens and grounds, surrounded by the magnificent North Yorkshire Moors National Park, yet only two miles from the seaside resort of Scarborough. Individually decorated bedrooms vary in either size or aspect; some have traditional Queen Anne four-posters, others ornate metal, French or high-backed sleigh beds. Ground floor rooms overlook a wisteria-covered courtyard, while others survey the well-kept gardens and woodland beyond. The courtyard lends its name to the restaurant, where chefs prepare dishes from the finest local and organic Yorkshire produce. On fine summer's days you can also take drinks on the terrace overlooking the beautiful gardens. If you prefer less formal dining, the brasserie, with its beamed ceiling, log burner and traditional bar, is a relaxed alternative to the main restaurant. Ox Pasture Hall simply couldn't be more perfect for a relaxing or romantic break.

Recommended in the area

Whitby; North Yorks Moors Railway; Cleveland Way

Palm Court Hotel

★★★ 79% HOTEL

Address: St Nicholas Cliff, SCARBOROUGH,
YO11 2ES
Tel: 01723 368161
Fax: 01723 371547
Email: info@palmcourt-scarborough.co.uk
Website: www.palmcourtscarborough.co.uk
Map ref: 6, TA08
Directions: Follow signs for town centre & town hall,
hotel before town hall on right Rooms: 40 (7 fmly)
S £50-£58 D £95-£120 (incl. bkfst) Facilities: Wi-fi ⊗ Parking: 40 Notes: ⊗ in bedrooms

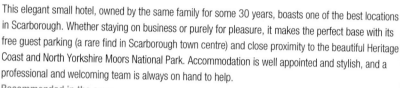

This elegant small hotel, owned by the same family for some 30 years, boasts one of the best locations in Scarborough. Whether staying on business or purely for pleasure, it makes the perfect base with its free guest parking (a rare find in Scarborough town centre) and close proximity to the beautiful Heritage Coast and North Yorkshire Moors National Park. Accommodation is well appointed and stylish, and a professional and welcoming team is always on hand to help.

Recommended in the area

North Yorkshire Heritage Coast; North Yorkshire Moors National Park; Castle Howard

The Cliffemount Hotel

★★★ 80% ⊛⊛ SMALL HOTEL

Address: Bank Top Lane, Runswick Bay, WHITBY,
TS13 5HU
Tel: 01947 840103
Fax: 01947 841025
Email: info@cliffemounthotel.co.uk
Website: www.cliffemounthotel.co.uk
Map ref: 6, NZ81
Directions: Exit A174, 8m N of Whitby, 1m to end
Rooms: 20 (5 GF) (4 fmly) S £70-£100 D £110-
£160 (incl. bkfst) Facilities: Wi-fi Parking: 25

This privately-owned hotel sits on the cliff-top above Runswick Bay, with spectacular views out to sea. Recently refurbished throughout, it has 20 individually designed rooms with all the modern must-haves. Premier rooms have added luxuries, balconies and even - in some cases - telescopes to bring you closer to the sweeping bay below. The hotel's two-Rosette restaurant has fine views of the bay and fine modern British food on the menu.

Recommended in the area

Runswick Bay; Whitby; North Yorkshire Moors National Park

Runswick Bay

Dunsley Hall

★★★ 71% ® COUNTRY HOUSE HOTEL

Address: Dunsley, WHITBY, YO21 3TL
Tel: 01947 893437
Fax: 01947 893505
Email: reception@dunsleyhall.com
Website: www.dunsleyhall.com
Map ref: 8, NZ81
Directions: 3m N of Whitby, signed off A171
Rooms: 26 (2 GF) (2 fmly) S £95-£120 D £149 (incl. bkfst) Facilities: Tennis Parking: 30
Notes: ⊗ in bedrooms

A Victorian shipping magnate built this mellow-stone hideaway in four acres of landscaped gardens, full today (and who knows, maybe then too) of beautiful rhododendrons. Dunsley Hall is now a family-run country-house hotel, with oak-panelling, stained glass windows and other surviving period gems to ensure a pleasing blend of the old with the best facilities a hotel of today can offer. In the main house, accommodation is available in traditionally designed, individually furnished bedrooms, some with four-posters; rooms in the ground floor extension are contemporary yet elegant, while a self-catering cottage provides all the amenities for an independent stay. Wherever you choose, you'll have a view of the grounds, countryside or coast. With Whitby so close you can expect seafood – trio of salmon, red snapper and king prawns, for example – to feature prominently on the Oak Room restaurant's menu, while lighter lunchtime and early evening alternatives are provided in the Pyman Bar. In addition to seafood, local produce is the foundation of all menus. Guests may visit the hotel's working farm at nearby Ramsdale, where 50 acres of farmland are available for outdoor pursuits and team-building events, so bring wellingtons and a warm coat.

Recommended in the area

North Yorks Moors Railway; Captain Cook Museum; Castle Howard

Estbek House

★ ★ ★ ★ @@ RESTAURANT WITH ROOMS

Address: East Row, Sandsend, WHITBY, YO21 3SU

Tel: 01947 893424

Fax: 01947 893625

Email: info@estbekhouse.co.uk

Website: www.estbekhouse.co.uk

Map ref: 8, NZ81

Directions: On Cleveland Way, within Sandsend, next to East Beck

Rooms: 4 (3 en suite) (1 pri facs) **S** £60–£90

D £90–£130 **Facilities:** Wi-fi **Parking:** 6 **Notes:** ⊗ in bedrooms ❌ under 14 yrs

Co-owners Tim Lawrence and David Cross run this restaurant with rooms with great skill and enthusiasm, and their attention to detail is evident at every meal and in every one of the bedrooms. Tim, and chef James, lead the team in the open-plan kitchen, and base their menus on local moorland produce and fresh, wild seafood. Not surprisingly, given its location in a pretty coastal village, there is always a large selection of fish, cooked simply and with a choice of sauces, plus seafood creations such as a trio of mornay, halibut in white wine, or whole lobster thermidor with crayfish and brown shrimp. Meat dishes might include Gressingham duck and black pudding, pan-seared and served with slow roasted figs in a balsamic sauce reduction, or loin of local spring lamb. The wine list reflects David's particular interest and expertise, with some unique varieties on offer and an emphasis on antipodean wines. The four rooms make good use of the spacious Georgian architecture, each with its own style and ambience. Contemporary furnishings and modern bathroom fittings blend with original features such as ships' timber beams and unique touches that include original works by local artists and hand-made patchwork quilts.

Recommended in the area

The Cleveland Way; Whitby Abbey; North York Moors

Best Western Dean Court Hotel

★★★★ 77% ◉◉ HOTEL

Address: Duncombe Place, YORK, YO1 7EF
Tel: 01904 625082
Fax: 01904 620305
Email: sales@deancourt-york.co.uk
Website: www.deancourt-york.co.uk
Map ref: 6, SE65
Directions: City centre opposite York Minster
Rooms: 37 (4 fmly) S £95-£135
D £120-£225 (incl. bkfst) **Facilities:** Wi-fi
Parking: 30 **Notes:** ⊗ in bedrooms

Standing in the very shadow of York Minster, the Dean Court has arguably the best location of any hotel in the city. Inside you'll find contemporary elegance, comfort and style, and genuinely friendly service. Bedrooms are all non-smoking and offer first-class comfort and facilities, with the deluxe and four-poster rooms boasting magnificent views of the Minster. Families are very welcome and a range of services are offered to ensure a stress-free stay, including a toy box for toddlers and a media library offering a wide range of entertainment. Locals speak highly of the food here, served in both the elegant and friendly restaurant, DCH, which has two AA Rosettes and Minster views; and the café-bistro and bar, The Court, a more informal setting with big sofas – just the place for a light meal, cocktails or supper with friends. Privately owned and personally run, the hotel has excellent conference, meeting and private dining facilities, and offers free Wi-fi throughout plus complimentary valet-parking. The hotel offers the opportunity to add extras to a normal stay, from champagne and chocolates to afternoon tea, as well as a wide variety of special breaks, from the Champagne Lovers' break to Christmas and Valentine's Day.

Recommended in the area

York Minster; National Railway Museum; Castle Museum; Castle Howard

The Grange Hotel

★★★★ 77% ◉◉ HOTEL

Address: 1 Clifton, YORK, YO30 6AA
Tel: 01904 644744
Fax: 01904 612453
Email: info@grangehotel.co.uk
Website: www.grangehotel.co.uk
Map ref: 8, SE65 **Directions:** On A19 York/Thirsk
road, approx 500yds from city centre
Rooms: 36 (6 GF) S £117-£188 D £160-£225 (incl.
bkfst) **Facilities:** STV Wi-fi **Parking:** 26

This superbly restored Regency townhouse is in the city but feels just like a warm country house. Top priority is given to attention to detail and efficient room service in the luxurious bedrooms, including three with four-posters. The award-winning Ivy Brasserie complements the hotel's stylish character, serving classic brasserie dishes, making good use of locally sourced produce wherever possible. The charming Cellar Bar is a popular informal dining venue with both guests and local residents. First class facilities for business meetings, private dining, weddings and receptions are available.

Recommended in the area

York Minster; National Railway Museum; Castle Howard

York Marriott Hotel

★★★★ 77% HOTEL

Address: Tadcaster Road, YORK, YO24 1QQ
Tel: 01904 701000
Fax: 01904 702308
Email: mhrs.qqyyk.pa@marriotthotels.com
Website: www.yorkmarriott.co.uk
Map ref: 6, SE65
Directions: From A64 at York 'West' onto A1036,
follow signs to city centre. Approx 1.5m, hotel on
right after church and lights **Rooms:** 151 (27 GF)

(14 fmly) **Facilities:** STV Wi-fi ⊛ Tennis Spa Gym Sauna **Parking:** 160 **Notes:** ⊗ in bedrooms

Surrounded by five acres of beautiful landscaped gardens, the York Marriott is ideally located within walking distance of York's many attractions. The hotel's stylish accommodation includes some suites with private balconies and views of the gardens and racecourse. The recently refurbished leisure club has a heated pool, sauna, steam room, Jacuzzi, gym and tennis court. The new Chase Bar & Grill serves up locally sourced food, along with more of those fabulous racecourse views.

Recommended in the area

National Railway Museum; York Minster; York Racecourse

Stream in Goit Stock Wood

Best Western Mosborough Hall Hotel

★★★ 80% HOTEL

Address: High Street, Mosborough, SHEFFIELD,
S20 5EA

Tel: 0114 248 4353

Fax: 0114 247 9759

Email: hotel@mosboroughhall.co.uk

Website: www.mosboroughhall.co.uk

Map ref: 6, SK49 **Directions:** M1 junct 30, A6135 towards Sheffield. Follow Eckington/Mosborough signs 2m. Sharp bend at top of hill, hotel on right **Rooms:** 43 (16 GF) (4 fmly) **S** £49-£89 **D** £49-£89 **Facilities:** Wi-fi **Parking:** 100 **Notes:** ⊗ in bedrooms

Mosborough Hall is an imposing manor house dating back to the 15th century with, some say, a resident ghost. It is surrounded by four acres of peaceful grounds, yet is only a short distance from the centre of Sheffield. The hotel was refurbished in 2008 and has a range of stylish bedrooms.

Recommended in the area

Peak District National Park; Sheffield Arena; Meadowhall Shopping Centre

Best Western Rombalds Hotel

★★★ 83% ⊛ HOTEL

Address: 11 West View, Wells Road, ILKLEY,
LS29 9JG

Tel: 01943 603201

Fax: 01943 816586

Email: reception@rombalds.demon.co.uk

Website: www.rombalds.co.uk

Map ref: 7, SE14

Directions: A65 from Leeds. Left at 3rd main lights, follow Ilkley Moor signs. Right at HSBC Bank onto Wells Rd. Hotel 600yds on left

Rooms: 15 (2 fmly) **Facilities:** STV Wi-fi **Parking:** 28

Following Colin and Jo Clarkson's caring, extensive refurbishment Rombalds is a gracefully furnished, classic country-house hotel. Day rooms include delightful lounges and a much commended restaurant, offering a pleasing selection of local and international cuisine, and wines from around the world. Ideal for a weekend country break. The hotel also has facilities for wedding receptions.

Recommended in the area

Ilkley Moor; Yorkshire Dales National Park; Harewood House

CHANNEL ISLANDS

St Peter Port, Guernsey

La Barbarie Hotel

★★★ 80%  HOTEL

Address: Saints Road, Saints Bay, ST MARTIN, Guernsey, GY4 6ES
Tel: 01481 235217
Fax: 01481 235208
Email: reservations@labarbariehotel.com
Website: www.labarbariehotel.com
Map ref: 13
Rooms: 26 (8 GF) (3 fmly) S £57.50-£75 D £75-£126 (incl. bkfst) **Facilities:** Wi-fi 🕸
Parking: 50 **Notes:** ⊗ in bedrooms

This fine hotel is named after the Barbary Coast pirates who kidnapped and held to ransom the house's owner in the 17th century. A hotel since 1950, it lies in a peaceful green valley close to some of the lovely bays, coves and cliffs in the south of the island, and retains all of its historic charm, not least in the lovely residents' lounge, with its old beams and open fireplace. The en suite accommodation comes with every modern comfort, and includes some two-room suites with inter-connecting doors, ideal for families with children. Some self-catering apartments are also available, most of which overlook the heated swimming pool. Dining here is serious but far from pretentious, with praise coming from many corners, including the producer of one of Rick Stein's TV series, who remarked that the lobster he enjoyed at La Barbarie was the best he'd tasted in 15 years of travelling the world making food programmes. The fixed-price four-course dinner menu is very good value, while for something lighter you can choose from the bar or poolside menu. The poolside patio is the perfect secluded spot for a lazy lunch or quiet aperitif before dinner. The hotel is ideally placed for walkers, cyclists, horse riders and joggers.

Recommended in the area

Saumarez Manor; Castle Cornet; South Coast Cliff Path

The Duke of Richmond Hotel

★★★ 79% HOTEL

Address: Cambridge Park, ST PETER PORT,
Guernsey, GY1 1UY

Tel: 01481 726221

Fax: 01481 728945

Email: manager@dukeofrichmond.com

Website: www.dukeofrichmond.com

Map ref: 13

Directions: On corner of Cambridge Park &
L'Hyvreuse Ave, opposite leisure centre

Rooms: 75 (16 fmly) S £65-£87.50 D £95-£115 (incl. bkfst)

Facilities: STV Wi-fi ⸙ Parking: 6 Notes: ⊗ in bedrooms

Overlooking a quiet park but right in the heart of Guernsey's capital town of St Peter Port, The Duke of Richmond provides the perfect base for both leisure and business visitors to the island. It's a modern, purpose-built hotel, with 74 comfortable bedrooms and suites equipped with satellite TV, direct-dial telephone, trouser press, hairdryer and facilities for making hot drinks. Rooms have lovely views of either the park or the sea, some have balconies and there are some penthouse suites. Wi-fi is available throughout the hotel and there's 24-hour room service. The Cambridge Room Restaurant is an elegant space, serving international cuisine from a daily-changing fixed price dinner menu, as well as a la carte. In the summer months guests can take a dip in the outdoor pool, or simply relax on the sun-trap terrace with a drink from the cocktail bar while enjoying the stunning views over a tree covered valley towards the harbour. The Terrace Lounge is the place to head to for morning coffee or afternoon tea, while bar snacks at lunchtime and in the evening are served on the terrace or in the conservatory.

Recommended in the area

St Peter Port marina; St Peter Port shopping; Candie Gardens

Fermain Valley Hotel

★★★★ 78% HOTEL

Address: Fermain Lane, ST PETER PORT,
Guernsey, GY1 1ZZ
Tel: 01481 235666 & 0800 316 0314
Fax: 01481 235413
Email: info@fermainvalley.com
Website: www.fermainvalley.com
Map ref: 13
Directions: Turn left from airport, follow Forest Rd,
turn right onto Le Route de Sausmarez, then right
onto Fermain Lane
Rooms: 45 (6 GF) (1 fmly) **S** £90-£145 **D** £120-£230 (incl. bkfst)
Facilities: STV Wi-fi ✥ Sauna **Parking:** 40 **Notes:** ✖ in bedrooms

Peaceful and secluded yet conveniently situated just five minutes from Guernsey's charming harbour capital, St Peter Port, the four-star Fermain Valley Hotel offers the perfect place for a relaxing break. The hotel has 45 exquisitely decorated bedrooms, all unique and designed with comfort in mind. A long list of thoughtful in-room extras includes bathrobes, fridge, flat-screen TV, wireless broadband, hairdryer, sherry decanter and complimentary tea and coffee. Some rooms even benefit from private balconies. The Palm Court is the hotel's fine dining restaurant, while the Valley Brasserie offers a more relaxed alternative and boasts an outside decking area with stunning views down the valley and out to sea. The hotel also has an indoor heated pool and sauna, a residents' private cinema showing the latest films, complimentary wireless broadband access throughout, and ample facilities for meetings and functions. The Fermain Valley's friendly staff are dedicated to providing the very highest standards of personal service, whether your stay is for business or pleasure. Special offers and breaks are also available.

Recommended in the area

Castle Cornet; tax-free shopping

The Farmhouse Hotel

★★★★ 80% ⊛ SMALL HOTEL

Address: Route Des Bas Courtils, ST SAVIOUR,
Guernsey, GY7 9YF
Tel: 01481 264181
Fax: 01481 266272
Email: enquiries@thefarmhouse.gg
Website: www.thefarmhouse.gg
Map ref: 13
Directions: From airport, left to 1st lights. Left then
left again around runway perimeter. After 1m left at

x-rds. Hotel 100mtrs on right **Rooms:** 14 (7 fmly) **S** £110-£200 **D** £140-£250 (incl. bkfst)
Facilities: STV Wi-fi ⌁ **Parking:** 80 **Notes:** ⊗ in bedrooms

Created from a 15th century farmhouse, this smart yet informal hideaway sits in extensive grounds
in the parish of St Saviour, in the heart of rural Guernsey. Now run by the second generation of the
Nussbaumer family, the emphasis here is on warm hospitality and fine service. The hotel has been
refurbished throughout in a contemporary country-house style, and each of the 14 rooms and suites is
beautifully furnished, with state-of-the-art bathrooms and all the modern luxuries you'd expect. There's
free wireless internet access available throughout the building, and in the summer you can work up
an appetite for dinner in the outdoor pool or on one of the many countryside or cliff walks nearby. The
pretty gardens are perfect for a pre or post prandial stroll, too. During the warmer months you can
dine al fresco on the patio, while in winter log fires blaze in the comfy lounges. The Farmhouse is a
destination in itself for dining on the island, and the head chef and his team present an adventurous
menu full of unexpected flavours along with traditional favourites. Ingredients are always fresh and
mostly local and organic, including plenty of local seafood.

Recommended in the area

Bruce Russell & Son goldsmiths; The Little Chapel; German Occupation Museum

Jerbourg Point, Guernsey

Somerville Hotel

★★★★ 77% ◉◉ HOTEL

Address: Mont du Boulevard, ST AUBIN, Jersey, JE3 8AD
Tel: 01534 491906
Fax: 01534 499574
Email: somerville@dolanhotels.com
Website: www.dolanhotels.com
Map ref: 13
Directions: from village, follow harbour into Mont du Boulevard
Rooms: 56 (4 GF) S £65-£145
D £80-£189 (incl. bkfst) **Facilities:** STV Wi-fi ⚲
Parking: 26 **Notes:** ⊗ in bedrooms ⌖ under 4 yrs

Nestling on the hillside, overlooking the yachting harbour, the village of St Aubin and the bay beyond, the views from the Somerville Hotel are breathtaking. The Somerville has an excellent reputation as one of Jersey's finest hotels, where a warm welcome is always guaranteed. Most of the comfortable and tastefully furnished bedrooms enjoy spectacular sea views, as does the Tides Restaurant. Jersey has earned a worldwide reputation for the quality of its dining and Tides Restaurant at the Somerville Hotel is no exception. Awarded two AA Rosettes for its cooking and with those panoramic views over the harbour, the Somerville offers a memorable dining experience. Lunch on the terrace is particularly popular. Enjoy a pre or post-dinner drink in the cocktail bar, or simply relax and unwind with coffee in the lounge. Following the completion of a two-year refurbishment, which included extending the Somerville's conference and banqueting facilities, the hotel now offers a choice of three meeting rooms, two of which benefit from natural light and have spectacular views as a perfect backdrop. The hotel is just five minutes' walk from the sandy expanse of St. Aubin's Bay and the sheltered cove of Belcroute Beach.

Recommended in the area

Durrell Wildlife Conservation Trust; Elizabeth Castle; Jersey War Tunnels

The Club Hotel & Spa

★★★★ ◎◎◎◎ HOTEL

Bohemia's Chefs Table

Address: Green Street, ST HELIER, Jersey, JE2 4UH
Tel: 01534 876500
Fax: 01534 720371
Email: reservations@theclubjersey.com
Website: www.theclubjersey.com
Map ref: 13
Directions: 5 mins walk from main shopping centre
Rooms: 46 (4 GF) (4 fmly) S £130-£215
D £130-£215 (incl. bkfst) **Facilities:** STV Wi-fi ⊠ �
Spa Sauna **Parking:** 30 **Notes:** ⊗ in bedrooms

This swish, townhouse hotel in the centre of Jersey's capital features stylish, contemporary decor throughout. The fully air-conditioned bedrooms and suites have large, full-height windows opening on to a balustrade, while the beds are dressed with Frette Egyptian cotton sheets and duck-down duvets. All rooms are equipped with safes, flat-screen TVs, DVD/CD players, Bang & Olufsen portable phones and private bars. Granite bathrooms include power showers, robes, slippers and aromatherapy products. Free Wi-fi access is available throughout the hotel. The dining choice includes the award-winning Bohemia Bar and Restaurant, where a typical main course might be roast local turbot with braised frog's leg, minted peas, herb gnocchi and chicken emulsion. Overlooking the outdoor pool is The Club Café, a contemporary New York-style restaurant offering breakfast, light lunches and dinner. Several hours might easily be spent in The Spa, starting with a swim in the salt pool, followed by mud treatment in the rasul (a traditional Arabian ritual cleansing) room, and finally a spell on one of the luxurious loungers. Two luxury meeting rooms with oak tables and leather chairs can accommodate 50 theatre style or up to 32 as a boardroom.

Recommended in the area

German Underground Hospital; Jersey Zoo; Mount Orgeuil

Grand Jersey

★★★★ 79% ◉◉◉ HOTEL

Address: The Esplanade, ST HELIER, Jersey,
JE2 3QA
Tel: 01534 722301
Fax: 01534 737815
Email: reservations@grandjersey.com
Website: www.grandjersey.com
Map ref: 13
Rooms: 123 (6 GF) (53 fmly)
Facilities: STV Wi-fi ⊗ Spa Gym Sauna **Parking:** 30
Notes: ⊗ in bedrooms

Grand Jersey, sitting in a prime spot on St Helier's seafront, is a stunning hotel and spa presenting guests with an exceptional experience. Having undergone a multi-million-pound refurbishment in recent years, it offers supremely comfortable accommodation, sophisticated restaurants, the exclusive and atmospheric Champagne Lounge, and a luxurious, award-winning spa. The hotel also has a dedicated and innovative business centre - the Park Suites - complete with private cinema, meeting rooms and flexible events spaces. Grand Jersey's glamorous fine dining restaurant, Tassili, holds three AA Rosettes and offers exquisite modern European cooking using the very best seasonal Jersey produce. For a more informal alternative, head to the hotel's main restaurant Victorias. Here, in a chic and relaxed setting, you can enjoy the perfect brasserie experience, from laid back Sunday lunches to high quality comfort food. If a spot of pampering appeals during your stay on the island, then you've come to the right place. Spa at Grand Jersey was recognised as 'UK Residential Spa of the Year' in the Professional Beauty Awards 2009. With its range of VIP, twin and single treatment rooms, indoor heated pool and experience showers, it's plain to see why.

Recommended in the area

St Helier shopping; St Aubin's Bay; Durrell Wildlife Conservation Trust

Longueville Manor Hotel

★★★★★ ◉◉◉ HOTEL

Address: ST SAVIOUR, Jersey, JE2 7WF
Tel: 01534 725501
Fax: 01534 731613
Email: info@longuevillemanor.com
Website: www.longuevillemanor.com
Map ref: 13
Directions: A3 E from St Helier towards Gorey.
Hotel 1m on left
Rooms: 30 (7 GF) **S** £185-£380 **D** £210-£600 (incl.
bkfst) **Facilities:** STV Wi-fi ⌇ Tennis **Parking:** 40

For more than 60 years this charming hotel has been run by the Lewis family, and is currently owned by Malcolm and Patricia Lewis. The refurbished 14th-century manor house is set in its own wooded valley, with 15 acres of grounds including vibrant flower gardens and a lake complete with black swans, yet is only five minutes from St Helier. The hotel is stylishly presented, with warm colour schemes, fine antique furnishings and lavish floral displays. The tranquil location, historic setting and excellent food invite complete relaxation, with a tennis court and a heated swimming pool to enjoy, plus a poolside bar and barbecue. The bedrooms are each named after a type of rose and come with a chaise longue, Egyptian cotton sheets, wide-screen TV and DVD/CD player, cordless phone, fruit, flowers and home-made biscuits. Additional in-room equipment includes a safe, hairdryer, iron and ironing board, and rooms on the ground floor have a private patio overlooking the garden. The hotel's restored Victorian kitchen garden provides abundantly for the dining room, including delicacies from the Victorian glass houses. The restaurant offers a fine dining experience with a Master Sommelier to advise on wines.

Recommended in the area

Royal Jersey Golf Club; Durrell Wildlife Conservation Trust; Mont Orgeuil Castle

SCOTLAND

Loch Katrine, Loch Lomond and the Trossachs National Park

Falls of Lora Hotel

★★★ 77% HOTEL
Address: CONNEL, By Oban, PA37 1PB
Tel: 01631 710483
Fax: 01631 710694
Email: enquiries@fallsoflora.com
Website: www.fallsoflora.com
Map ref: 9, NM93
Directions: From Glasgow take A82, A85. Hotel
0.5m past Connel sign, 5m before Oban
Rooms: 30 (4 GF) (4 fmly) S £47.50-£59.50
D £55-£139 (incl. bkfst) Facilities: Wi-fi Parking: 40

This Victorian owner-run hotel enjoys views over the hotel gardens (across the road), Loch Etive and the Connel Bridge. The ground floor includes a comfortable traditional lounge and cocktail bar with open log fires, offering more than 100 whiskies. Well-equipped bedrooms come in a variety of styles, ranging from cosy standard doubles to high quality luxury suite-type rooms. Guests may eat in the comfortable and attractive Bistro and in the evening there is an exciting and varied menu.
Recommended in the area
Oban Distillery; Iona Abbey; Ben Nevis

Taychreggan Hotel

★★★ 85% ⬡⬡ COUNTRY HOUSE HOTEL
Address: KILCHRENAN, Taynuilt, PA35 1HQ
Tel: 01866 833211 & 833366
Fax: 01866 833244
Email: info@taychregganhotel.co.uk
Website: www.taychregganhotel.co.uk
Map ref: 9, NN02 Directions: W from Crianlarich
on A85 to Taynuilt, S for 7m on B845 (single track)
to Kilchrenan Rooms: 18 S £85-£167 D £110-£274
(incl. bkfst) Facilities: Wi-fi Parking: 40

Taychreggan Hotel is a romantic 300-year-old drover's inn situated on the shores of Loch Awe. The hotel's 18 comfy rooms have breathtaking views of Scotland's longest inland loch from most windows. Enjoy cuisine to tempt the robust appetite, fine wines and a dram or two from Taychreggan's shamefully large selection of malt whiskies. Snooker, sailing (boats are available on site), fishing rights, clay pigeon shooting and hawk handling are all available. Or you could just relax in an overstuffed armchair looking out across the loch and enjoy a spot of afternoon tea.
Recommended in the area
Inverary Castle; Cruachan Power Station; Oban War Museum

Manor House Hotel

★★★ 83% ⊛ HOTEL

Address: Gallanach Road, OBAN, PA34 4LS
Tel: 01631 562087
Fax: 01631 563053
Email: info@manorhouseoban.com
Website: www.manorhouseoban.com
Map ref: 9, NM93
Directions: follow MacBrayne Ferries signs, pass
ferry entrance for hotel on right
Rooms: 11 (1 GF) **S** £95-£160 **D** £108-£193 (incl.
bkfst) **Facilities:** Wi-fi **Parking:** 20

Built in 1780, the Manor House was the principal residence of the Duke of Argyll's Oban estate.
Featuring late Georgian architecture, great consideration has been given to preserving its elegance,
charm and atmosphere. All bedrooms have been tastefully decorated in the period style and include
every modern amenity. The beautifully restored Dining Room is open both to residents and non-
residents each evening. This, and the Drawing Room have magnificent views over Oban Bay.

Recommended in the area
Morvern Mountains; Isle of Mull

Balcary Bay Hotel

★★★ 86% ⊛⊛ HOTEL

Address: AUCHENCAIRN, DG7 1QZ
Tel: 01556 640217 & 640311
Fax: 01556 640272
Email: reservations@balcary-bay-hotel.co.uk
Website: www.balcary-bay-hotel.co.uk
Map ref: 7, NX75 **Directions:** On A711 between
Dalbeattie & Kirkcudbright, hotel 2m from village
Rooms: 20 (3 GF) (1 fmly) **S** £71 **D** £126-£156 (incl.
bkfst) **Parking:** 50

The hotel lawns run down to the edge of the beautiful bay from which it takes its name, and from many
rooms there are magnificent views; either across the Solway Firth to the beautiful peaks of the Lake
District, or over the gardens. No longer a haunt of smugglers, as it was in the 17th century, the hotel
still retains much of its old character. The award-winning cuisine is based on local Scottish ingredients
such as prime Galloway beef, lamb, lobsters, prawns and Balcary Bay salmon. A bistro-style lunch
menu is available every day, and the wine list is extensive.

Recommended in the area
East Stewartry Coast; Threave Garden (NT); Loch Ken

Best Western Station Hotel

★★★ 79% HOTEL

Address: 49 Lovers Walk, DUMFRIES, DG1 1LT
Tel: 01387 254316
Fax: 01387 250388
Email: info@stationhotel.co.uk
Website: www.stationhotel.co.uk
Map ref: 7, NX97 **Directions:** A75, follow signs to Dumfries town centre, hotel opp railway station
Rooms: 32 (2 fmly) **S** £50-£75 **D** £80-£120 (incl. bkfst) **Parking:** 34

So-named because it's just across the road from the train station, this friendly, traditional Victorian hotel makes the perfect base for exploring beautiful Dumfries and Galloway. The Best Western Station Hotel is just five minutes' walk from the town centre and within easy reach of stunning coastal and countryside scenery, castles, golf courses and tourist attractions. There are 32 comfortable en suite rooms. Home-cooked food is on offer in the restaurant, an impressive single malt whisky collection in the bar, and in the summer you can relax in the patio garden complete with pretty fountain.

Recommended in the area

Gretna Green's Smithy; Tullie House Museum & Art Gallery; Carlisle Castle and Cathedral

Cavens

★★ ◉ COUNTRY HOUSE HOTEL

Address: KIRKBEAN, DG2 8AA
Tel: 01387 880234
Fax: 01387 880467
Email: enquiries@cavens.com
Website: www.cavens.com **Map ref:** 5, NX95
Directions: Enter Kirkbean on A710, hotel signed
Rooms: 5 (1 GF) **S** £80-£150 **D** £80-£240 (incl. bkfst) **Parking:** 12 **Notes:** ⚞ under 12 yrs

Set within six acres of beautiful grounds, this rural retreat is in a charming village just minutes from the picturesque Solway coast and perfectly placed for exploring the attractions of south-west Scotland. Cavens has stylish and comfortable bedrooms that provide total relaxation, and there's a choice of two peaceful lounges in which to relax and soak up the charming country house atmosphere. Chef-proprietor Angus Fordyce offers daily-changing menus of unpretentious dishes that are full of flavour, based on such quality local produce as Galloway beef and lamb, served in a spacious and elegant dining room overlooking the front lawn.

Recommended in the area

Threave House and Gardens; Dumfries House; Kirkcudbright Artists' Town

Corsewall Lighthouse Hotel

★★★ 78% HOTEL

Address: Corsewall Point, Kirkcolm, STRANRAER,
DG9 0QG

Tel: 01776 853220

Fax: 01776 854231

Email: info@lighthousehotel.co.uk

Website: www.lighthousehotel.co.uk

Map ref: 5, NX06

Directions: A718 from Stranraer to Kirkcolm
(approx 8m). Follow hotel signs for 4m

Rooms: 10 (2 GF) (4 fmly) **S** £130-£150 **D** £150-£250 (incl. bkfst & dinner)

Parking: 20

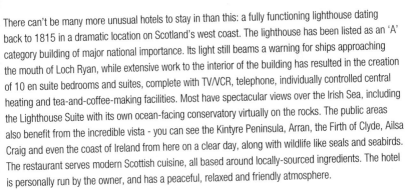

There can't be many more unusual hotels to stay in than this: a fully functioning lighthouse dating back to 1815 in a dramatic location on Scotland's west coast. The lighthouse has been listed as an 'A' category building of major national importance. Its light still beams a warning for ships approaching the mouth of Loch Ryan, while extensive work to the interior of the building has resulted in the creation of 10 en suite bedrooms and suites, complete with TV/VCR, telephone, individually controlled central heating and tea-and-coffee-making facilities. Most have spectacular views over the Irish Sea, including the Lighthouse Suite with its own ocean-facing conservatory virtually on the rocks. The public areas also benefit from the incredible vista - you can see the Kintyre Peninsula, Arran, the Firth of Clyde, Ailsa Craig and even the coast of Ireland from here on a clear day, along with wildlife like seals and seabirds. The restaurant serves modern Scottish cuisine, all based around locally-sourced ingredients. The hotel is personally run by the owner, and has a peaceful, relaxed and friendly atmosphere.

Recommended in the area

Coastal walks; golf; bird watching

Edinburgh Royal Mile, the crown spire of St Giles Cathedral

The Balmoral

★★★★★ 88% ◉◉◉ HOTEL

Address: 1 Princes Street, EDINBURGH, EH2 2EQ
Tel: 0131 556 2414
Fax: 0131 557 3747
Email: reservations.balmoral@
roccofortecollection.com
Website: www.roccofortecollection.com
Map ref: 10, NT27 **Directions:** follow city centre
signs. Hotel at E end of Princes St, adjacent to
Waverley Station **Rooms:** 188 (22 fmly) **S** £305-
£2000 **D** £360-£2000 **Facilities:** STV Wi-fi ⊗ Spa Gym Sauna **Parking:** 100 **Notes:** ⊗ in bedrooms

The Balmoral is more than a hotel, it's an Edinburgh landmark, thanks to the majestic clocktower
that is a feature of the city skyline. Built as a traditional railway hotel, its public areas, conference and
banqueting suites, and stylish bedrooms have been beautifully refurbished to designs by Sir Rocco
Forte's sister, Olga Polizzi. Each room is individually decorated in the muted hues of Scottish moors,
mists and heathers. All are equipped with two phone lines, fax-modem, broadband, interactive national
and satellite TV, in-room refreshments, air conditioning, and spacious marble and ceramic bathroom
with fluffy towels, robes and other luxuries. Some look towards Edinburgh Castle, some the Old Town,
and some over the courtyard. When it comes to eating and drinking, guests can choose between
the attentive but non-intrusive service in number one, with outstanding cuisine by chef Jeff Bland;
Hadrian's Brasserie for chic and informal dining; The Bollinger Bar at Palm Court for champagne or
afternoon tea, or The Balmoral Bar for a relaxing whisky or cocktail. Enjoy the facilities in the award-
winning Balmoral Spa including a 15-metre swimming pool and fully equipped gym, as well as ESPA,
Ytsara and ghd spa treatments.

Recommended in the area

Palace of Holyroodhouse; St Giles Cathedral; Royal Mile

Edinburgh Castle and St Cuthbert's Church

Prestonfield

★★★★★ ⚜⚜ TOWN HOUSE HOTEL

Address: Priestfield Road, EDINBURGH, EH16 5UT
Tel: 0131 225 7800
Fax: 0131 220 4392
Email: reservations@prestonfield.com
Website: www.prestonfield.com
Map ref: 10, NT27
Directions: A7 towards Cameron Toll. 200mtrs beyond Royal Commonwealth Pool, into Priestfield Rd
Rooms: 23 (6 GF) **S** £225-£275 **D** £225-£275 (incl. bkfst)
Facilities: STV Wi-fi **Parking:** 250

Many commentators have sprinkled their reviews of this celebrated city centre hotel, a 17th-century mansion, with words such as 'opulent', 'indulgent' and 'Baroque extravaganza'. So when James Thomson, the creative force behind Prestonfield and other prestigious Scottish restaurants, calls it the 'ultimate retort to minimalism', a picture begins to take shape. Interiors are gilded, brocaded and velvet-covered, and to the fine art and antique furnishings Thomson has added a quixotic assortment of finds from European auction rooms. Bedrooms and suites have discreet technology, including air conditioning, high-speed internet, Bose sound system and flat-screen TV. Bed linen is by Frette and there are luxurious bathrobes, fresh flowers and exclusive toiletries. The unusually named Rhubarb restaurant is split between a pair of grand oval Regency rooms. Here, exceptional cooking might include smoked salmon with Beluga caviar, fillet of Black gold beef, and Lindisfarne oysters, not to mention the famed rhubarb desserts, and a choice of wines from the much-praised cellars.

Recommended in the area

Museum of Scotland; Scottish Parliament (Palace of Holyroodhouse); Edinburgh Castle

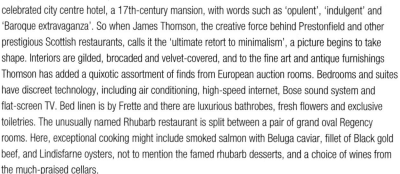

The Witchery by the Castle

★★★★★ 🏵 RESTAURANT WITH ROOMS
Address: 352 Castlehill, The Royal Mile,
EDINBURGH, EH1 2NF
Tel: 0131 225 5613
Fax: 0131 220 4392
Email: mail@thewitchery.com
Website: www.thewitchery.com
Map ref: 10, NT27 **Directions:** Top of Royal Mile
Rooms: 8 (1 GF) **S** £295 **D** £295 (incl. bkfst)
Facilities: STV **Notes:** ⊗ in bedrooms

Many hotels purport to be unique, but nowhere lives up to the claim quite like The Witchery. Standing at the gates of Edinburgh Castle, it is totally unlike any other hotel and the term 'fantastic' can be used in its most literal sense here, with rooms that are both dramatic and decadent. Gothic excess is all around, in features such as velvet-lined bedroom walls, antique four-poster beds, tapestries and deeply sensuous colour schemes. Bathrooms, clearly designed for togetherness, are stunning too, perhaps oak-panelled or lacquered; chapel-like in the Old Rectory suite; book-lined and hidden behind a secret door in the Library room. Little wonder that this is a favourite place to stay for A-list UK and Hollywood celebrities. In the restaurant the emphasis is on the very best Scottish produce, such as fully traceable Angus beef, game and seafood. Lunch, dinner and theatre suppers are available. Main courses on a typical menu might include saddle and smoked haunch of Speyside venison with squash purée, turnip and potato gratin and chocolate oil; braised Borders oxtail with seared foie gras, Savoy cabbage and celeriac mousseline; and fillet of monkfish with picante chorizo, baby octopus and Loch Fyne mussel stew. The renowned wine list numbers almost 1,000 expertly chosen wines.

Recommended in the area

Edinburgh Castle; National Museum of Scotland; National Gallery Complex

Moorings Hotel

★★★ 80% ◉ HOTEL

Address: Banavie, FORT WILLIAM, PH33 7LY
Tel: 01397 772797
Fax: 01397 772441
Email: reservations@moorings-fortwilliam.co.uk
Website: www.moorings-fortwilliam.co.uk
Map ref: 12, NN17
Directions: take A830 (N from Fort William), cross Caledonian Canal, 1st right
Rooms: 27 (1 GF) (1 fmly) **S** £43-£116 **D** £86-£142 (incl. bkfst) **Facilities:** STV Wi-fi **Parking:** 60

Alongside the famous Neptune's Staircase on the Caledonian Canal, this hotel offers high standards of accommodation and panoramic views, which take in not only the canal, but also Aonach Mor and the UK's highest mountain, Ben Nevis. Each of the bedrooms is individually designed, and an upgrade has created some superior rooms, all of which have wonderful views and spacious living areas. All the bedrooms have satellite TV channels, a hospitality tray and direct-dial telephones, and videos and video players are available in the family rooms. The formal Jacobean Restaurant has also been refurbished, and its team of chefs offer a menu featuring fresh west coast seafood and Highland game. More casual dining is offered in the split-level Upper Deck Lounge Bar, which overlooks the canal and Ben Nevis. The extensive bar menu ranges from simple snacks to hot dishes such as fisherman's creel pie, salmon with penne pasta, and chicken stuffed with haggis. On summer evenings guests can mingle with the loyal local clientele that frequent the Mariners Cellar Bar, which has a lively and informal pub atmosphere and nautical decor. Summer also sees the hotel's secluded garden at its best.

Recommended in the area

West Highland Museum; Ben Nevis Distillery; Jacobite Steam Train

Kincraig Castle Hotel

★★★★ 78%  COUNTRY HOUSE HOTEL

Address: INVERGORDON, IV18 0LF
Tel: 01349 852587
Fax: 01349 852193
Email: info@kincraig-house-hotel.co.uk
Website: www.kincraig-house-hotel.co.uk
Map ref: 12, NH76
Directions: off A9 past Alness towards Tain. Hotel on left 0.25m past Rosskeen Church
Rooms: 15 (1 GF) (1 fmly) **S** £65-£150 **D** £80-£300 (incl. bkfst) **Facilities:** STV Wi-fi **Parking:** 30

Kincraig Castle Hotel is proud to be one of the most elegant country houses in the Highlands, set in the beautiful countryside with views of the Cromarty Firth. There is much to enjoy in the area, which boasts some of Scotland's finest golf courses, distilleries, castles and beaches. Special golf breaks are available at Kincraig, including two nights' dinner, bed and breakfast with two rounds of golf at Tain and/or Fortrose and Rosemarkie. The hotel, which is just off the A9, is also within striking distance of Inverness, capital of the Highlands, and the world famous Loch Ness. Moulded ceilings, fireplaces and oak panelling create a warm, inviting atmosphere inside the hotel. Three styles of bedrooms are offered - Premier, Executive and Classic, with the larger Premier rooms overlooking the gardens. A turreted room with a colonial bed or a four-poster room is the ideal choice for a special occasion; this has a fully tiled en suite bathroom with a corner bath and separate shower. The beautifully appointed restaurant serves locally caught seafood, game dishes and other local produce, and from here there are views across the gardens to the Cromarty Firth.

Recommended in the area

Dunrobin Castle; Falls of Shin; Tain and Dornoch golf courses

Glenmoriston Town House Hotel

★★★★ 74% ◉◉◉ HOTEL
Address: 20 Ness Bank, INVERNESS, IV2 4SF
Tel: 01463 223777
Fax: 01463 712378
Email: reception@glenmoristontownhouse.com
Website: www.glenmoristontownhouse.com
Map ref: 12, NH64
Directions: On riverside opposite theatre
Rooms: 30 (6 GF) (1 fmly) **Facilities:** STV Wi-fi
Parking: 40 **Notes:** ⊗ in bedrooms

The Glenmoriston Town House is close to the city centre and enjoys charming views of the River Ness. The hotel's bold contemporary designs blend seamlessly with its original classical architecture. The smart, well-proportioned and refurbished bedrooms all have Wi-fi access and many of the rooms look out towards the river, as does the one Rosetted Contrast Brasserie. The refined French restaurant Abstract has three AA Rosettes and gives top priority to Scottish produce prepared by international award-winning chefs.

Recommended in the area
Culloden Battlefield; Loch Ness; Cawdor Castle

Grants at Craigellachie

★★★★ ◉ RESTAURANT WITH ROOMS
Address: Craigellachie, Ratagan, GLENSHIEL,
IV40 8HP
Tel: 01599 511331
Email: info@housebytheloch.co.uk
Website: www.housebytheloch.co.uk
Map ref: 11, NG91 **Directions:** From A87 turn to
Glenelg, 1st right to Ratagan, opp Youth Hostel sign
Rooms: 4 (3 GF) D £150-£220
Facilities Wi-fi **Parking** 8 **Notes** ⚫ under 12 yrs.
Closed Dec-mid Feb. Reservations only Oct-Apr

Sitting on the tranquil shores of Loch Duich and overlooked by mountains, including the famous Five Sisters of Kintail, this popular restaurant with rooms has a stunning location. With a well deserved reputation for fine wine and excellent food, and bedrooms that are stylish and equipped with all the creature comforts, Grants makes the perfect base for exploring the local area and the rest of the Scottish Highlands beyond. The menu changes daily and is rooted in fantastic, fresh local produce.

Recommended in the area
Eilean Donan Castle: Glenelg Brochs; Camusfearna

Dunrobin Castle

The Glenmorangie Highland Home at Cadboll

★★★ ◉◉ COUNTRY HOUSE HOTEL

Address: Cadboll, Fearn, TAIN, IV20 1XP
Tel: 01862 871671
Fax: 01862 871625
Email: relax@glenmorangieplc.co.uk
Website: www.theglenmorangiehouse.com
Map ref: 12, NH88

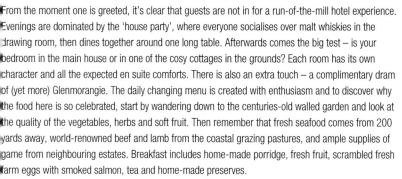

Directions: From A9 onto B9175 towards Nigg. Follow tourist signs
Rooms: 9 (3 GF) (4 fmly) **Facilities:** Wi-fi **Parking:** 60 **Notes:** ⊗ in bedrooms ⊁ under 14 yrs

From the moment one is greeted, it's clear that guests are not in for a run-of-the-mill hotel experience. Evenings are dominated by the 'house party', where everyone socialises over malt whiskies in the drawing room, then dines together around one long table. Afterwards comes the big test – is your bedroom in the main house or in one of the cosy cottages in the grounds? Each room has its own character and all the expected en suite comforts. There is also an extra touch – a complimentary dram of (yet more) Glenmorangie. The daily changing menu is created with enthusiasm and to discover why the food here is so celebrated, start by wandering down to the centuries-old walled garden and look at the quality of the vegetables, herbs and soft fruit. Then remember that fresh seafood comes from 200 yards away, world-renowned beef and lamb from the coastal grazing pastures, and ample supplies of game from neighbouring estates. Breakfast includes home-made porridge, fresh fruit, scrambled fresh farm eggs with smoked salmon, tea and home-made preserves.

Recommended in the area

Dunrobin Castle; Falls of Shin; Dornoch Cathedral

Culdearn House

★★ 85% 🏵 SMALL HOTEL

Address: Woodlands Terrace,
GRANTOWN-ON-SPEY, PH26 3JU
Tel: 01479 872106
Fax: 01479 873641
Email: enquiries@culdearn.com
Website: www.culdearn.com
Map ref: 12, NJ03
Directions: from SW into Grantown on A95,
left at 30mph sign, hotel opposite

Rooms: 6 (1 GF) **S** £89 **D** £126 (incl. bkfst) **Parking:** 12 **Notes:** ⊗ in bedrooms 🚼 under 12 yrs

This Scottish Victorian granite house is set in its own grounds on the edge of woodland, yet is within walking distance of the centre of Grantown-on-Spey. There are just six bedrooms here; each is individually and elegantly styled to combine antique and contemporary features. The relaxing lounge has a collection of more than 60 specially selected malt whiskies to sample, perhaps after a meal beside the log fire in the candlelit dining room, where the finest Scottish fare is served.

Recommended in the Area

The Whisky Trail; Cairngorms National Park; Strathspey Railway

Inver Lodge Hotel

★★★★ 🏵🏵 HOTEL

Address: LOCHINVER, IV27 4LU
Tel: 01571 844496
Fax: 01571 844395
Email: stay@inverlodge.com
Website: www.inverlodge.com
Map ref: 12, NC02
Directions: A835 to Lochinver, through village, left
after village hall, follow private road for 0.5m
Rooms: 21 (11 GF) **S** £110 **D** £200 (incl. bkfst)
Facilities: Wi-fi Sauna **Parking:** 30

The Inver Lodge offers a tranquil retreat in spectacular surroundings. A blazing log fire warms the residents' lounge during afternoon tea, a card game, or the inevitable 'post mortem' following a day's fishing. The kitchen takes full advantage of abundant local produce, preparing such topographically named dishes as Kyle of Tongue scallops, Lochinver-landed sea bass or Stornoway black pudding. Head for bed in one of the comfortably equipped rooms, all named after local mountains and lochs.

Recommended in the area

Eas Caul Aulin Waterfall; Handa Island (RSPB); Knockan Cliff Nature Trail

Cairngorms National Park

Dalmunzie Castle Hotel

★★★ 81% ◉◉ COUNTRY HOUSE HOTEL

Address: SPITTAL OF GLENSHEE, Blairgowrie, PH10 7QG
Tel: 01250 885224
Fax: 01250 885225
Email: reservations@dalmunzie.com
Website: www.dalmunzie.com
Map ref: 10, NO17
Directions: on A93 at Spittal of Glenshee, follow signs to hotel
Rooms: 17 (2 fmly) **S** £65-£125 **D** £140-£270 (incl. bkfst & dinner)
Facilities: STV Wi-fi Tennis Golf **Parking:** 40 **Notes:** ⊗ in bedrooms

Scott and Brianna Poole had been searching for a quintessential Scottish property for years; in 2004 they found Dalmunzie. With circular turrets and pointed roofs, this Scottish Baronial-style, former laird's manor house stands proudly at the head of a 500-year-old, 6,500-acre estate. Magnificent Highland scenery surrounds it, yet Edinburgh, Glasgow, Aberdeen and Inverness are only about two hours' drive away. Peace is guaranteed in the various lounges, library and bar. The bedrooms are spread throughout the castle – in the Hunting Lodge, the Tower, and the Victorian and Edwardian wings. Breakfast is taken in either the sun-room, with Ben Earb visible through its windows, or in the Dining Room, overlooking the front lawn; lunch may be eaten more or less wherever you like. Dinner is a deliberately slow-paced affair to enable full appreciation of the 'traditional estate/country house' cuisine. Ingredients are extensively drawn from the surrounding area, and the menu changes daily. Wine list descriptions are insightful, and the whisky enthusiast can choose from over 80 single malts. The active can try golf, tennis, mountain-biking, fishing, stalking and walking, for which the options are infinite.

Recommended in the area

Balmoral; Glamis Castle; Edradour Distillery

The Four Seasons Hotel

★★★ 83% ◉◉ HOTEL

Address: Loch Earn, ST FILLANS, PH6 2NF
Tel: 01764 685333
Fax: 01764 685444
Email: info@thefourseasonshotel.co.uk
Website: www.thefourseasonshotel.co.uk
Map ref: 9, NN62
Directions: on A85, towards W of village
Rooms: 18 (7 fmly) S £55-£90 D £110-£130 (incl. bkfst) **Facilities:** Wi-fi **Parking:** 40

Of countless highly desirable hotel settings in Scotland, this is unquestionably in the upper echelons. Looking south west down beautiful Loch Earn, the views are almost too good to be true – they include spectacular sunsets, morning mists and snow-covered mountains. Built in the 1800s for the manager of the local limekilns, the house has been extended over the years to become today's small but exceedingly comfortable hotel, with several individual sitting rooms, a choice of bedrooms and, out on the wooded hillside at the rear, six comfortable and well-equipped chalets. All bedrooms are spacious, most with bath and shower, and many have uninterrupted views down the loch. The chalets have a double or twin room and a bunk room making them ideal for family use. When eating, choose between the more formal Meall Reamhar Room or the Tarken Room. Both offer the same high standard of contemporary Scottish cuisine, with much, as you might expect, coming from local sources. Rabbit and pistachio terrine, Scrabster king scallops, Angus Limousin beef, and pressed dark chocolate cake are typical of the fare. A large selection of malts is stocked in the bar. Dog owners will be gratified to know that resident canine Sham welcomes his cousins; he'll even tolerate cats, parrots and gerbils, depending on his current humour.

Recommended in the area

Loch Lomond & the Trossachs National Park; Stirling Castle; Famous Grouse Experience

The Horseshoe Inn

★ ★ ★ ★ ❀ ❀ ❀

RESTAURANT WITH ROOMS
Address: EDDLESTON, Peebles, EH45 8QP
Tel: 01721 730225
Fax: 01721 730268
Email: reservations@horseshoeinn.co.uk
Website: www.horseshoeinn.co.uk
Map ref: 10, NT24
Directions: A703, 5m N of Peebles
Rooms: 8 (6 GF) (1 fmly) **S** £70 **D** £100 (incl. bkfst)
Facilities: Wi-fi **Parking:** 20

Just half-an-hour from Edinburgh, this former blacksmith's (smiddy in the local vernacular) is situated in the quiet village of Eddleston in the beautiful Scottish Borders. It was transformed some four years ago into one of the most appealing restaurants in the area. In the Lodge (formerly the village's Victorian primary school) at the rear of the inn, are the individually designed bedrooms. There are five double rooms, two twin rooms and a family room – each one delightfully appointed and very chic. Co-owner (with wife Vivienne) and head chef Patrick Bardoulet revels in having his own restaurant, where he and his team use the freshest local ingredients to create regularly changing lunch and dinner menus. The result? Award-winning, high quality classical French cuisine, typified by wild grouse fillet soufflé with Scottish mushroom, confit root vegetables and Cassis jus and Valrhona chocolate soufflé, mandarin espuma and mandarin sorbet. Over 100 European and New World wines are offered in both the restaurant and the bar/bistro. Guests come back time and time again to this gem of a place.

Recommended in the area

Edinburgh Castle; Edinburgh Crystal Visitor Centre; Scottish Textiles Museum

Lochgreen House Hotel

★★★★ ◉◉◉ COUNTRY HOUSE HOTEL

Address: Monktonhill Road, Southwood, TROON, KA10 7EN
Tel: 01292 313343
Fax: 01292 318661
Email: lochgreen@costley-hotels.co.uk
Website: www.costley-hotels.co.uk
Map ref: 9, NS33 **Directions:** From A77 follow Prestwick Airport signs. 0.5m before airport take B749 to Troon. Hotel 1m on left
Rooms: 38 (17 GF) **S** £125-£170 **D** £190-£250 (incl. bkfst)
Parking: 50 **Notes:** ⊗ in bedrooms

Lochgreen House Hotel, the flagship of family-run hotel and restaurant group Costley and Costley, is situated in 30 acres of secluded woodland and gardens. Following a loving restoration it opened its doors in 1991 and is still considered one of the best places to stay in Ayrshire. Located on Scotland's beautiful west coast, it offers magnificent views over Royal Troon golf course and the Irish Sea. From the moment you walk through the doors of Lochgreen you'll experience the highest standards of luxury and elegance found only in an AA four-red-star hotel. A meal in the Tapestry Restaurant, overlooking the fountain garden, really shouldn't be missed. The restaurant is acclaimed as one of the finest dining experiences in Scotland. Executive chef director Andrew Costley, youngest son of proprietor and master chef Bill Costley, has led his team to achieve three AA Rosettes, and his personal supervision ensures every meal is prepared and served to the highest international standards. Menus have a distinct Scottish influence, making optimum use of the excellent seafood, meat, game and cheese that are synonymous with the west coast of Scotland.

Recommended in the area

Culzean Castle; Burns National Heritage Park; Scottish Maritime Museum

View across Whiting Bay to Holy Island

Best Western Kinloch Hotel

★★★ 80% HOTEL

Address: BLACKWATERFOOT, Isle of Arran,
KA27 8ET

Tel: 01770 860444

Fax: 01770 860447

Email: reservations@kinlochhotel.eclipse.co.uk

Website: www.bw-kinlochhotel.co.uk

Map ref: 9, NR92

Directions: Ferry from Ardrossan to Brodick, follow
signs for Blackwaterfoot, hotel in village centre

Rooms: 37 (7 GF) (7 fmly) **S** £40-£65 **D** £80-£130 (incl. bkfst)

Facilities: STV Wi-fi ⊗ Gym Sauna

Parking: 2 **Notes:** ⊗ in bedrooms

Well known for providing an authentic island experience, this stylish, long-established seafront hotel
is perfect for exploring, and indeed seeing, the beauty of Arran. Smart public areas include several
lounges, popular bars and appealing leisure facilities. Bedrooms vary in size and style, with most
enjoying panoramic views of Kilbrannan Sound. The spacious restaurant provides a wealth of choice,
though it closes during winter; a creative menu, however, is still offered in the comfortable bar, where
you can savour some of the local produce from land and sea, then finish with an Island cheese platter.
Too much to eat? Never mind, there's an indoor pool, sauna, squash court, snooker room, gym, horse
riding, quad biking and a golf course nearby.

Recommended in the area

Machrie Moor Stone Circle; Balmichael Visitor Centre; Shiskine Golf Club

Loch Long, Loch Lomond and the Trossachs National Park

Scarista House

★ ★ ★ ★ ◉◉ RESTAURANT WITH ROOMS

Address: SCARISTA, Isle of Harris, HS3 3HX
Tel: 01859 550238
Fax: 01859 550277
Email: timandpatricia@scaristahouse.com
Website: www.scaristahouse.com
Map ref: 11, NG09
Directions: On A859, 15m S of Tarbert
Rooms 5 (2GF) **S** £125-£140 **D** £180-£200
Parking 12 **Notes** Closed Xmas, Jan & Feb

Scarista House has to be one of the most beautiful and remote places to stay in Britain. The hotel is surrounded by heather covered hills and looks out onto a three-mile sandy beach, with stunning views of the Atlantic Ocean beyond. This Georgian former manse isn't a grand house, but it is elegant and comfortable. There are just five bedrooms, while the two guest sitting rooms, both with open fires, are ideal for relaxing with a drink before dinner – perhaps hand-dived scallops, followed by local lamb. As one guest put it in 2009, it's "the best place anywhere to enjoy doing as little as possible".

Recommended in the area

Beach; Harris Golf Club; mediaeval church

Highland Cottage

★ ★ ★ ◉◉ SMALL HOTEL

Address: Breadalbane Street, TOBERMORY,
Isle of Mull, PA75 6PD
Tel: 01688 302030
Email: davidandjo@highlandcottage.co.uk
Website: www.highlandcottage.co.uk
Map ref: 9, NM55 **Directions:** A848 Craignure/
Fishnish ferry terminal, pass Tobermory signs,
straight on at mini rdbt across narrow bridge, turn
right. Hotel on right opposite fire station **Rooms:** 6 (1
GF) **S** £120-£135 **D** £150-£185 (incl. bkfst) **Facilities:** Wi-fi **Parking:** 6 **Notes:** ⚫ under 10 yrs

David and Jo Currie designed and built this small hotel. Both are career hoteliers and bring to it many
years of experience. The hotel stands above Tobermory, the Isle of Mull's pretty 'capital', in the town's
quiet conservation area, yet only minutes from the hustle and bustle of Main Street and Fisherman's
Pier. With just six individually designed bedrooms, staff rarely need to ask guests for their room
number. This relaxed policy continues in the rooms themselves, where the Curries have deliberately
avoided decor that screams 'Hotel!' All are provided with flat-screen TV with Freeview, DVD, CD player
and i-Pod dock, and an en suite bathroom with full-size bath and thermostatic shower, while some
have four-posters. There are two inviting lounges – the Sitting Room upstairs, with views across the
bay to the mainland; and downstairs the Sun Lounge, an extension of the Dining Room and the ideal
place for pre- or after-dinner drinks. Breakfasts are described as 'memorable', dinners as 'splendid'.
Whenever feasible, the kitchen uses only the freshest of locally-sourced ingredients, such as scallops
from Tobermory Bay, crabs from Croig on the island's west coast, mussels farmed at Inverlussa on
Loch Spelve, and venison reared at Ardnamurchan.

Recommended in the area

Duart Castle; Fingal's Cave (Staffa); Whale-watching

Bosville Hotel

★★★ 81% ◉◉ HOTEL

Address: Bosville Terrace, PORTREE, ISLE OF SKYE,
IV51 9DG
Tel: 01478 612846
Fax: 01478 613434
Email: bosville@macleodhotels.co.uk
Website: www.macleodhotels.com
Map ref: 11, NG44
Directions: A87 signed Portree, then A855 into
town. After zebra crossing follow road to left

Rooms: 19 (2 fmly) **S** £69-£130 **D** £88-£240 (incl. bkfst) **Facilities:** STV Wi-fi **Parking:** 10

Overlooking Portree's harbour and the Sound of Raasay, this elegant place blends the chic contemporary style of a boutique hotel with traditional Isle of Skye hospitality. Guests and locals mingle in the Merchant Bar, once the village bank, where you can sip a cappuccino, sample one of the malt whiskies, or enjoy the evening entertainment. The cuisine at the Bosville is Scottish with a French twist, featuring locally caught seafood, fresh game and meat, and organic Skye vegetables and berries. Chef John Kelly, author of Flavours of Skye, who trained at London's Savoy among other places, demonstrates his considerable flair in dishes such as pan-roast fillet of organic salmon on a cauliflower and potato purée with tempura battered oyster, and a little stew of mussels and clams in a saffron, white wine and cream nage. As an alternative to the Chandlery Restaurant, there's simpler but no less interesting and accomplished fare on offer in the Bistro, and the Merchant Bar offers good-value lunches such as roasts, pasta, sandwiches and dishes such as cajun-spiced salmon with avocado salsa and roasted chilli sauce. The supremely comfortable bedrooms feature stylish modern decor with quality fabrics and furnishings.

Recommended in the area

Dunvegan Castle; Talisker Distillery; The Aros Experience

Duisdale House Hotel

★★★★ 76% ⊛⊛ SMALL HOTEL

Address: ISLEORNSAY, Isle of Skye, IV43 8QW
Tel: 01471 833202
Fax: 01471 833404
Email: info@duisdale.com
Website: www.duisdale.com
Map ref: NG71
Directions: 7m S of Bradford on A851 towards
Armadale. 7m N of Armadale ferry
Rooms: 18 (1 GF) (1 fmly) **S** £65-£150 **D** £65-£115
(incl. bkfst) **Facilities:** STV Wi-fi **Parking:** 30 **Notes:** ⊗ in bedrooms ⫟ under 5 yrs

Duisdale House is a luxurious, romantic hotel in the south of the Isle of Skye, with panoramic views across the Sound of Sleat. Recently refurbished in contemporary style, the hotel's bold design features blend beautifully with the grand exterior. The sleek bedrooms – including some with four-poster beds – are mostly decorated in a colour scheme of black, mushroom and cream, but some come in reds and aubergines. All rooms have either sea or garden views and are equipped with flat-screen TVs and all the luxury amenities you would expect in a hotel of this quality. Complimentary Wi-fi is available throughout the hotel. A meal at Duisdale House shouldn't be missed. The talented, award-winning chef's signature dishes include Loch Sconsor hand-dived scallops, saddle of wild forest hare, Sound of Sleat lobster ravioli and dark chocolate veloute with liquorice root ice cream and black olive syrup. Blazing open fires and candlelight create the perfect atmosphere for a romantic evening, and there is a well stocked bar and extensive wine list. Exclusive daily sailing excursions are available onboard the hotel's own luxury yacht, and guests can also relax in the garden hot tub.

Recommended in the area

Talisker Distillery; Dunvegan Castle; Portree Town

Kinloch Lodge

★★★ 88% ◎◎◎ COUNTRY HOUSE HOTEL
Address: ISLEORNSAY, Skye, IV43 8QY
Tel: 01471 833214 & 833333
Fax: 01471 833277
Email: reservations@kinloch-lodge.co.uk
Website: www.kinloch-lodge.co.uk
Map ref: 11, NG71
Directions: 6m S of Broadford on A851, 10m N of Armadale on A851
Rooms: 14 (1 GF) **S** £130-£250 **D** £260-£360 (incl. bkfst & dinner) **Facilities:** STV Wi-fi **Parking:** 40

Named 'Romantic Hotel of the Year' at the Scottish Hotel Awards in 2009, Kinloch Lodge on the Isle of Skye is the perfect retreat to escape to for a dose of rest and relaxation at any time of the year. Set in the unrivalled beauty of the 'Misty Isle', the former hunting lodge of the Macdonald clan is nestled between the rugged mountains of Skye and the waters of Loch na Dal. The luxuriously appointed 15 double bedrooms each have spectacular views of the dramatic surrounding landscape, and the three drawing rooms with ancestral portraits of the Macdonald family, book-lined walls, roaring log fires and deep sofas provide a cosy haven away from the elements. The award-winning fine dining restaurant at Kinloch offers some of the best food in Scotland. Head chef Marcello Tully uses locally sourced, seasonal ingredients to incredible effect, whether it's a full Scottish fry-up or a sumptuous six-course feast. Be it spring, summer, autumn or winter, the changing scenery and seasonal larder on the Isle of Skye will delight even the weariest of visitors, and the owners and staff at Kinloch Lodge make it their mission to send each of their guests home relaxed, revived and plotting their return.

Recommended in the area

Clan Donald Castle and Visitors Centre; Talisker Whisky Distillery; Bella Jane boat trip on Loch Coruisk

Toravaig House Hotel

★★★ 80% ◉◉ SMALL HOTEL

Address: Knock Bay, TEANGUE, Isle of Skye,
IV44 8RE
Tel: 0845 055 1117 & 01471 833231
Fax: 01471 833231
Email: info@skyehotel.co.uk
Website: www.skyehotel.co.uk
Map ref: 9, NG71
Directions: From Skye Bridge, left at Broadford onto A851, hotel 11m on left. Or from ferry at Armadale take A851, hotel 4m on right
Rooms: 9 D £100-£190 (incl. bkfst) **Facilities:** STV Wi-fi
Parking: 15
Notes: ⊗ in bedrooms ⋇ under 12 yrs

Glorious sunsets are a frequent bonus at this romantic Isle of Skye hideaway, set in two acres of grounds with magnificent views over the Sound of Sleet. Such seclusion needn't mean remoteness from the mainland, however, as Toravaig House is just a short drive from the Skye Bridge and Armadale ferry port. There's plenty to explore on the island and in summer guests can take a trip on the hotel yacht - Solus na Mara - personally crewed by the owners. The bedrooms at Toravaig House are individually furnished with beautiful fabrics and wall coverings. Each has an en suite bathroom with power shower (some also have a bathtub), and luxurious Arran Aromatic toiletries. The cosy lounge with its open fire is the perfect place to relax and sample the large selection of fine wines and malt whiskies. Only the finest local ingredients, such as Loch Snizort scallops and wild Skye sea trout, find their way onto the menu at Toravaig House, voted 'Highlands and Islands Restaurant of the Year 2009'.

Recommended in the area

Armadale Castle; Gardens and Museum of the Isles; Cuillin Hill; Skye Serpentarium

WALES

Cribyn, Pen-y-Fan, Corn Du mountains

Cardiff Bay

Cardiff Marriott Hotel

★★★★ 80% [@] HOTEL

Address: Mill Lane, CARDIFF, CF10 1EZ
Tel: 029 2039 9944
Fax: 029 2039 5578
Website: www.cardiffmarriott.co.uk
Map ref: 2, ST17 **Directions:** M4 junct 29/A48M
E follow signs city centre & Cardiff Bay. Continue on
Newport Rd for 3m then turn right onto Mill Lane
Rooms: 184 (68 fmly) **S** £125 **D** £125
Facilities: STV Wi-fi [@] Gym Sauna **Parking:** 146
Notes: [@] in bedrooms

A fabulous location on the doorstep of the new St David's 2 shopping development, in the heart of
Cardiff city centre, makes this luxury hotel the perfect base for business or leisure. Bedrooms are
elegantly appointed and come with air-conditioning, luxurious bedding and high-speed internet. Get
active in the hotel's fitness club with heated indoor pool, relax with a cocktail on the terrace at Chats
Bar, and sample Anglo-French cuisine along with European wines in buzzy Brasserie Centrale.
Recommended in the area
Cardiff Bay; Millennium Stadium; Cardiff Castle and Civic Centre

Ivy Bush Royal Hotel

★★★ 75% HOTEL

Address: Spilman Street, CARMARTHEN, SA31 1LG
Tel: 01267 235111
Fax: 01267 234914
Email: reception@ivybushroyal.co.uk
Website: www.ivybushroyal.co.uk
Map ref: 1, SN42
Directions: M4 onto A48 W, over 1st rdbt, 2nd rdbt turn right. Straight over next 2 rdbts. Left at lights. Hotel on right at top of hill
Rooms: 70 (4 fmly) S £55-£95 D £75-£140 (incl. bkfst)
Facilities: STV Wi-fi Gym Sauna **Parking:** 83 **Notes:** ⊗ in bedrooms

Once a favoured retreat of Lord Nelson and Lady Hamilton, this friendly family-run hotel has been sympathetically modernised to blend its old-world charm with up-to-date facilities. The en suite accommodation is spacious and well-equipped, and includes some family rooms, a four-poster suite, executive suites and the Merlin suite with its own whirlpool bath. Dine in style in the restaurant, where the produce is locally sourced and the a la carte menu changes with the seasons. Welsh black beef is a particular speciality, and carvery lunches are extremely popular on Sundays. For guests looking for a more informal dining experience, the cosy bar and lounge area is open all day, every day, serving a full range of traditional meals. For those wanting to get active during their stay, the gym has all the latest cardiovascular equipment, and you can ease your tired muscles after a workout with a relaxing session in the sauna. The hotel is licensed for weddings and has four meeting and conference rooms with facilities to accommodate up to 200 people. Whether your stay is for business or pleasure, the Ivy Bush Royal Hotel can cater for all your needs.

Recommended in the area

National Botanic Garden of Wales; Aberglasney House and Gardens; Oakwood Theme Park

The Cliff Hotel

★★★ 77% HOTEL

Address: GWBERT-ON-SEA, Cardigan, SA43 1PP
Tel: 01239 613241
Fax: 01239 615391
Email: reservations@cliffhotel.com
Website: www.cliffhotel.com
Map ref: 1, SN14
Directions: off A487 into Cardigan, follow signs to Gwbert, 3m to hotel
Rooms: 70 (5 GF) (6 fmly) **S** £59-£85 **D** £75-£135 (incl. bkfst) **Facilities:** ⓧ ↘ Spa Gym Sauna **Parking:** 150

Built in 1850 and originally known as the Gwbert Inn, this coastal retreat was renamed the Cliff Hotel in the early 1900s in a bid to become a seaside getaway to rival the holiday resorts of southern England. Whether the name change was enough to persuade holidaymakers away from the south coast and across into Wales, we don't know, but The Cliff Hotel and Spa is certainly in a prime sea-facing spot. The 70-bedroom hotel sits in 30 acres of land along South Ceredigion's beautiful coastline, with stunning views of Cardigan Island, Cardigan Bay and Poppit Sands. Most rooms benefit from those views and all are en suite and have tea-and-coffee-making facilities. In the last three years a new state-of-the-art gym has been added to the hotel, along with a hydro spa, sauna, Jacuzzi, steam room, heated loungers, and a beauty therapy suite offering a range of treatments. A day spent on the par 3, nine-hole golf course, which stretches along the clifftop, should give you a good appetite for dinner in the a la carte restaurant or the Island Bar. The food at The Cliff Hotel & Spa is locally sourced and freshly prepared, and a meal here comes with the added bonus of watching the sun set over Cardigan Bay.

Recommended in the area

Clifftop walks; golf; dolphin, porpoise and seal watching

Conwy Castle

Quay Hotel & Spa

★★★★ 82% @@ HOTEL
Address: Deganwy Quay, DEGANWY, LL31 9DJ
Tel: 01492 564100
Fax: 01492 464115
Email: info@quayhotel.com
Website: www.quayhotel.com
Map ref: 5, SH77
Directions: M56, A494, A55 junct 18, straight
across 2 rdbts. At lights bear left into The Quay.
Hotel on right

Rooms: 74 (30 GF) (15 fmly) **Facilities:** Wi-fi ⊗ Spa Gym **Parking:** 96 **Notes:** ⊗ in bedrooms

Soon after being built on the site of some redundant railway sidings, this boutique hotel was named
'AA Hotel of the Year for Wales 2007–08'. Occupying a marvellous position beside the Conwy estuary,
its interior uses space and light to create a very stylish feel. Spacious bedrooms, many with balconies
and wonderful views, are decorated in neutral colours and offer plenty of extras, plus state-of-the-art
communication systems. The restaurant combines modern fine dining with first-class service.
Recommended in the area
Conwy Castle; Great Orme Heritage Coast; Snowdonia National Park

St George's Hotel

★★★★ 79% ⓦ HOTEL
Address: The Promenade, LLANDUDNO,
LL30 2LG
Tel: 01492 877544 & 862184
Fax: 01492 877788
Email: sales@stgeorgeswales.co.uk
Website: www.stgeorgeswales.co.uk
Map ref: 5, SH78
Directions: A55-A470, follow to promenade,
0.25m, hotel on corner
Rooms: 75 S £70-£120 D £95-£180 (incl. bkfst)
Facilities: STV Wi-fi Sauna **Parking:** 36 **Notes:** ⊗ in bedrooms

St George's Hotel is situated in a stunning position on the North Wales coast, overlooking the Llandudno seascape and the Great and Little Orme Mountains. It's also very close to the A55, with Chester and Wrexham less than 45 minutes' drive and Liverpool and Manchester easily accessible. The hotel is proud to maintain many of its original architectural features and traditional service values, and is just a five-minute walk from Venue Cymru, one of the largest theatres and conference centres in Wales. All 75 elegant bedrooms have air-conditioning, sumptuous bathrooms and all the luxuries expected from a hotel of this quality. The restaurant, which has been awarded an AA Rosette, uses only the best, freshest, local Welsh produce – all traceable, and organic wherever possible - and is the perfect place to sample some fine home-cooked cuisine. Guests can also enjoy light lunches, tea and coffee in the Terrace Lounge, with its stunning seafront views. During the evening this room becomes a haven where guests congregate, perhaps to sample the range of malt whiskies or enjoy a gin and tonic before dinner.

Recommended in the area

Great Orme Mines; Snowdonia National Park; Bodnant Gardens; Llandudno dry ski slope

Osborne House

★★★★ ❀ TOWN HOUSE

Address: 17 North Parade, LLANDUDNO, LL30 2LP
Tel: 01492 860330
Fax: 01492 860791
Email: sales@osbornehouse.com
Website: www.osbornehouse.com
Map ref: 5, SH78 **Directions:** Exit A55 junct 19. Follow signs for Llandudno then Promenade. Continue to junct, turn right. Hotel on left opposite pier entrance **Rooms:** 6 S £145-£200 D £145-£200 (incl. bkfst) **Facilities:** STV Wi-fi **Parking:** 6 **Notes:** ⊗ in bedrooms 🐾 under 11 yrs

Built in 1832, this Victorian house, which makes an excellent touring base for visiting North Wales, has been restored to a grand design by the Maddocks family, with original art, antiques and beautiful drapes in abundance. Today, this all-suite luxury townhouse provides a gloriously romantic retreat, and guests can enjoy stunning views of the bay and promenade from each bedroom. All of the spacious suites offer unrivalled comfort and luxury, combining antique furnishings with state-of-the-art technology, and free Wi-fi is available throughout. In addition, all of the bedrooms are air-conditioned and feature king-size canopied beds and sitting rooms with a large sofa and an original Victorian fireplace; each room also boasts an Italian marble bathroom with double-sided clawfoot bath and monsoon walk-in shower. Dining at the award-winning Osborne's Café/Grill is a sumptuous experience not to be missed. This is an all-day venue with brasserie-style menus and an emphasis on fresh, local produce, and fish is a speciality. In the evening, it is transformed by a multitude of candles, reflecting the gilt-edged mirrors and crystal chandeliers. As an added benefit, guests at Osborne House may also make full use of the spa at the Empire Hotel just 100 yards away.

Recommended in the area

Bodnant Gardens; Snowdonia National Park; Portmeirion Italianate village

Royal Oak Hotel

★★★ 83% ⊕ HOTEL

Address: Holyhead Road, BETWS-Y-COED,
LL24 0AY
Tel: 01690 710219
Fax: 01690 710603
Email: royaloakmail@btopenworld.com
Website: www.royaloakhotel.net
Map ref: 5, SH75
Directions: On A5 in town centre, next to St Mary's
church **Rooms:** 27 (1 fmly) **S** £75-£95
D £100-£170 (incl. bkfst) **Facilities:** STV Wi-fi **Parking:** 90 **Notes:** ⊗ in bedrooms

The wonders of Snowdonia National Park are right on the doorstep of this former Victorian coaching inn, which nestles at the foot of a wooded hillside in the heart of the picturesque village of Betws-y-Coed, overlooking the River Llugwy. Rooms have been designed with the heritage of the hotel in mind, with stylish fabrics and feature beds offering contemporary luxury in a period setting. For a special occasion book one of the four-poster rooms with Jacuzzi bathroom. Guests can benefit from complimentary membership of the nearby Dukes Leisure Complex, while broadband is available in all rooms and Wi-fi in the lounge bar. The award-winning Llugwy Restaurant, with its crisp white linen and splendid period features, offers modern Welsh cooking via an a la carte or four-course tasting menu. Dishes might include locally smoked halibut or a trio of Welsh mountain lamb, and, if you're lucky, the bara brith-and-butter pudding with Welsh whisky ice cream. Alternative dining options are the relaxed and modern Grill Bar, serving the finest Welsh produce, or the Stables Bistro which has a rather special atmosphere with its regular music nights, plenty of cask ales, and al fresco dining when the weather allows.

Recommended in the area

Snowdon Mountain Railway (or a walk to the summit); Conwy Castle; Llechwedd Slate Caverns

Castle Hotel Conwy

★★★★ 81% ◎◎ TOWN HOUSE HOTEL

Address: High Street, CONWY, LL32 8DB
Tel: 01492 582800
Fax: 01492 582300
Email: mail@castlewales.co.uk
Website: www.castlewales.co.uk
Map ref: 5, SH77
Directions: A55 junct 18, follow town centre signs, cross estuary (castle on left). Right then left at mini-dbts onto one-way system. Right at Town Wall Gate, right onto Berry St then High St

Rooms: 28 (2 fmly) **S** £79-£98 **D** £120-£265 (incl. bkfst) **Facilities:** Wi-fi **Parking:** 34

The distinctive building that houses the Castle Hotel hints at its long and fascinating history. Built on the site of a Cistercian abbey, it has welcomed many famous people through its doors, including Thomas Telford (who built the town's famous bridge), railway pioneer George Stephenson, William Wordsworth and the Queen of Romania. The current owners, the Lavin family and partner/head chef Graham Tinsley, have been very mindful of this important heritage while giving the place an attractive facelift. All of the bedrooms have en suite bathrooms and modern facilities. Deluxe rooms have spa baths, one has an ornately carved four-poster bed, and another enjoys a good view of the castle. Graham Tinsley MBE, and his award-winning kitchen team, have gained a reputation for serving excellent Welsh produce. Food is available in both Dawson's Restaurant and the bar, where the atmosphere is relaxed and the emphasis is on locally sourced ingredients. There's a real seasonal feel to the menu, with Conwy mussels featuring in the winter months, and Conwy Valley lamb in spring and early summer. There's also a good selection of vegetarian and organic food on the menu.

Recommended in the area

Conwy Castle; Caernarfon Castle; Snowdonia National Park; Bodnant Garden (NT); Anglesey

Empire Hotel & Spa

★★★★ 73%  HOTEL

Address: Church Walks, LLANDUDNO, LL30 2HE
Tel: 01492 860555
Fax: 01492 860791
Email: reservations@empirehotel.co.uk
Website: www.empirehotel.co.uk
Map ref: 5, SH78
Directions: From Chester, A55 junct 19 for
Llandudno. Follow signs to Promenade, turn right at
war memorial & left at rdbt. Hotel 100yds on right
Rooms: 54 (2 GF) (1 fmly) **S** £65-£85 **D** £95-£120 (incl. bkfst)
Facilities: STV Wi-fi ⊗ ⊀ Spa Gym Sauna **Parking:** 40 **Notes:** ⊗ in bedrooms

Privately owned and personally run by the Maddocks family, the Empire is a stylish and elegant hotel
in an excellent central location close to the promenade, pier and shops. The en suite bedrooms are
attractively furnished, with smart bathrooms and all the modern amenities you'd expect, plus a host
of thoughtful extras. Indulge in the stunning newly renovated spa with indoor heated pool, Jacuzzi,
sauna and steam room, along with a fully equipped gym. The beauty therapy suite offers a wide range
of treatments, from mud wraps in the special wet room to facials and massages in the 'his and hers'
treatment room. There is also a small outdoor pool and a patio with sunbeds for the warmer months.
Dine on fine local produce in the award-winning Watkins & Co restaurant, with its traditional menu and
loyal, long-serving staff. Alternatively, the new contemporary style Poolside restaurant offers great value
for money.

Recommended in the area

Portmeirion; Conwy Castle; Bodnant Gardens

Dunoon Hotel

★★★ 81% HOTEL

Address: Gloddaeth Street, LLANDUDNO, LL30 2DW
Tel: 01492 860787
Fax: 01492 860031
Email: reservations@dunoonhotel.co.uk
Website: www.dunoonhotel.co.uk
Map ref: 5, SH78
Directions: Exit Promenade at war memorial by pier onto wide avenue. 200yds on right
Rooms: 49 (7 fmly) **S** £72.50-£89 **D** £114-£145 (incl. bkfst)
Parking: 24

Close to the promenade in this well preserved Victorian seaside resort, the Dunoon has a certain old-world grace about it. Hushed and stuffy it isn't, though. In fact, the Williams family, who have been here a good while, make sure it offers a happy antidote to what they regard as anodyne modern living. For example, they treat returning guests like old friends, and first-time customers as new ones. Their approach is evident too in the way they have styled the bedrooms, with no two alike, and in their attention to detail, with crisp Egyptian cotton bedlinen, and Molton Brown toiletries in every bathroom. The same is true of the restaurant, where silver rings contain freshly pressed linen napkins, and white porcelain is used on the tables. Food and wine are the Williams' abiding passions. Cooking is unpretentious, using fresh ingredients sourced locally as far as the seasons allow, with specialities such as terrine of game, medley of local fish, ragout of Welsh lamb with mint dumplings and asparagus mousse. Their taste in wines is adventurous, with a list that, in their words, 'offers more than you would expect from a modest hotel in the sleepy outer reaches of Britain'.

Recommended in the area

Great Orme; Bodnant Gardens; Snowdonia National Park

A barge travels high above the River Dee across Telford's Poncysyllte Aqueduct of 1796

Ruins of Castle Dinas Bran at Llangollen

Ruthin Castle

★★★ 85% ◉◉ HOTEL

Address: RUTHIN, LL15 2NU
Tel: 01824 702664
Fax: 01824 705978
Email: reservations@ruthincastle.co.uk
Website: www.ruthincastle.co.uk
Map ref: 5, SJ15
Directions: A550 to Mold, A494 to Ruthin, hotel at end of Castle St
Rooms: 61 (14 GF) (6 fmly) **S** £60-£95 **D** £60-£290 (incl. bkfst) **Facilities:** Wi-fi Gym **Parking:** 200 **Notes:** ⊗

Full of history, romance and impressive architecture, this ancient hotel stands in a walled dry moat in 30 acres of parkland and gardens. Prince Charles stayed here en route to his Investiture in 1969, as did Edward VII. Marble lions recline on plinths in the wood-panelled entrance hall and big open log fires help to make the public rooms cosy, despite their scale. Many of the bedrooms enjoy views towards the Welsh mountains. Chandelier-hung Bertie's restaurant offers award-winning modern British cuisine.

Recommended in the area

Snowdonia; Llangollen; Portmeirion; Chester

Bron Eifion Country House Hotel

★★★ 87% ◉ COUNTRY HOUSE HOTEL

Address: CRICCIETH, LL52 0SA
Tel: 01766 522385
Fax: 01766 523796
Email: enquiries@broneifion.co.uk
Website: www.broneifion.co.uk
Map ref: 5, SH43
Directions: A497 between Porthmadog & Pwllheli, 0.5m from Criccieth, on right towards Pwhelli
Rooms: 19 (1 GF) (1 fmly) **S** £95-£120
D £130-£180 (incl. bkfst) **Facilities:** Wi-fi **Parking:** 50 **Notes:** ⊗ in bedrooms

Bron Eifion, a delightful Grade II listed country house hotel set in extensive grounds to the west of Criccieth, enjoys breathtaking views of the sea. Golfers are particularly well catered for here, with five of the best courses in North Wales in close proximity to the hotel; special golf packages can be arranged. Inside, guests will find a tranquil and relaxing atmosphere, with attentive and friendly service, and the interior style highlights the many retained period features. There is a choice of restful lounges, warmed by log fires, and the very impressive central hall features a minstrels' gallery. The en suite bedrooms have been individually decorated to combine luxury and elegance, and tea-and-coffee-making facilities as well as flat-screen TV, Wi-fi access and hairdryers all come as standard. Deluxe rooms also provide bathrobes and slippers. The Orangery Restaurant, overlooking the spectacular gardens, is fresh and bright by day, candlelit and relaxed in the evening. The emphasis is on fresh Welsh produce, with dishes such as Llyn Peninsula Seabass, Criccieth spider crab and roast rack of Welsh lamb, followed by seasonal desserts, home-made ice creams and pastries. Afternoon tea includes a delicious selection of sandwiches and home-made sweet treats.

Recommended in the area

Portmeirion; Snowdonia National Park; Blaenau Ffestiniog Railway

Dolserau Hall Hotel

★★★ 81% ◉ HOTEL

Address: DOLGELLAU, LL40 2AG
Tel: 01341 422522
Fax: 01341 422400
Email: welcome@dolserau.co.uk
Website: www.dolserau.co.uk
Map ref: 2, SH71
Directions: 1.5m outside Dolgellau between A494 to Bala & A470 to Dinas Mawddy
Rooms: 20 (3 GF) (1 fmly) **S** from £71 **D** £142-£176 (incl. bkfst) **Parking:** 40 **Notes:** ✾ under 10 yrs

This lovely privately owned Victorian country-house hotel offers peace and quiet, even at the height of the season. Set in five acres of well established gardens, it has beautiful views from every window. Spacious lounges to relax in lead off the galleried hall, and there are 20 comfortable bedrooms complete with all the little luxuries that make you feel spoilt. Dinner in the Rosetted restaurant really is something to look forward to, as is the complimentary tea and cakes served every afternoon.

Recommended in the area

Portmeirion; Harlech Castle; Welsh Highland Heritage Railway

The Crown at Whitebrook

★★★★★ ◉◉ RESTAURANT WITH ROOMS

Address: WHITEBROOK, NP25 4TX
Tel: 01600 860254
Fax: 01600 860607
Email: info@crownatwhitebrook.co.uk
Website: www.crownatwhitebrook.co.uk
Map ref: 2, SO50
Directions: 4m from Monmouth on B4293, left at Whitebrook sign, 2m on unmarked rd, Crown on right
Rooms: 8 **S** £80–£100 **D** £125–£150 (incl. bkfst)
Parking: 20 **Notes:** ⊗ in bedrooms

The Crown at Whitebrook lies just 5 miles from Monmouth in the beautiful Wye Valley. Set in 5 acres of landscaped gardens, this establishment offers a peaceful haven. The contemporary bedrooms all come with luxury en suite bathrooms, and some have power showers or double-ended baths. Other features include flat-screen TVs and individually controlled heating. The modern restaurant lies at the heart of the Crown. Guests may enjoy an aperitif while perusing chef James Sommerin's award-winning menu.

Recommended in the area

Tintern Abbey; Offa's Dyke; Chepstow Castle; Chepstow Racecourse

The Celtic Manor Resort

★★★★★ 85% ◉◉◉ HOTEL

Address: Coldra Woods, NEWPORT, NP18 1HQ
Tel: 01633 413000
Fax: 01633 412910
Email: postbox@celtic-manor.com
Website: www.celtic-manor.com
Map ref: 2, ST38
Directions: M4 junct 24, take B4237 towards Newport. Hotel 1st on right
Rooms: 400 (34 fmly) S £198-£1500
D £198-£1500 **Facilities:** STV Wi-fi ⊗ Tennis Spa Gym Sauna **Parking:** 1300 **Notes:** ⊗ in bedrooms

The Celtic Manor Resort is two hotels, one old, one new, that stand together in 1400 acres of parkland in the beautiful Usk Valley. The 19th-century Manor House was where the resort's owner, Sir Terence Matthews, was born when it was a maternity hospital. Original character is all around – admire, for example, the leaded windows, wood-panelled walls and sweeping wooden staircase. Traditionally styled bedrooms include three with four-posters. There's a choice of places to eat or drink: The Patio Restaurant, serving Italian-style dishes, the Cellar Bar and the Manor Lounge. The five-star resort hotel opened in 1999, with a soaring atrium and 330 individually decorated and beautifully appointed bedrooms. One of the two Presidential Suites even has a baby grand piano. Guests in both hotels may make complimentary phone calls to national landlines. Eating options include fine-dining in The Crown; the informal Olive Tree offering contemporary Mediterranean cuisine; Merlins piano bar serving afternoon teas; and the Forum Café providing light refreshments. The resort also offers a convention centre, 31 function rooms, three championship golf courses including The Twenty Ten, a golf academy, two health clubs and two spas. Quite a venue for The 2010 Ryder Cup.

Recommended in the area

Caerleon Roman Town; Tintern Abbey; Raglan Castle

Best Western Lamphey Court Hotel

★★★ 80% HOTEL

Address: Lamphey, PEMBROKE, SA71 5NT
Tel: 01646 672273
Fax: 01646 672480
Email: info@lampheycourt.co.uk
Website: www.lampheycourt.co.uk
Map ref: 1, SM90 **Directions:** A477 to Pembroke. Turn left at Milton Village for Lamphey, hotel on right **Rooms:** 38 (6 GF) (7 fmly) S £82-£105 D £110-£160 (incl. bkfst) **Facilities:** Wi-fi ⓢ Tennis Spa Gym Sauna **Parking:** 50 **Notes:** ⊗ in bedrooms

Lamphey Court Hotel & Spa is a Georgian mansion with an up-to-the-minute feel but plenty of period charm. It's friendly yet fastidiously run, as you'd expect of a hotel that's been under the same private ownership for 30 years. The bedrooms and suites are well proportioned and elegantly furnished. All guests have access to the superb leisure club and spa, with a good-sized heated indoor pool, Jacuzzi, sauna, gym and a wide choice of soothing treatments. There are also some floodlit tennis courts and a jogging trail in the grounds. Food is taken seriously at Lamphey Court, with a choice of more formal dining in the candlelit Georgian restaurant, or a slightly more laid-back, casual affair in the Conservatory, and the option to eat on the patio during the summer. Whichever route you take, expect imaginative cooking using lots of local produce, including Freshwater Bay lobster, salmon from the River Teifi, and lamb from Pembrokeshire's green Preseli Hills. With a great choice of outdoor activities on the doorstep, a medieval bishops' palace as a neighbour, and the south Pembrokeshire coastline so close at hand, Best Western Lamphey Court is a hotel with year-round appeal.

Recommended in the area

Lamphey Bishop's Palace; Pembrokeshire Coast; Tenby and Saundersfoot

Carew Castle at low tide

Warpool Court Hotel

★★★ 79% 🏵🏵 COUNTRY HOUSE HOTEL

Address: ST DAVID'S, SA62 6BN
Tel: 01437 720300
Fax: 01437 720676
Email: info@warpoolcourthotel.com
Website: www.warpoolcourthotel.com
Map ref: 1, SM72
Directions: At Cross Square left by The Bishops
Restaurant (Goat St). Pass Farmers Arms pub, after
400mtrs left, follow hotel signs, entrance on right
Rooms: 21 (2 fmly) S £125 D £150-£350 (incl. bkfst)
Facilities: Wi-fi ⊗ Tennis Parking: 100

A privately-owned hotel in large grounds on St David's peninsula, overlooking the gentle sweep of
St Bride's Bay. Bedrooms are well equipped and attractively furnished, and many have sea views.
The spacious restaurant, overlooking the gardens and the sea, offers an extensive menu. A heated
swimming pool opens from Easter to 31st October and there is an all-weather tennis court.

Recommended in the area

Pembrokeshire Coast National Park; St David's Cathedral; Pembroke Castle

Stack Rocks, Pembrokeshire Coast National Park

Three Cliffs Bay, Gower

Maes-Yr-Haf

★★★★★ ◉ RESTAURANT WITH ROOMS

Address: PARKMILL, SA3 2EH
Tel: 01792 371000
Fax: 01792 234922
Email: enquiries@maes-yr-haf.com
Website: www.maes-yr-haf.com
Map ref: 2, SS59
Rooms 5 S £65-£120 D £95-£160 Facilities Wi-fi
Notes Closed 11-31 Jan

An award-winning restaurant with rooms, Maes-Yr-Haf nestles quietly in the peaceful rural village of Parkmill, just a gentle stroll from the renowned Three Cliffs Bay. There are five luxuriously appointed en suite double bedrooms, each tastefully furnished with pure cotton linens and the latest technology including flat-screen TV, DVD player and iPod dock. Complimentary Wi-fi is available throughout the building. In the contemporary and spacious restaurant, top quality produce is used to create an inspired modern European menu with a distinctly local flavour. The wine list is carefully selected and there's an excellent range of aperitifs and digestifs.

Recommended in the area

Three Cliffs Bay and Gower coastline; Gower Heritage Centre; Mumbles and Swansea

MAPS

KEY TO ATLAS PAGES

Shetland Islands

13

Orkney Islands

11   **12**

Inverness

Aberdeen

Fort William

●	Bed & Breakfast
○	Town name
Ⓜ	Motorway junction
Ⓡ	Restricted motorway junction

Perth

9   **10**

Glasgow   Edinburgh

Stranraer

Carlisle

Newcastle upon Tyne

Kendal

Middlesbrough

5   **6**   **7**   **8**

Leeds   York

Liverpool   Manchester   Kingston upon Hull

Holyhead

Sheffield

Nottingham   Lincoln

Norwich

Aberystwyth

Birmingham   Cambridge

Carmarthen   Gloucester   Colchester

Cardiff   Bristol   Oxford

1   **2**   **3** LONDON **4**

Guildford

Barnstaple   Taunton   Maidstone   Dover

Dorchester   Southampton   Brighton

Exeter

Plymouth

Isles of Scilly

Penzance

13

Channel Islands

© Automobile Association Developments Limited 2009

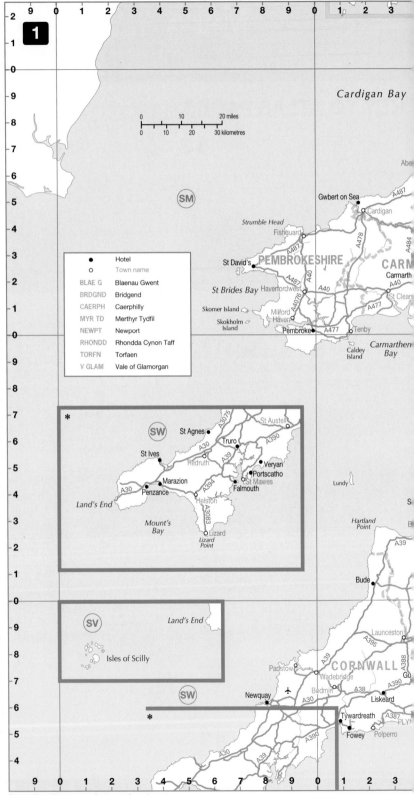

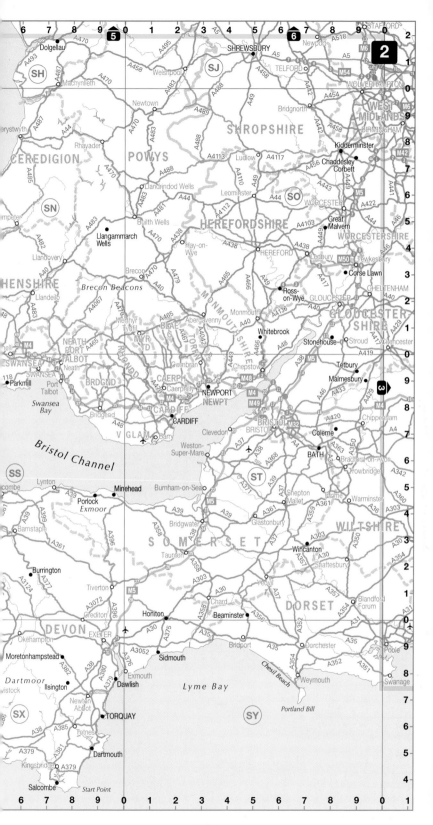

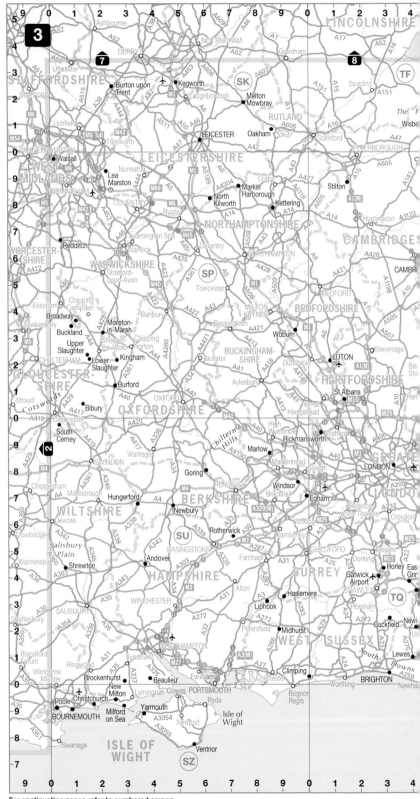

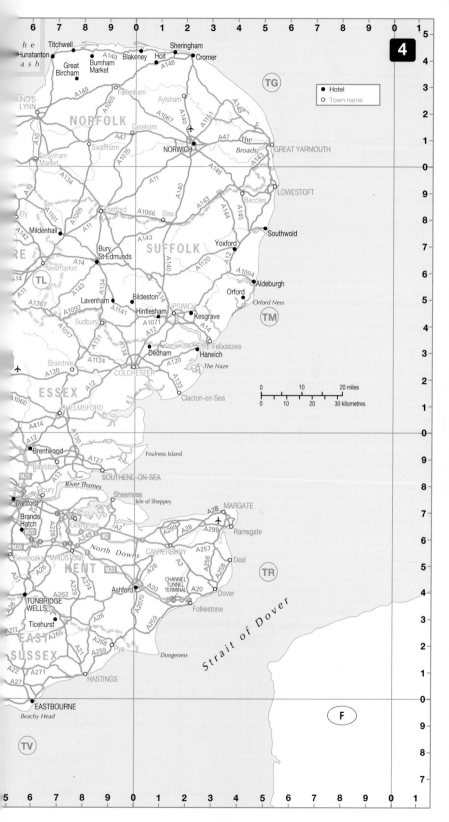

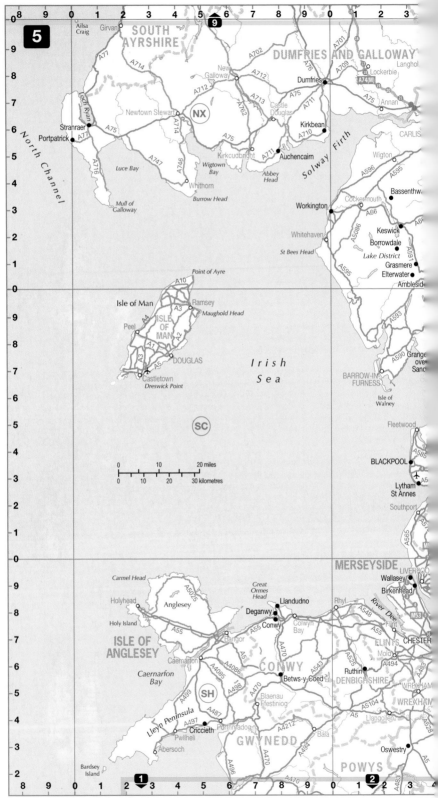

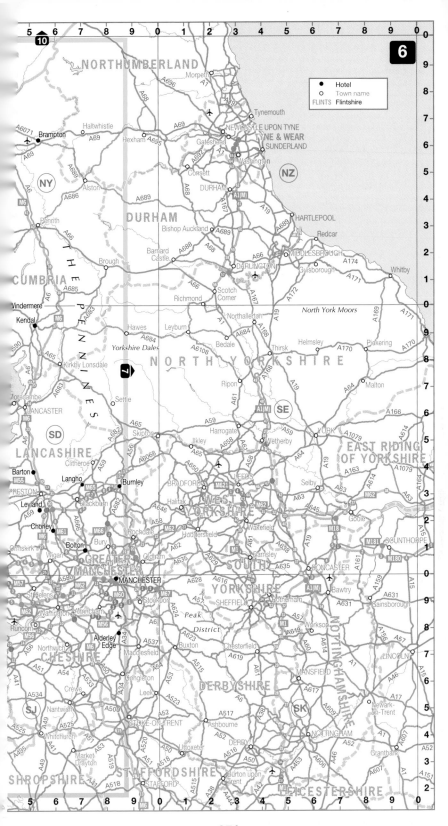

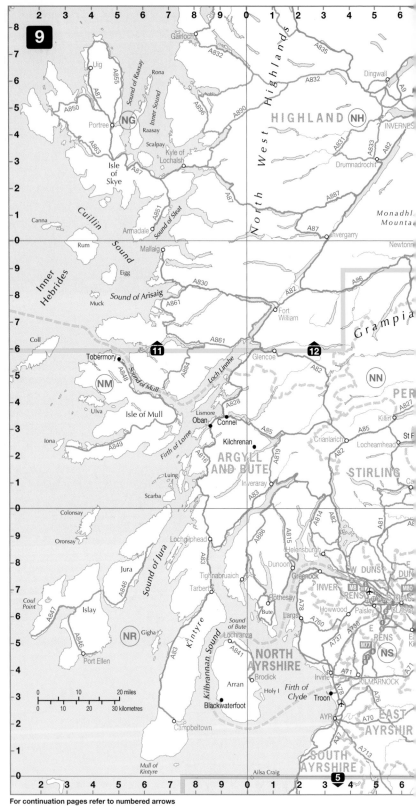

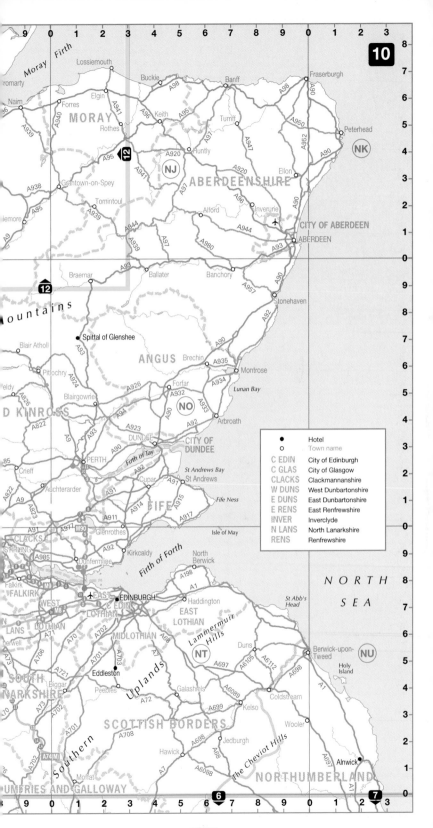

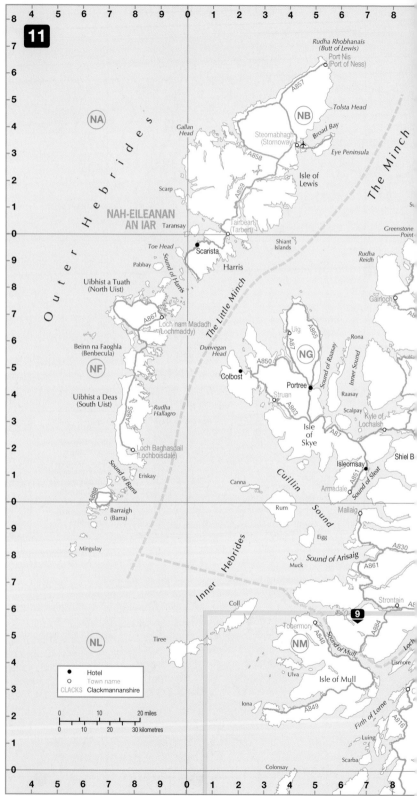

For continuation pages refer to numbered arrows

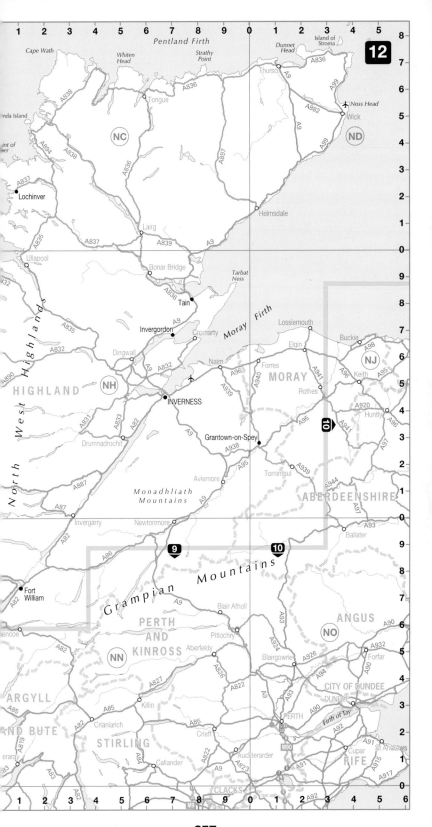

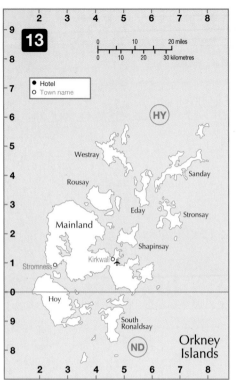

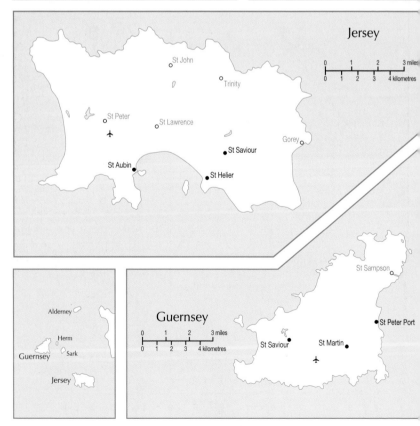

County Map

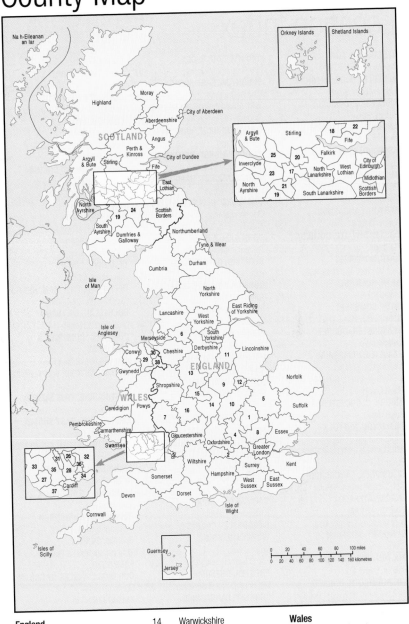

England

1	Bedfordshire
2	Berkshire
3	Bristol
4	Buckinghamshire
5	Cambridgeshire
6	Greater Manchester
7	Herefordshire
8	Hertfordshire
9	Leicestershire
10	Northamptonshire
11	Nottinghamshire
12	Rutland
13	Staffordshire
14	Warwickshire
15	West Midlands
16	Worcestershire

Scotland

17	City of Glasgow
18	Clackmannanshire
19	East Ayrshire
20	East Dunbartonshire
21	East Renfrewshire
22	Perth & Kinross
23	Renfrewshire
24	South Lanarkshire
25	West Dunbartonshire

Wales

26	Blaenau Gwent
27	Bridgend
28	Caerphilly
29	Denbighshire
30	Flintshire
31	Merthyr Tydfil
32	Monmouthshire
33	Neath Port Talbot
34	Newport
35	Rhondda Cynon Taff
36	Torfaen
37	Vale of Glamorgan
38	Wrexham

Location Index

Location Index

Location Index

Location Index

Hotel Index

Hotel Index

Hotel Index

366

Hotel Index

Credits

The Automobile Association would like to thank the following photographers, companies and picture libraries for their assistance in the preparation of this book.

Abbreviations for the picture credits are as follows: (t) top; (b) bottom; (l) left; (r) right; (c) centre; (AA) AA World Travel Library.

4 Stockbyte Royalty Free; 5 AA/N Jenkins; 7 Royalty Free Photodisc; 8 Royalty Free Photodisc; 9 Imagestate; 11 Photodisc; 12/13 Feversham Arms Hotel; 14t Best Western Castle Green Hotel; 14l Best Western Castle Green Hotel; 15t Chewton Glen; 15cr Chewton Glen; 15bl Andy Spain Photography; 15bc St James's Hotel & Club; 16t Kinloch Lodge; 16cl Kinloch Lodge; 16cr Milsoms; 16b Milsoms; 18/19 AA/R Coulam; 20AA/M Birkitt; 23 AA/V Bates; 27 AA/M Birkitt; 28t AA/J Tims; 30 AA/M Birkitt; 33t AA/T Mackie; 34 AA/J Beazley; 35t AA/T Marsh; 37 AA/C Jones; 43t AA/J Wood; 47t AA/R Moss; 48 AA/T Mackie; 54t AA/S Day; 59 AA/A Mockford & N Bonetti; 61t AA/E A Bowness; 63 AA/T Mackie; 64t AA/J Beazley; 68 AA/G Edwardes; 72 AA/N Hicks; 74t AA/C Jones; 76 AA/N Hicks; 82 AA/H Williams; 83t AA/A Burton; 85t AA/R Fletcher; 91t AA/A Burton; 92 AA/C Lees; 94 AA/N Setchfield; 98 AA/D Hall; 100t AA/H Williams; 103t AA/D Hall; 106 AA/C Molyneux; 111 AA/M Moody; 118t AA/A Burton; 122t AA/S&O Mathews; 123 AA/H Palmer; 125 AA/M Moody; 128 AA/N Setchfield; 130t AA/D Forss; 132t AA/M Busselle; 133 AA/J Beazley; 134t AA/C Jones; 139t AA/C Jones; 140 AA/J Tims; 141t AA/P Baker; 146 AA/J Tims; 148t AA/T Mackie; 149 AA/J Tims; 153t AA/B Smith; 164t AA/J Tims; 171t AA/M Jourdan; 178 AA/S Day; 179t AA/S Day; 181 AA/T Mackie; 182t AA/T Mackie; 186t AA/T Mackie; 190t AA/T Mackie; 191 AA/M Birkitt; 193 AA/D Forss; 195 AA/J Tims; 199 AA/W Voysey; 202 AA/M Birkitt; 203 AA/M Birkitt; 204t AA/M Birkitt; 207 AA/C Jones; 211 AA/S Day; 212t AA/C Jones; 214t AA/C Jones; 217 AA/C Jones; 219t AA/A J Hopkins; 220 AA/T Mackie; 223t AA/T Mackie; 229 AA/H Williams; 232t AA/P Davies; 233 AA/J Tims; 236 AA/J Miller; 240 AA/J Miller; 243 AA/J Miller; 247 AA/J Miller; 251t AA/J Mottershaw; 252 AA/R Coulam; 254 AA/C Jones; 255t AA; 256 AA/R Surman; 258 AA/M Moody; 260 AA/M Moody; 261t AA/C Jones; 263 AA/C Jones; 264t AA/M Moody; 267t AA/M Moody; 268 AA/M Moody; 269t AA/F Stephenson; 270 AA/M Kipling; 277 AA/R Newton; 282 AA/J Tims; 284 AA/S Abraham; 289 AA/W Voysey; 294/295 AA/D W Robertson; 300 AA/J Smith; 302 AA/J Smith; 308 AA/E Ellington; 311 AA/M Hamblin; 316 AA/K Paterson; 318t AA/D W Robertson; 324/325 AA/N Jenkins; 326t AA/N Jenkins; 329t AA/N Jenkins; 336 AA/C Jones; 337t AA/N Jenkins; 342t AA/C Warren; 343 AA/C Molyneux; 344t AA/N Jenkins;

Every effort has been made to trace the copyright holders, and we apologise in advance for any accidental errors. We would be happy to apply any corrections in the following edition of this publication.